ALPHA GEEK
BY CHRIS 51

ALPHA GEEK
Copyright 2017 by Chris Rohaley, Chris 51
All original text by Chris 51
All art by Chris 51, unless otherwise noted
All photography by Chris 51, Bob Williams, and Celeb Photo Ops, unless otherwise noted.
All toy photography by Chris 51, and taken from his private collection, with special appreciation to Kenner, Mattel, LJN, Playmates, Kidrobot, Hasbro, Galoob, Powell Peralta, Sims, G&S Skateboards, and Topps.
All right reserved. No part of this book may be reproduced or transmitted in any form or by any means, electronic or mechanical, including photocopying, recording, or by any information storage and retrieval system, without written permission of the publisher.
ISBN 978-1-5136-1817-3
ALPHA GEEK PUBLISHING
3585 Main St.
Springfield, OR 97478
CHRIS 51
email-Chris@chris51.com

This book is dedicated to the fans and friends of Epic Ink. Your support has changed my life and allowed me to live what most artists can only dream of. I appreciate each and every one of you and hope that I can continue to instill artistic inspiration, expression, hope, and happiness in you and serve as a positive role model to your children. I love you all.
Stay Epic.

PREFACE

Like me, this book follows little rhyme or reason. It has run-on sentences and random tangents that probably go off in some weird direction that has little to do with the subject at hand. There will probably be tonz of spelling errors because I can write like a motherfucker but can't spell worth a shit. I threw in random quotes that may totally interrupt the flow of the literature, but for some reason I thought they were relevant or important so there they stayed.

The chapters are barely in order. Some chapters are too short and most sentences and paragraphs are probably too long. I even made up a shitload of words (noted by *), which can be found in the DICKtionary at the end of the book. Anyone can follow all the literary rules and self-publish a book. They can carefully plan the entire layout from point A to B, but what fun is that? That is the same old stale boring shit, and if you are a friend of mine, you know that we don't play that normal game very well! I am here to make a statement and do shit my way like I always have. In the immortal words of Dale Doback, I am here to fuck shit up!

I am here to motivate you to put down this stupid-ass book and get out there and make a difference, take some risks and try something new.

I feel like a pretentious dick for writing about myself anyway, so we might as well have some fun on the journey. Ohh I love Journey, such a good band.

So, why the hell is a guy like me writing a book anyway? I am as normal as they come. I lived in a trailer park when I was young and have been married three times. I never had any money or anything given to me. And, that is precisely why I am one of you! I am a regular dude who just outworked all the other regular dudes to break the mold of mediocrity. I outsmarted the masses and followed my heart. I took risks and never held back. I went from a plumber's punk-ass son climbing out of ditches in a polluted logging town to climbing the Great Wall of China after hosting tattoo symposiums. I beat all the odds and got my fifteen minutes of fame on TV, and I did it with honor, integrity, and respect. Somewhere in the mix I found myself and the meaning of life, and I want to share that with you so maybe you can find yours. I didn't find it through God or some fantastic spirit animal; I simply saw past the bullshit and paved my own path. I want to help mix the asphalt that paves your road. I will be your motivation for domination.

I speak for the geeks!

☆ THE GUTS ☆

0 INTRODUCTION page...1

1 GEEKS DO IT BETTER page...5

2 MY 1970s page...13

3 WHAT'S YOUR MOTIVATION FOR DOMINATION? page...18

4 RISKS (THE SAFEST WAY TO LIVE HAPPILY) page...22

5 EPIC INK (Take 1) page...25

6 MY 1980s page...31

7 HARD WORKING-MOTHER-FUCKIN MACHINE page...38

8 HARD WORKING-MOTHER-FUCKIN ARTISTS page...48

9 EPIC INK (Take 2) page...55

10 DO YOUR BUSINESS page...58

11 MY 1990s page...80

12 THE ART OF COLLECTING page...86

13 EPIC INK (Take 3) **page...90**

14 INSIDE THE HUDDLE page...98

15 THOSE LIFE-CHANGING MOMENTS page...102

16 MY 2000s page...109

17 EPIC INK (Take 4) **page...119**

18 THE HATE SCALE page...129

19 COATTAILS page...136

20 THE KLINGONS WERE RIGHT page...140

21 EPIC INK (Take 5) page...143

22 SPONSORSHIPS, ENDORSEMENTS, AND GETTING FREE SHIT page...154

23 GEEKSTERINK LEGENDS TOUR page...172

24 EUGENE COMIC CON page...182

25 EPIC INK (Take 6) page...190

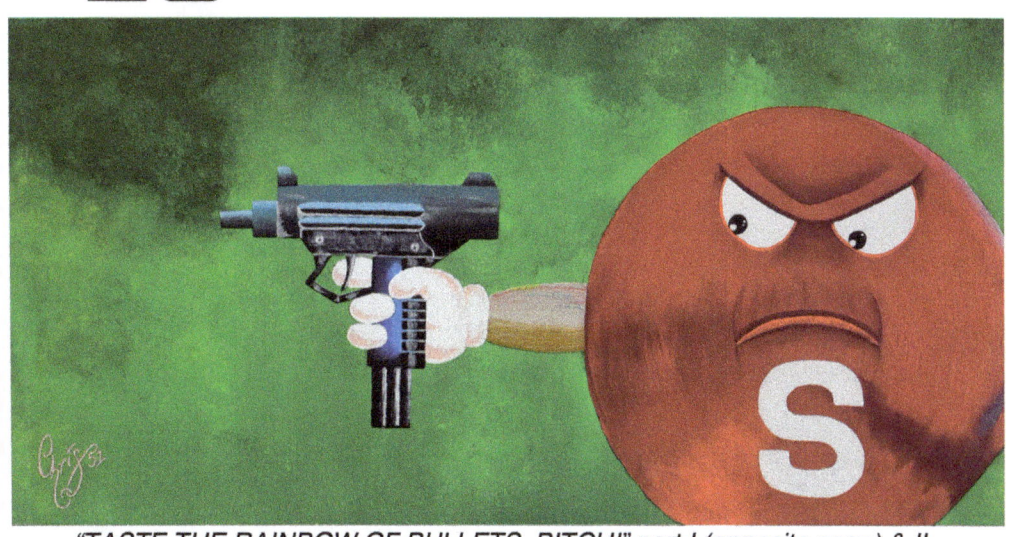

"TASTE THE RAINBOW OF BULLETS, BITCH!" part I (opposite page) & II

37 JUST THE TIP (FOR TATTOOERS) page...320

38 MY SUPPORTING CAST page...332

39 MY ART, YOUR ART page...346

51 FAR FROM PERFECT page...368

SPECIAL THANKS page...370

DICKTIONARY page...373

INTRODUCTION

Just a decade ago, being called a geek or nerd was viewed as derogatory. Now those of us who have endured the bullying persecution wear it as a badge of honor. We fight aliens and villains with it, win Epic battles, and create the world's entertainment for the unimaginative. I am proud to be a geek and your self-proclaimed geek ambassador to the tattoo reality generation, a term I use to define today's twenty-five- to forty-five-year-old geek-cultural demographic.

There were two types of boys born in the 1970s: those who liked *Star Wars* and those who lived *Star Wars*. I once heard that there might have even been some weird kids who never saw *Star Wars*, but that would be incomprehensible, and I would not have associated with those fools on the monkey bars anyway.

Boys who liked *Star Wars* played with the expensive toys until the battery-powered sounds ran out, and then moved on to *G.I. Joe* or *Masters of the Universe* packaged play sets, preconstructed for their uncreative cure for boredom. If you were a child who needed bright, flashy stimuli to pull you away from the television, and couldn't get lost in a world of good vs.

evil and love shall overcome fear, then you were already lost. Welcome to flipping burgers and pumping gas forever.

Boys who lived *Star Wars* were usually broke and happy with a few dozen figures and half-broken TIE fighter. They created entire planetary systems throughout the backyard and used mom's spare Tupperware and dad's garage treasures to construct to-scale rebel hideouts and imperial weaponry for their prized figures. If you wanted to recreate the perfect Hoth environment you sat in the snow and froze your ass off. Obsession sparked imagination and imagination fueled creativity. I strongly believe that the Epic trilogy single-handedly shaped the future of a generation, harvesting young minds that grew into artists, scientists, and anyone building, designing, or creating something out of nothing.

Analogies are only as good as the culture or times they represent, so if you are too old or too young to understand my comedic and nostalgic point of references then I suggest that you stop reading now and don't waste your time, because you will never catch this Road Runner's message, Wile E.

What is all this shit about anyway? Is it about good vs. evil? Maybe it's about love overcoming fear? Could it be a nonreligious spiritual journey to finding confidence and direction? An encouraging self-help advisement on business and life in general? Or is it about maximizing your potential to entrepreneurial greatness? Maybe it's just some alpha geek telling you secrets about his success and life, and how important it is to have a good toy collection. Actually, it just may be more about being proud to

be a geek or nerd, and standing tall in your beliefs. So, you could say it's a little of all of the above, saturated with profanity, reality, optimism, and positivity. In a short version of the long crap I just put you through, this book is about spitting truths and not swallowing pride, and inventing your own path for life, business, and fatherhood in the tattoo reality generation. In shorter short, it's about growing huge balls and loving your life . . . and your new big balls.

Not only will I make up random words that just sound better than proper literary terms, I will do so without giving a single fuck. (*See the Chris 51 Dicktionary at end of book for full definitions.) I will cuss like a motherfucker to get my point across. I will be totally politically incorrect and be all anticonformity* up in here. I will try and motivate you to get off your ass and do great things and take great risks. I will take you and your future seriously, but rarely myself, because if you can't make fun of yourself then life is way too serious . . . and you're missing the whole point of living. I will geek out, a lot! I will do all this with absolute justification. And why is it justified? Because I said so. It's my book; therefore I make all the rules up in this bitch. Please do not misinterpret my confidence for arrogance, although you might get a little of the latter with a lot of the other. You can have it all and get it all and still maintain your humility. If it seems like I am bragging, then you are missing the whole point. I am simply telling you of my own experiences and how I worked hard in life, love, and employment to make shit happen and get through hard shit, and how I benefited from all that shit in the end. I hope that you can too.

I am proud to say that I have pretty much done it all, or at least tried it all, when it comes to work. You cannot be considered a quitter when you try out new things in the first place; I call that a tryer. It's those that don't open themselves up to new experiences that are the quitters; they've already quit on life's opportunities.

I have been everything from a reality TV star and producer to an electrical engineer. I was a Pizza Hut pie maker to

Domino's delivery driver. A licensed journeyman plumber to arborist and landscaper. I built houses, both as a framer and finish carpenter. I was a handyman and maintenance guy. I washed dishes at the Holiday Inn and cooked at a local hamburger joint. I bagged groceries at Safeway and unloaded trailers at UPS on the dreaded graveyard shift. I installed water filtration systems and was a cliché tanned pool-cleaner guy in Florida. I owned a music store, a sports photography business, and a plumbing company all before I was thirty. I even did fuckin telemarketing. I was a nightclub bouncer and part-time DJ. The list goes on like a bad case of eczema. I was as blue-collar as they come, but I never accepted that as my fate.

As you can see, my work experience log is bigger than a young Ron Jeremy cock. I always had two attitudes when it came to employment. One, you must stay employed to support yourself and family. Unemployment is for lazy losers. Two, if you don't like your job, quit, as long as you have another one lined up. Being happy is a priceless emotion in the workforce since you spend most of your life forced to work, but not working holds no ethical code whatsoever.

I really don't give two shits what you think about me or what I have accomplished, but I do genuinely care about helping you if I can. In the end, people are the most important thing life has to offer, and if you aren't interested in helping others then you are again missing the point to life itself.

I don't want to just tell you my story; I want to show you how I made it, and how to make a story of your own. How hard work beats talent every day. How risking everything is the only way to get anything. In other words, please let me help you help yourself. Resistance is futile. I speak for the geeks.

1

GEEKS DO IT BETTER

Let's get one thing straight: you need to be proud to be a geek. In all my travels and all my conventions worked, I have found that Geeks are the nicest and most supportive collective in human culture. They work hard and play hard, and mostly do so together regardless of age, race, or religion. They are intelligent and well mannered, typically nonviolent and respectful of others, even if others don't share their affinity for fucking awesomeness. Geeks don't judge, and like the superheroes they idolize, have good morals and values. In short, geeks are the shit! I am proud to be a geek. I can only hope that you might consider me your geek ambassador to the mainstream television and tattoo reality generation world.

I have gone where few geeks have gone before. I have obtained celebrity-type success by doing what I am passionate for, all while staying strong in my beliefs and morals and not selling out like a punk bitch. Wil Wheaton did it through an acting career; I've done it through a tattoo and business career. Am I bragging? Fuck no! I am proud of my hard work and want to share my experiences so you can take from it and find your own success. I don't want anybody to have to go through the struggles I went through if there is a better way.

So why am I writing this book? Probably because I have an insatiable love for all that is geeky pop-culture, whether it's toys, comics, collectibles, fanboy shit, or movies. I bleed an O-Positive passion for science fiction and cartoons, and all of this motivates me in life and business.

So why am I writing this book really? I'm a fuckin businessman and entrepreneur who doesn't sleep for shit and whose brain won't shut down, so why the hell not? If I can give just one thing back or contribute my positive ideas to a culture and fandom that has given me so much joy and drive in life, then why wouldn't I jump at the opportunity? Plus, I'm a geek, and geeks create shit, that's what we do.

Allow me to give you a quick rundown of my qualifications to do this project . . . there it is! It doesn't matter what they are cause I don't care and neither should you. A good motivational book by a geek for geeks is all the resume I need, because we are untied strong! But if you still need more, allow me to tell you my story in a brief literary teaser that will be explored more thoroughly throughout the project. Here are the highlights and spoilers to my success.

I became a tattoo artist after I owned a used music and memorabilia store and the bottom dropped out on the market because of Napster. The rise of downloading was the fall of fuckin awesome mom and pop record stores, which I still miss to this day. I had to get creative so I decided to put a tattoo area in my alternative-type store. This of course was way before tattooing went mainstream and television made it a lucrative enterprise. Only problem was that all of my tattoo artist classifieds were answered by ex-convicts and tweekers that I didn't want anywhere near my life. I was always a good artist, spending more time doodling in textbooks than reading them, so I adopted the axiom, if you want it done right just do it yo damn self. I found the first old-school shitty apprenticeship that took me, and scrubbed toilets for months before I was even allowed to draw a tattoo, let alone apply one. I didn't learn shit, but I did take with me the most important thing I found . . . myself! I realized that tattooing was what I was meant to do in this life, the sole purpose that I escaped the womb. I was gonna give it my all and be happy, whether it made me rich or poor. And that attitude and passion is why I became good, not because of natural talent, but because of hard work and dedication to my craft and the unyielding love it embedded in my soul.

Fast-forward a couple years of self-instruction and trial and error. I wasted no time to let the world know that I was better than I actually was. You see, it's all in your confidence and branding capabilities. Marketing is the key to success, not the ink in the skin. I'm sure a lot of tattooers will argue with that, saying their work speaks for itself, but guess what, work doesn't say shit if it doesn't have an audience to see and hear it. You can be the best artist in your town, but if you don't extend your reach outside of your town, that is all you will ever be. I aspired for greater, and so should you.

I promoted and thanked many companies for putting out good products and told aspiring artists what I used to create my art. Then one day I realized that I should trade this wisdom for free products if I am helping them sell more (right?). I started contacting companies and endorsing products before sponsorships were a prevalent thing. I even taught a company or two how a sponsorship could work to benefit their brand with no advertising cost to them, only a little product write off. I wrote old-fashioned pen and paper letters to old-fashioned companies. MySpace came around and I digitally promoted new companies. Rather than buying new cars and unproductive shit I spent my money driving and flying to meet with business owners face-to-face about endorsements. I literally hit the pavement to help companies help me. I knew that if they could see that fire and passion in my eyes, they couldn't turn me away.

I began writing stories for tattoo magazines from an industry insider's perspective because I was tired of the same fluff and fill I was seeing copy after copy. You could say that I had issues with their issues (okay that was bad). I did it all for free, seeing the bigger picture that the exposure would only grow my "brand." And grow it did. Before I knew it I was writing monthly columns for one, two, and three magazines, from here in the states to Germany to the UK. Articles turned to artist interviews and those turned into my own interviews. My interviews led to teaching business seminars at tattoo conventions and foreign sympo-

osiums. Teaching seminars abroad led to teaching continued education seminars at home for Oregon artists through an accredited college.

Meanwhile, in my spare time between midnight and being a single dad rising early, I managed to create my own tattoo ink company. I started from scratch and researched and learned. I used my reputation as a well-respected artist and businessman to recruit some great artists to sponsor and help me promote my ink since I had zero budget for advertising. I gave them exactly what I sought out years before, but with more. I included them in every facet of the goings-on and tried to promote them as much as they promoted me. They in turn felt like it was their company too, really taking pride in it and defending it to the end. It was a good strategy, and I made lots of friends and contacts doing it. My brand, as an artist and business owner, continued to grow.

The next logical step for me was television. I (along with most tattoo artists) had grown very weary of how we were portrayed on TV. Very few of us were these violent and argumentative brutish thugs that Suzy Homemaker thought we were. Most of us were actually quite the opposite, and got into tattooing in the first cause we were geeks that drew comics and cartoons. I knew that it was time for something fun and different. I had an idea to intertwine my love for everything geeky and pop-culture with a drama-free format for a refreshing, comedic twist on tattoo reality TV. I expanded to a new tattoo shop that I specifically designed to cater to a filming scenario, complete with tall ceilings and an open floor plan. I used to be an electrical engineer and carpenter, so I calculated and remodeled it in hopes to attract and encourage a network to help my dream turn reality TV. I wrote episode story lines in my spare time and already had a cast of my best friends in mind for when the time was right.

When you work at conventions and comic cons around the world, your brand grows exponentially, but you gotta work it, and work it hard to get noticed. I worked my fuckin ass off for years traveling and missing my family. My tattooing was heavily influenced by pop-culture. My shop was called Area 51 Tattoo, and it was a geek's dream, full of arcade games and collectible memorabilia. And my ink company, Formula 51, had quickly grown into a big-time competitor in the ink market. Formula 51 was marketed primarily with fun product names and illustrative graphics all with science fiction and pop-culture references. Apparently, somebody noticed all the combined geekery within my brands. A production company contacted me out of the blue. They had seen my body of work and heard of my reputation and presented me with an idea for a sci-fi themed tattoo reality TV show. Ironically, I got the e-mail on a layover on my way to *Star Wars* Celebration Germany. I replied with an enthusiastic "No fuckin way, I have a plan in place for a pop-culture themed tattoo reality show, very similar to your idea, just encompassing a broader geek spectrum." Needless to say, our two ideas fused into one solid vision of explosive orgasmic geekiness. I contacted my cast of friends that day because I just knew this was destined to happen. They all agreed to make the sacrifice to move out west to Oregon for a period of time if it was to come to fruition. I then wrote essays to the production company on how they were the best of the best at tattooing this specific genre, and why their personalities would "work" on TV.

    Later, after months of planning with a show creator and many cast Skype interviews, my perfect puzzle of friends all proved me right. They shined and dazzled the powers that be, and the puzzle was complete. I knew that only this puzzle would work; it was all or nothing. Nobody was better or more or less important than the next. We were a close family of friends long before the show and that showed on camera. You can't fake love and mutual respect. You just can't fake that shit! Three grueling months later, filled with sixteen-hour days, six days a week, we had OUR show. We made ten magical, wanted, which is unheard of in Hollywood. We kept it positive, family friendly, respectable, talented, and drama free like we initially envisioned. We made the show that raised the GEEK flag

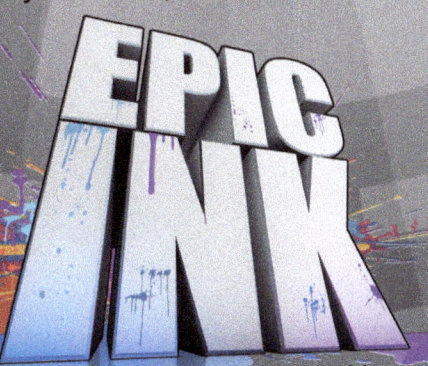

proudly, and waved it every minute of every episode. A&E Networks gave us the faith and freedom to do so, and supported us every step of the way. The show here brought the spotlight to the small town of Springfield, OR. It showed the public that it is cool to be a geek or nerd and that you should wear that badge with honor. It portrayed good values and we became role models, proud that children could watch this program with their parents as a family. Lastly, it showed that tattoos and geek-culture were accepted by all, whether you were black or white, skinny or fat, nerd or jock, girl or boy! #EpicInkforLife.

That brings us up to the current. I am writing this book because I love everything and everyone involved in geek-culture, and I've learned a thing or two in life and business that I want to give back to the world. I want to teach through peace what I learned through hardship. I'm hoping that my simple story will help motivate you to make one of your own. Finally, I just love talking geekery. My fans have been very kind to me, so I owe them one too! Geeks unite.

(Below) *My son Ryker knows what's up.*

2

MY 1970s

I was born in Fort Myers, Florida, in the 1970s. My early years were a steady diet of *Star Wars*, toys, football, classic rock, and Cocoa Puffs. I was lucky enough for my mom to protect my innocence with a formidable wall of love and education, so I grew up very happy and properly spoiled with attention. My dad's belt whippings kept me in line and respectful, and even though I hated them then, I understand their leather lessons now.

Spending my developing years in the Deep South taught me several lessons. It showed me segregation and racism were normal and rampant on both sides of the color barrier. On the flip side, I learned that large families could love and thrive just by being together. I realized that having a brother and a vast imagination are what every young boy truly needs.

My parents were young and in love, and it showed. Being eighteen years old with a new child goes only one of two ways. Luckily for me, it brought my parents closer, and they would stay that way for the the next forty years. I was ex-

posed to flirting, love, and affection as early as I can remember, and I love remembering that spell. If more children grew up today watching their parents navigate through a loving relationship, the world might find more serene ways to coexist. But instead, we navigate through our touch screens, ignoring most of the love our lives have to offer.

Just before I headed west I lived on the beach, and the sand was always a different playground if you believed it could be. Although I got stung by stingrays five times, I never feared going back in the water alone. I learned strength. Life was simple for me and I cherished my early childhood. When I was six years old we moved across the country, then I really started learning about the grandeur and greatness that life outside of my comfort zone had to offer.

I quickly realized that Oregon was the beauty to Florida's beast. The happy Barney Rubble to the crabby Fred Flintstone. There was little anger and racism and life seemed to move at a more peaceful and logical pace. Of course, I didn't understand any of this then, but the environment quickly grew to become part of me. I immediately found two best friends

(Left) My most favorite childhood memory. My brother Kevin (right) and I getting our dream Star Wars toys. My parents were so broke that my mom had to make the PJ's we were wearing, but they still managed to surprise us.

(whom I still have). We three amigos ruled the neighborhoods on our Huffys (the poor-kid's Diamondback). Joe, Jeff, and I were Oregon Goonies before Hollywood actually came to Astoria. We had it all and knew it all until we saw *Star Wars*. That single movie forever changed our lives and how we played and imagined, especially for me. *Star Wars* changed every kid on different levels; some just wanted the toys and wore the Underoos, and some wanted greatness and defined purpose. For me, it was the latter. That's how I still am, and proud of it.

Two years old in 1975 and already had a football in hand.

My dad worked hard so my mom could raise her boys from home. I wholeheartedly believe that the time and energy my mom spent on me during those years shaped my positive personality and set my moral compass pointing true north from the beginning.

I was introduced to team sports and my life again changed. Don't ever underestimate the power of winning and losing as a team of brothers. I learned some of life's most crucial lessons through sports, and experienced camaraderie unmatched in society. Parents that keep their kids out of sports for fear of injury are only hurting their kids' minds in the process and depriving them an education that could never be learned from books or schoolteachers. Coaches are some of the most important teachers your child will ever have.

Sports. Music. Art. Probably the three most integral pieces to a child's piece of a bright future's pie. In the 1970s I discovered the sweet sound of the electric guitar. It blew my mind by age five, and I was listening to bands like Led Zeppelin, ELO, KISS, Black Sabbath, AC/DC, and whatever other eight-tracks and records I heard my dad jamming to. I couldn't soak up enough gold in those old gold rock 'n' roll records. I was a sponge and my dad was the liquid priest to the Rock Gods. He didn't just tell me what song came on the transistor radio, but what year it was produced, the album name, what former band the singer was in, and when he saw them in concert. He was the Rockopedia of 1970s' music until the day he passed.

I found art in everything I saw and that has never changed. After I watched the *Hulk* I would draw the Hulk. While football was on TV I would be lying on my tummy drawing the helmets and immortalizing the scenes as they played. When I listened to Led Zeppelin I would recreate the blimp on paper along with other album covers. KISS and Boston covers were pure art. I filled pads of paper with imaginary worlds based around my beloved pop-culture, sports, and music. But, nothing captivated me like cartoons. They were art brought to life on TV and in comic pages. I found that I could even create my own characters right there on the pages without any rules or wrongs. Then the sculpting began. Play-Doh soldiers quickly turned to the more technical. I would build the *Battle of the Planets* ship from Legos like a work of science fiction wonder. I constructed

This Hulk was my favorite thing ever! It was a sculpture, toy, and bank all in one. I have been searching for a replacement for years.

Lego *Star Wars* Star Destroyers decades before the company's teams of plastic engineers imagined them, even painting my yellow-only mini figs white to become proper Stormtroopers.

I feel so lucky to have spent my most formative years in that era. You were forced to use your imagination for everything, so the world was the art you created in your mind, not what a company thought it should be. I feel sorry for children that don't get to experience all that I did, the way I did. Today, impressionable kids get all of their (lack of) imagination, music, and visual stimuli from a digital demon screen, stunting their artistic growth. Not my kids! I feed them a steady diet of imagination for educational and instrumental purposes and allow the video games only as a reward or privilege. Sure the video games are fun, I mean I am a *Mike Tyson's Punch Out* master, but they didn't rule my life and make me a Mountain Dew-addicted, socially inept shut-in who couldn't use a wrench to save his life. Being able to build the biggest house on Minecraft won't teach you to use a hammer to build an actual house for your family when the zombie apocalypse actually does happen.

I was lucky enough to be shielded from war and politics, chaos, and mayhem in the 1970s. I was brought up to love life and chase happiness. My parents weren't hippies, but they weren't conservative prudes either. We were a hardworking, church-going, blue-collar unit. I was taught that intelligence was limitless and that for the most part, the Earth was a good place.

3

WHATS YOUR MOTIVATION FOR DOMINATION?

We all have our ambitions and dreams; some of us just get off of our lazy asses more than others and do something about them. We are driven for different reasons and motivated by different morals.

I can tell you this, if you are driven by money alone, you will fail, be miserable, or lose every person in your life that really matters. People driven by money usually only care about that bottom line, and the bottom line is a low place to live.

Those driven by passion stay happy because it is what they love that fuels them. When you are fueled by love it will show in your work, and the money will come.

Then there are people driven by people. Those who are ambitious out of necessity to provide substance or sustenance for their families are relentless and unstoppable. When your love for your family or children guides you, you are selfless, and selfless people have little fear.

Finally, there are those driven by revenge or hate. Although this can kick-start a fiery work ethic under your ass, it can also be a double-edged sword if not extinguished along the way. When you do get your satisfaction you have nothing left to push or cure you, and feeling that sense of rage and negativity for so long can leave you so alone at the top.

Personally I have experienced a little of each of the motivational engines. I never cared about the money part for anything I do. As long as I can provide for my family, and I am doing the right thing in their eyes, then I have all that I need.

I have been fueled by hate, betrayal, and negativity on a couple occasions that you will probably figure out by reading more of this shit. But, I have embraced listening to my wife and close friends on how and when to let hatred go and focus on the bigger picture. My wife Katie, and friends Josh Bodwell, Kyler Shinn, and Rob Smead have been instrumental in shoring my calm and refocusing my thoughts on kindness and grandeur. I look back now and I'm actually disappointed in myself for giving some individuals the time of day to warrant negative behavior in me. There is so much more I could have done with that time than worrying about their opinions of me. It kills me now that they even know they got to me emotionally. I can assure you that won't happen again.

I want to leave a positive legacy for my children. Sure it's nice to have some fame and notoriety, but the more important lesson is showing my kids that you can have that and more if you work hard enough and do it the right way. I want them to be proud of daddy. I want them to outdo daddy and accomplish great things using my career as a model and then kicking its ass by surpassing it!

I want you to really search your soul. You already know what you are most passionate about in this life by now. You need to exploit that and let it guide you. If you don't, you will always feel incomplete and never truly be happy. It is better to fail at doing what you love then succeed at being who you hate, so why not try? It doesn't matter how ridiculous your passion is, I guarantee you that there are others out there who share it. The only difference is that they won't have the balls to pursue it and you will!

Welcome to your first Alpha Geek lesson. You don't need me to tell you what motivates you because you already know. You need me to help push you to do it! I am here to push you, nag you, and maybe even annoy you a little. But I do it because I know you can do it. It's just a little easier to do when you know someone who has taken leaps, and landed successfully. Your hesitant eyes can rest assure that you are not alone.

What do you want to do most in this life, what do you love to do? Think about that while you read this book, and by the end you will be motivated to at least try it.

Remember you're already a winner, you beat out all the other sperm. All of us are born winners. You can do it again.

INCOMPLETE RANDOMNESS

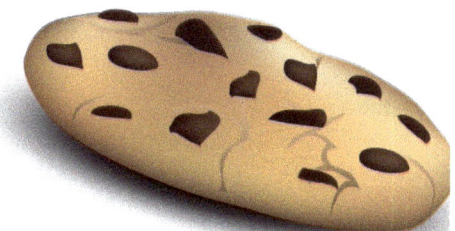

I once broke up with a chick for eating my cookie dough. For reals, some things you just don't fuck with. Before you think I'm a total asshole let me explain.

When I purchased the log of Pillsbury golden goodness I told her in advance that it was the only thing off limits in my home. I take my cookies very seriously. They are my reward for hard work. I mean, I have a tattoo of a giant monster cookie on my ass for shit's sake! Anyway, I further explained that I had a ritual cookie-baking night that I looked forward to all damn week while I was being good and keeping clear of the sugary temptations the rest of the time. For a sugar addict this is no different than a smoker going all week cigarette free knowing that he gets to smoke a fuckin carton on Sunday night if he chooses.

Needless to say that when she was going to bake my only cookies (the day of my cheat night) for her and her daughter, it erupted into a yelling match, which led to her throwing the cookie dough log at me like some sort of ninja turtle attack, which led me to telling her to get the fuck out of my life if you can't respect my wishes. Never saw her again. She was a crazy ex-stripper bitch anyway.

The life lesson here is that you never fuck with a person's sweets, especially cookies.

The bigger picture is about not wasting your time on a partner who isn't going to value your values.

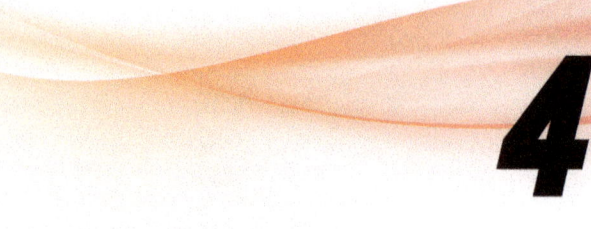

RISKS
(The Safest Way To Live Happily)

What happens without taking a risk? Nothing! And nothing is the worst thing that can happen! I say this line in virtually every interview I do, and I live by it daily. I will never be that dude who says "what if" or "I wish I would've tried or done that." Regret is death in slow, excruciating increments. It's torture. Travel to that place, try that food, go for that job, ask that girl out; what have you got to lose? Some might say you can lose your pride with rejection or failure; well, I disagree. I say that you lose way more than pride by not taking those risks; you lose confidence and courage and the educational experience from failing and approaching said risk from a different perspective the next time. To put it in a classier and more philosophical way: don't be a sheepish little bitch, be a fuckin man and tell yourself you're gonna be a fuckin man, and it's her loss if she doesn't want to go out with you, or it's their loss if they want to hire some douche bag over you.

Here are a couple examples of risks that I have taken, and thank God I did, because they forever changed my life. I hope they can help you.

I had major back surgery in my early twenties, which forced me to reevaluate my career choices. Physical labor was no longer a viable long-term option, nor a desire. I saw what plumbing and landscaping did to my father's and uncle's bodies, and I wanted no part in it anymore. I needed a challenge for my brain, not my back. So, I revisited what I started in college and put myself back through school, post-surgery back brace and all. No more salary = huge risk number one.

Getting my degree didn't mean shit—hitting the pavement every day until I found a firm that would give me a low-level entry position did. A little resume lying and a lot of bullshitting and I was in. Before I knew it I was an electrical engineer designing complete electrical systems for beachside condominiums. I went to school for architecture, so I didn't know shit about this stuff, but if you just listen to people and have common sense you can quickly learn. I was in. A suit and tie guy with a 401(k) plan and secure future! Only problem was, the job was boring as shit! Sitting in a cubicle all day is a slow death, and a coffin of repetitious stagnancy. I felt more like a drone and less like a man. There was no spirit or fire in it, no soul or sense of accomplishment by my own two hands. I lasted eleven months. It didn't even take me a year to realize what was most important: happiness. Happiness is worth way more to me than stability, otherwise why live life? You'd just be going through the motions, already dead inside long before dying. I quit = risk number two.

I was broke but happy. Happiness allowed me to dream. Dreams motivated me for change. Change was the beginning of my real life.

If I could give up a steady job as an electrical engineer in little more than the snap of my fingers after years of schooling for it, then you can follow your dreams too. Is it scary, fuck yes. Is it worth it, fuck yes. Do what makes you happy. Remember it's not just you who suffers—it's the people around you too. You are your best you when you are happy.

Turns out, the biggest risk is taking no risks at all (oh snap that's a good line!). It is in our nature to conquer; some do it with guns, some do it with keyboards. Those who end up being the rulers and making the new rules are the ones who took the biggest risks.

People will warn you, caution you, and try and hold you back. Most of those people are ones that took a small risk and failed miserably and are afraid to try it again. Don't listen to those sheep.

Athletes risk career-ending injuries every time they take to the field or court. That's why they make the big money and why we pay to watch them. It's the risk that makes the game exciting. A player's career could span ten years or ten seconds. But you can't think about that when you strap on that helmet. Athletes strap it on for the passion and excitement, and that's why they endure the pain and risk everything. You need to strap on your proverbial helmet and get in the game too. Do it now before it's too late or someone behind you straps theirs on faster and runs past you. Whether it's in business, labor, or serving careers, we all have our helmets to strap on. Time to go in headfirst and fight.

5

EPIC INK
(Take 1)

I had this crazy idea. A geeky comedy reality tattoo TV show with a bunch of the world's best artists and biggest nerds who actually love each other and have zero hate drama! That is about as far-fetched of an idea you will ever hear for a pitch. But guess what? There just so happened to be a production company out there with a similar idea that was willing to listen to my crazy, geek-laden idea.

The idea first sparked in me when I was tattooing on this little comic con circuit. I did a few comic cons and a couple horror fests and witnessed the shock and admiration that the pop-culture fans had when they saw us tattooing there among them.

I was already the biggest geek that I knew, so I fancied myself an expert in the modern pop-culture genre, at least enough to have a tangible grasp on the demographic and fan base. I started seeing a bigger picture of grandeur and realized that there could be so much more to

offer my fellow geeks than just this little tour that was really going nowhere. I envisioned people bonding over the joy and excitement of their newfound fandoms. They just needed to experience the art, atmosphere, and childhood nostalgia that the pop-culture world had to offer. Much of the population didn't even know that this subculture was blossoming and attracting all walks of life. Masses of closeted geeks needed to have their doors ripped off and be shown that it was not only okay—but actually cool—to be a geek or nerd!

I was tattooing iconic images from geek-culture onto people's skin that would brand them as geeks for eternity. Short guys were walking tall, and quiet women were talking loud about their favorite cartoon, video game, and movie characters that they were getting tattooed. I wanted everyone to feel the passion and exuberance that my clients were feeling. That I was feeling. Even if they didn't care to feel it, I was about to shove it down their throats.

My tattoo shop was already heavily geekified, and I had a popular name in the industry, known as an aficionado of the genre. My ink company was marketed completely by pop-culture influence, and all my endeavors were tied to the culture in some way. I had lived the geek life all my life, and through ridicule or support it was what I understood and excelled at. It was time to take it to the next level. Wonder Twins, activate . . . form of . . . a TV show!

(Photos) I was always changing collections to adorn the walls at Area 51 Tattoo. It became a tribute to geeks everywhere and a landmark in the pop-culture community.

With the overwhelming presence of the reality tattoo TV boom, it was the perfect time to imagine my dream more strategically. How would my show make it and compete against these big dogs in big cities with big-named artists? How would it be any different, other than collecting a better artist arsenal than the other shows currently offered? How could I keep it respectful in my industry's eyes, which had such a disdain for the present portrayal of "us" on the boob tube? After a few of these questions, I basically answered them on my own. I wouldn't worry about any of that shit! I would take the risks and just do it my way and appeal to myself, my peers, and my fellow geeky friends out there. If I didn't adopt that truth, then the whole thing would have never happened.

First priority, location! Without a unique, kick-ass shop, I knew I had nothing. Being a geek is largely based on visual

stimuli, so my shop had to be big, colorful, and mesmerizingly awesome. The shop alone had to get people talking and excited before they even saw the personalities or tattoos. That would be the first thing to set me apart from the rest.

I'd had Area 51 Tattoo for over a decade, and it was one of the oldest and most popular shops in the area. I had continuously upgraded throughout the years and finally settled into a nice 2,000-square-foot retrofit house on a busy main road. I was happy there, but I wanted more. I wanted a TV show done my way. I just knew that my idea had value and, given the chance, could have success. So, I had to put myself in a position to get that chance.

Area 51 Tattoo, Oregon. From house to warehouse.

I took the risk. I packed up my seven employees and everything I owned and moved to a giant location. I scouted out spots all over town, but when I saw this one I knew it was perfect. It was way out of my price range, but guess how many fucks I gave? That's right, zero fucks were given. It was more than double what I was currently paying, plus there would be new construction costs, permits, licenses, and all that shit. But, I never thought twice about it. It had sixteen-foot-tall ceilings, perfect for lighting and overhead camera mounting. There was a huge warehouse in back for staff and filming equipment, and there was even an enormous parking lot. It was perfect! I did the construction myself, carefully planning walls, partitions, and rooms for optimal filming ease. It took every penny that I had, and then some borrowed from my parents. I made it work by doing the work myself. Step one complete. Huge risk and a long way from a reward.

Second on project getting-a-TV-show agenda...the cast. Like any great television program out there, it's the cast that makes the show, not necessarily the plot. If people love the personalities then they will keep watching to experience empathy, admiration, lust, or laughter. This was actually the easiest part for me. I instantly thought of four other artists who were not only amazing tattoo artists, but they had the giant personalities and the looks to make this dream of mine become reality.

I'd met and befriended Chris Jones, Josh, Jeff, and Heather through tattoo conventions and comic cons. They are the type of people you fall in love with instantly, with infectious personalities and kind souls. I wrote a complete essay on each one of them describing how both their art skill and personality would be perfect for this project. Josh was the kind and responsible one, Heather the funny and loud chick, Jeff the young and suave newcomer, and Jones was just Jones the exotic foreigner with a smile of gold (literally).

(Above) Me, Chris Jones & Josh Bodwell taking time off from a convention in Rio De Janeiro.
(Left) Jones, myself, and Heather Maranda in Brazil long before Epic Ink TV.

Soon after, I started writing show plots, stories, and scenarios. They outlined what type of shenanigans we could do and how to tie storyboards to particular tattoos.

I was completely ready. I had the shop. I had the cast. I had the ideas and stories. I had the talent and drive. I had the professional resume to back me. Now, all I needed was an ear to listen and a list of production company e-mail addresses to address!

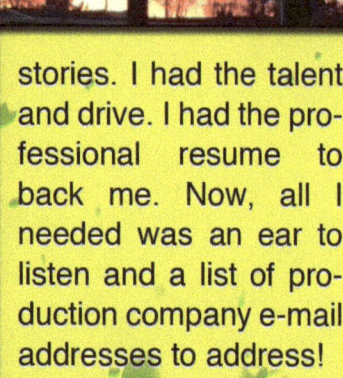

6

MY 1980s

Starting a decade off with *The Empire Strikes Back* is about as good a launch as you could dream of. The Force made my love for all things pop-culture grow even stronger. Infatuation for the continued *Star Wars* saga only led to an appetite for more geek-laden treasure hunting. *G.I. Joe, Transformers, Indiana Jones, He-Man, PAC-MAN, Ultraman,* and *Superman* all started shaping this man. The WWF turned sports into pop-culture for geeks and aspiring jocks alike, and you didn't bleed red American blood if you didn't like Hulk Hogan, Roddy Piper, "Hacksaw" Jim Duggan, Jake "The Snake," and the Macho Man. A few toys turned into serious action figure collections, traded in high-stakes neighborhood negotiations with friends, and envied by enemies. Football

and baseball players now came to life on cards that even came with awesome gum. I could trade away all of my stupid Dallas Cowboys and 49ers cards for those larger-than-life Seahawks stars and those coveted Dan Marino and Eric Dickerson rookies. Smurfs made the boring forest cool. Pole Position accelerated my desire to get a driver's license. Transformers were way more than meets the eye. John Hughes introduced me to girls, parties, and teenage issues I wasn't ready to face but felt more prepared for with his classic teachings of *Sixteen Candles, Pretty in Pink, Weird Science,* and a certain Club of Breakfast misfits. Ronald Reagan kept me safe from nuclear war, so I could keep playing war with my plastic army men and blowing up my G.I. Joes with firecrackers. Happy Meals made us all happy, but we weren't obese because we went outside and played until our parents called us in at dark from down the street. We would skateboard home as fast as we could like Marty McFly to a mall parking lot. We had school the next morning; well, all except for that lucky cool kid Ferris Bueller.

    I picked on my brother a lot, like all older brothers did, but I definitely did it out of love. I am still friends with most of his friends as well. Don't worry; my dad paid me back ten-fold when I was tattled on. My bare ass still fears the belt, and "if you cry like a baby it will only continue," my dad use to warn me.

(2nd from right, bottom row) Monroe Mustangs bench warmer (Eugene, OR)

I got absolute straight As throughout elementary and middle school. I am not bragging; in fact, I could have never done it on my own. It was only thanks to my mom helping me understand my homework every single night. A lesson to parents: school comes much easier when you teach your children by relating the material to subjects and ideas that only you know they understand. My mom put things in sport numbers or science-fiction movie terminology. Way to go mom—you're still smarter than all of us!

We moved to Bethel, Alaska, for a couple years in the early eighties. The family had to go where the work was, and my dad was a plumber, so to the pipeline boom we ventured. It was my first experience at trailer-park living, which I didn't mind. We even built rafts out of the garbage in the dump lake behind the park where everyone threw their trash, including dead pets and bio waste. I was the only white kid in my school—a "Gussuk," the Eskimos called me, which is a racial slur the equivalent to wetback or nigger. It was a harsh initiation into the cruel world of racism. Only my charm and awesome *Star Wars* collection kept me from getting my ass

(Left) My brother, mom, and I at our luxurious double-wide trailer in Bethel, Alaska, dressed in Goodwill's finest.

kicked daily. My brother and I grew even closer because we were all each other had in the village. That, and the beginning of MTV! Video truly killed the radio star for me. My dad worked his ass off, and eventually we left the trailer park in the rear view to resume life in Oregon like we never left.

Like most preteens of the eighties, I quickly discovered rock 'n' roll. My love for the sweet sounds of classic and classy electric guitar quickly turned to lust for the heavy, raunchy riffs of hair metal solos. No band would ever define me more than Mötley Crüe. They were the epitome of cool and rebellious. They got the hottest chicks and had tattoos and motorcycles. Every Mötley Crüe clipping that I could find became my new wallpaper. Ratt went "Round and Round" my eardrums and burned my hair-metal torch even brighter. Hall & Oates gave way to Guns N' Roses. I even adopted a crazy new sibling, a Twisted Sister! My priest was named Judas, and I was a powerslave to the sounds and artistic record covers of Iron Maiden. I broadened my musical horizons with the funky sounds of pouring "Purple Rain" and discovered my first sex symbol in Madonna. Duran Duran made me hungry for more new wave. And Yo, MTV rapped!

My first read of *How to Eat Fried Worms* led to Choosing my Own Adventures, which led to wanting to write my own adventures. And comic books just got cooler and darker!

I found skateboarding, which probably kept me out of a lot of trouble, as I treated it more like a sport than an excuse to hang out with the stoners and smoke cigarettes. I wanted to be the best and ride a half-pipe like the masters Tony Hawk, Steve Caballero, and Mark Gonzales.

In middle school my entrepreneurial spirit was born. I was heavy into skateboarding and already had a reputation for building the sickest skate ramps. My dad helped me at first, then I quickly caught on and would crank them out solo. I would find scrap wood around the yard or behind buildings, even steal from construction sites (don't tell my mom or try this, kids) to create the vert ramps to pull off Method Airs or Rocket Airs. We didn't have the luxury of skate parks back then; we had to make our own! I even built them for my friends. I was the architect for skateboarding aggression. At school I organized the first ever skateboard competition. I even planned it to happen during class hours like an assembly in the parking lot. My dad and I brought all the ramps and set them up. I scheduled the times with the principal and the rules for the skaters. I even drew pictures with my friends Steve Burnett and Dan Garriot to promote the event in the school newspaper (*pictured below*). We learned advertising by hanging flyers everywhere. It was so successful that we did it the next year too. It was the birth of my entrepreneurial inner self. It gave me the rush I needed to stay off drugs and realize that anything was possible.

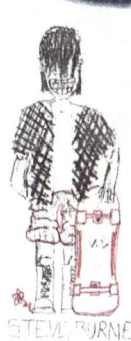

Later in the decade, I started working after school and on weekends for my dad. Not even a teenager yet, I learned the value of hard work and pride in a job well done. I had no choice in that matter; my dad made sure I possessed those ethics early on. I was an expert plumber before I hit middle school.

The end of the eighties delivered two pivotal moments in my own personal pop-culture geek life. The first crucial happening at the decade's end was the introduction of my brain to *The Simpsons*. It was not just a new TV show; it was a groundbreaking phenomenon that helped shape me as an artist, fanboy, and geek and made me a bit of a smart-ass. It helped me see that a lower-middle class family can still be cool, loving, and funny and accomplish great things despite their circumstances. The show was also more "real life" than just about any sitcom out there, and that's why it worked. People could relate to it because it was based around topics in their daily lives, packed with bratty kids, beer-drinking dads, and unappreciated stay-at-home moms. At first my parents, like most, wouldn't even let me watch it, but that just made it all the more appealing. Thank God they caved, because nothing since has single-handedly shaped my career and art style like that little Springfield family.

(Left) Simpson's creator Matt Groening signed this script for me with an original drawing and inscription about my tattoos that made life complete!

The second pivotal moment in my 1980s was when my favorite football player and my idol from my entire childhood, Steve Largent, retired. He was forever an underdog, undersized and slow. It was his never-give-up attitude and work ethic that made him the best. He outworked everyone else and gained that advantage. Seeing his dedication and work ethic was a precursor to the rules I would live my life by. Nobody again would live up to the idolization I harbored for that man.

I played football, baseball, and basketball. I did wrestling and karate. Those sports and teams laid the foundation of what and who I was to become. Football was my true love, but I was always too small to be any good. That never detoured me from trying my ass off though. I did karate for years. By age twelve I was the youngest brown belt in the state of Oregon, and my teacher had me poised for the junior Olympics. The only problem was that my dad constantly forced me to practice karate since I was so good at it, so naturally I hated it and wanted nothing more to do with it. A lesson to parents: forcing your child to play a sport will only push them further away from it.

I loved the 1980s. I still do. I think part of my soul will always be left in that time period. My childhood, my family, and the vibrant new pop culture were all exactly what I needed at the time to forge the mold of manhood.

(Right) Stylin' with my sweet Touch-of-Sun sprayed in blonde tips, 7th grade school photo.

7

HARD WORKING-MOTHER-FUCKIN MACHINE

There is only one way to get anywhere in life, and that's hard work. Luck is for the lucky and inheritance is for the spoiled, and both are assholes! The only destiny you have is the one you create for yourself. You can become a hard-working mother-fuckin machine, or settle for just being a robot!

Call it arrogance or bragging, I don't give a shit. I'm gonna call it truth. The reason I am where I am and what I am is because I outworked all the robots around me. I started earlier and stayed later. I dreamed bigger and aimed further. While they jacked each other off playing drinking games and building fake video game empires, I built my brand.

I actually wrote most of this book on

plane flights to tattoo and do TV appearances around the world. Simultaneously, I was writing two other books, starting a geek internet-dating site, building the nation's biggest tattoo comic con tour, and courting new networks for another TV show. You can't be a multitasker if you want to succeed; you need to be a supertasker.

First thing you need to secure is your home life. You will never finish first if you don't put your family first. Any distractions at home will turn your domination into fermentation. Being a hard-working mother-fucking machine (HWMFM) will ruin any relationship, so you either need to have the ultimate supportive partner, or be single. It's the harsh and selfish truth, and you can't do it somewhere in the middle. It's also not fair to a loved one who doesn't share your vision and passion. You can only be your best version of you if you are true to being the real you and not worried about someone hating or resenting you for it. The best version of me is only put forward when my wife (*pictured below*) is standing behind me.

Machines don't shut off until somebody shuts them down. You need to be more than a machine, and the only way to do that is by putting in the hours. The best athletes are the first at practice and the last to leave.

Case in point: when I won my prized Best in Show award, I was the first one at the convention and the last one finished! The guy I beat, Matt "Oddboy" Jones, was the second one at the show and finished just before me. We both put in the time, and it paid off.

Next, you need to notice local needs, demands, and voids, and be prepared on providing solutions for them. Be so prepared that you don't give people the option to say no to your new ideas! Warm up that machine before it needs to run hard.

When I owned a music store, I noticed that nobody really knew what new music was coming out and when. There was an informational void. I call that the ancient pre-iTunes time. So, I contacted the local newspaper and asked if I could write a weekly album review column with new-release- and top-selling lists included. Since I offered to do it for free and sent some samples of my writing, they would've been foolish to turn it down. I didn't give them the option to do so. Not only did this spark my writing career, but it was free advertising for my music store, which was all I wanted to begin with. You can have an angle behind any offer; you just can't expose

it or have it be your driving force. When I wasn't writing or working the counter, I was managing local bands to further spread my business network to include other local business and bar owners, thus forming relationships for cross-promotional opportunities.

When I read countless tattoo publications and saw very little to no stories actually written by tattoo artists from their industry-insider perspectives, I saw a need and an opportunity to expand my branding empire. I asked myself why there was so much shit by writers who had no idea what it was like to actually tattoo. Most of these reporters were covering conventions from the outside, never having stepped foot inside a booth and felt that pressure. How could they truly capture the essence and drama of the experience without having the experience? So, I fixed the problem. I sent a couple stories to the nation's leading magazine, Tattoo, and offered my writing services and experiences free of charge. I explained to them that they could get a much-needed insider perspective and coverage on topics that they might not have thought of. I'd also write to the general public about what tattoo artists were thinking and wanting and expecting from them. Once again this only built my brand bigger and solidified my reputation as a hard-working mother fucker in the industry.

One magazine company quickly spread to two, then three. Stories turned into regular monthly columns. Free columns turned into paying jobs. Before long I was writing for Germany's (and central Europe's) leading magazine Tattoo Spirit. For a year I had my own six- to eight-page centerfold spread called "Uncensored with Chris 51." I left the stories behind and started strictly interviewing other famous artists, asking them funny, raw, and risqué questions that nobody else would dare ask. And they answered because I was one of them, not just some nosy reporter who was gonna twist their responses to try and make something out of nothing. When the magazines hit the racks, I had famous artists with huge followings sharing their interviews. This of course totally helped spread my brand and reputation. That was the best cross proomotion that no amount of money could buy. *(Pictured)* below is a sample of Das Verhor, which translates to "The Interrogation."

My writing career was consuming nearly as much time at night as my tattoo career was by day. Before long I was putting out my own books.

The connections I made through all my traveling and writing allowed me the opportunity to publish my own book on nature-themed tattoos. It had never been done before. All tattoo art books up to that point were on the same old skulls and portraits. Nobody had ever focused on the softer side of the art, like flowers. Again, I saw a void and I filled it. I wrote *When Nature Calls* and my friend Bill Rhine did all the graphics. He killed it visually and made such a beautiful work of art. For a year I'd collected work from all kinds of artists and wrote stories on each of them. It was the first tattoo book to feature not just tattoos but also drawings, paintings, photography, and bios from any artist specializing in the genre. That book was actually my third, joining a poetry book that I wrote as a teen-

-ager and a football trivia book I self-published in 2008. The football book, Four Downs to a Pro Football Trivia Champion, was even a game that I invented while playing with my football card collection one night on the toilet. I wrote that book while I was writing my first letters to obtain sponsorships from tattoo companies and planning to open a second tattoo shop, all simultaneously.

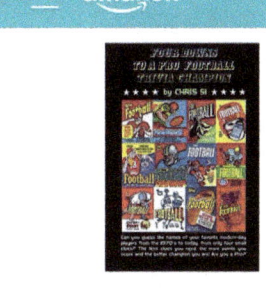

These are just some examples of what I have done in my free time while always having a full-time career. If you are satisfied with just having a job, then that is all it will ever be to you. But, if you put in the extra time to research, educate, and practice your craft, then you have the passion for a career, and it will always progress. Life will then always progress too.

You must also understand that everything you put out into the world will affect you down the road. If you want to waste your time screwing off or being lazy, then you will always have plenty of time being poor, unimportant, and unemployed in the future. If you want to constantly create art, music, or literature, then you create a symbiotic circle of production and income that will all feed off each other and maybe feed your family when you're old.

(Left) Due to release in 2017 will be my first comic book, adapted from a science fiction novel I wrote twenty years ago. It's brilliantly illustrated by my good friend Eddie Van Camp. and colored by the amazing James Mullin.

SLINGING INK

TATTOOS IN THE NEWS • REVIEWS • MUSIC • FASHION • RESOURCES • AND OTHER INTERESTING STUFF

TATTOO

I wrote a column for over a year for Tattoo magazine. My topics were based on everyday occurrences, problems, drama, business, and education around a tattoo shop and the industry itself. They were fresh and different and came from an actual artist's perspective; that's why they worked. It was all fuckin peachy until they wanted to start censoring my content, then it was time to part ways. Homie don't play by those rules!

Married To The Craft
By Chris 51

Tattooing is a relationship not a profession. It is the matrimony of monogamous dedication and motivation. There is no cheating. There is no separation or vacation from your vows. There is only a lifelong commitment to the addiction of creation, and that unfortunately can be a solitary road.

This conundrum is nothing new. I would like to think that there are plenty of other professions around the world that offer as much gratification as ours does, but who would I be kidding? Nothing is better than tattooing. Do you get pissed off when you have a sick day? Do you not know what to do with yourself when you are not tattooing, painting, or drawing? Do you spend more time at your shop than at your home? If you answered yes to any of these queries then you may have the same problem that I do. Let's call it what it really is. Tattooing is an addiction for some of us, and it can have dramatic side effects.

Chris 51 is about to get all emotional on yo ass, so if you are an overly sensitive, hopeless romantic, quasi-pussy like me, read no further. Otherwise, enjoy the pity of my ridiculously honest rant and please learn from my brilliant retardation.

Until the birth of my son two years ago, my life was consumed by one thing. I would like to say it was my wife, but after the embers suffocated, I saw what really propelled me. It was tattooing. My love, my passion, and my heart all belonged to my craft first and my partner second. I succeeded in everything I wanted to do in tattooing and much more, but I didn't realize that I was failing miserably at being a husband. Even if I had noticed my addiction, I probably wouldn't have cared. Tattooing had me by the balls, and I liked the way that mistress felt. Miss Tattoo gave me satisfaction beyond compare and fueled a drive that couldn't be matched by flesh and blood. She allowed me escape and stimulation that I couldn't find anywhere else, nor wanted to. The job was enough for me. It fed me, sheltered me, loved me, and praised me. Soon, it was the only one doing such things.

Then reality hit. My son showed me that there was more to life than just living for tattooing, but it was too late for my marriage. My addiction drove her away, and I hardly cared after so many years of putting her second anyway. The funny thing about addiction, though, is that it can graduate to a new high. My son provided the euphoria that I never knew existed in life. Tattooing for me turned into providing for my son. Painting by myself late at night morphed into teaching him to paint. My seduction by fame, fortune, and respect flat-lined and gave way to a new inspiration. All I care about now is that my son is one day proud of me. Every tattoo I do and bottle of ink I make is for his future, not mine. What a refreshing way to live. What a lesson learned. And the first thing I will teach my son is to never put your career ahead of your family.

SLINGING INK
TATTOOS IN THE NEWS • REVIEWS • MUSIC • FASHION • RESOURCES • AND OTHER INTERESTING STUFF

Building a Strong Clientele 101
By Chris 51

Are you tired of hearing baby artists today bitch about not having any work or not having all the fuller clients of a business rep that you have ensured through years of flight? Well this hard workin', good lookin', hope shoutin', candy lickin' son bitch is. So, I figured I would help the problem rather than feed the problem any longer. Mama tried to share spanking out the worms of jealousy into baby body beats.

Don't get me wrong. I'm not here to dog the younger pups of the industry in fact, a lot of the old school legends hate the fact that my procreations of education may offer the next generation of involved procreation a federation de futura illumination. Plus I'm all for artists. I'm not out of this very young class (over who I made it up alone to shop for, it's hot. Without further BS, I give you: Building a Strong Clientele 101.

First and foremost, hit the pavement! Tattooing old school dude. Your feet should have more blisters than Fred Flintstone after night hour. Nothing beats eye contact and social interaction when you are trying to sell a product. The product, which is yourself and your personality. YOU are the one that your work. If they like you, they will like you in your work. If they hate you, they won't even look at. Make a flyer or spring for particularly with photos of your work and a resume. Try 50% off of your first tattoo with me or something strong that will catch their attention and just set them in the door. At you have to do is get them in the door once and hit your personality and spirit sell the rest. If you are socially inept, good luck, go work for city bar with the rest of the card sucks. Walk up and blush your sexual history every supermarket, gas station, outhouse, doghouse, crack house, and whorehouse you come across. Make the public notice you and plans that seat that will one day grow in to a Venus fly trap. People remember grovelling and repetitions obsessions much more than, well, if you sit on your ass in the shop and get a late bag of doritos that they have never met. Plus, you will gain the respect of your coworkers for your crippling work ethic.

Yes Facebook is helpful, but a lot of us built a customer base bigger than Paris Hilton's without the use of any social media, so it is not a necessity. Do, it is a bonus if used and abused correctly. The biggest mistake community made is using just bad to convey your advertisement. And don't kick yourself, every year you make shitty tattoning is an advertisement for your product, too. You are an artist, act like one. Instead of slapping half off any tour this week, draw a dope tour that you want to do. If you take the time to draft and color a rose, people will take the time to look at it because it is now lovely art, if they can actually picture how it will look on their bodies, or maybe have friends that love who have the same tattoo about a rose and they can show their picture. Or, if you are limited on time, put together a portfolio type page of several things you have tattooed and say that you are dying to tattoo another one to your portfolio

and are offering a special deal on the first person to message you. All of a sudden it has become a sweepstakes and a challenge. Never post the same publicly though, or you will be expected to match that price all the time.

Thirdly, pick up the damn phone. Call your clients a few weeks after their procedure and ask them how it has healed. Don't ask if they were in urgent need money with you, just make sure their anxiety was well spent. Don't hype your office members do it, they want to hear your voice, this is the tattoo, the back the time out of your busy day to call them. A little time goes a long way and they will never forget it. People like nice people, and will resort or refer for the experience just as much as they will the artwork.

Take my words of advice for what they are. All artists aside, they do work and they will help you live your dream to the fullest.

SLINGING INK
TATTOOS IN THE NEWS • REVIEWS • MUSIC • FASHION • RESOURCES • AND OTHER INTERESTING

Keep Your Text Outta My Art!
By Chris 51

You know what drives Chris 51 crazier than Snickers using the term Fun Size to describe a mini candy bar (when we all know a true fun size would model a sofa) is when customers ask me to jack up a beautiful work of art by sticking writing in the middle of it. Did you see Monet put his girlfriend's or kids name in all of his Water Lilies? Did Picasso put the woman's initials in the Crying Woman's tears? I think not. And why you ask? Well I am here once again to drop a pound of knowledge on you (and I have plenty to spare). I will not just adhere to my standard scuttlebutt of bitching and complaining, but to offer some fresh alternatives to help persuade your clients otherwise, or at least a taste of bullsh-t to feed them, but it works. Please keep in mind that I am a realism artist, and test in traditional tattooing goes hand in hand like Oreos and milk.

It is scientific fact that the human eye focuses on text first in any picture. And this statement is one first thing I always tell my customers. I ask them why they would want a soft, beautiful, and colorful piece of art passed over by onlookers targeting in on the text. I further feed them the delicious question that entails going in to a museum and asking if they ever noticed writing in the middle of the paintings they liked. Some things just don't go together — chocolate and peanut butter do, text in realism tattooing doesn't. Next, I explain to the client that there is no way to be redrawn. I can almost guarantee that the flowers or butterflies they are getting (this scenario) are dedicated to a loved one). The art is enough said. You are already creating a part of your body and all of this story to put the thought of them on your body for the remainder of your life, and that is the purest and most sincere statement of love and remembrance you could ever offer anybody. Further question their motives of who is this for, them or the public. If it is for you then it doesn't need to be written out for everybody to see because you know what it means, and that is all that really matters, isn't it?

If they still don't concede, I take a final

drastic measure. I offer to do the desired writing or initials anywhere else on their body for free, as long as it stays out of my art. I have never made it past this option, but then again, I am a convincing son of a bitch. If my client still refused and was adamant about their desires, they would no longer be my client. I would kindly refer them

to an artist who didn't care about how shit looked. Snobby? Maybe. But I will never my artwork for a paycheck. I am in this because I love to create beautiful art, the is just a bonus that gets me by. If a client respect that kind of honesty and integrity, you really want them for a client? Just say...

SLINGING INK
TATTOOS IN THE NEWS • REVIEWS • MUSIC • FASHION • RESOURCES • AND OTHER INTERESTING STUFF

Tats & Talk

How To Not Be One Of "Those Guys" At A Convention
By Chris 51

And, by "those guys," yes, I do mean douchebags! The old Chris 51 is back with a new rant fresher than a Subway $5 Footlong!

I learned more going to conventions questioning and spying on artists that I admired then I ever did from my mentors. My stealthiness earned me more education than my apprenticeship ever did—and cost a lot less. I quickly learned that you must train like the gazelle before you can run like a lion. That being said, I have devised a douche-proof guide on to how to *not* be at a convention. Whether working or lurking, there are several types of artists that warrant this convention attention. Don't be one.

The Fashion Tool
This type of cute kitten belongs more in a Good Charlotte video than in a tattoo booth. You have definitely seen this cat before; he makes sure of it. With the ironed bandana fitted underneath the perfect 45-degree cocked hat, his carefully planned ensemble is completed by just-washed skate shoes and sparkly things that make me wanna go fishing. To complete the tool-time, he insists on wearing his sunglasses indoors because it is so damn bright inside the facility that it burns his retinas and the coolness will seep out of his eyeballs if they aren't well protected. We don't want to see this guy and we don't want to answer his questions because he looks like he is in it only to get laid or get paid.

The Trophy Whore
This slut of the silver and digger of the gold insists on proudly displaying all his trophies won at every show he has ever attended. Although it may be a beautiful buffet of acclaim, we don't give a sh-t unless it was won at the show we are currently at. Guess what else? Everyone is an award-winning artist, so quit printing it on your banner. I once won an award for a high school architecture project, so maybe I should brag about that on my banner, too. Put it in your portfolio if you must, or better yet, just put up the

picture of the award-winning piece and let the public judge for themselves so your fellow artists quit judging you.

The Apocalypse Packers
These herds are of the younger, less-traveled breed. After you show up with your one suitcase you can sit back on it, grab some delicious popcorn, and be entertained. It is like a U-Haul made love to an ant farm; lots of little worker ants marching in box after crate after chest full of sweet picnic treasures.

These bugs use more time setting up gadgets and gizmos (not the lovable gremlin variety) than they do tattooing. Unless they flew Southwest, I would like to see if their baggage fees equaled their profit margin.

Please don't mistake my (attempt at) comedy for bashing. As usual, Mr. 51 has a moral justification stronger than Mr. T's neck muscles. I simply want to drop some knowledge to help the younger players not make the same mistakes that so many of us have in this game. It takes a long time and a lot of hard work to earn the respect of your peers. You might as well know a few things that will help speed up that process. Always remember; like a Steve Largent or Barry Sanders' touchdown (non) celebration, act like you've been there to get there.

SLINGING INK
TATTOOS IN THE NEWS • REVIEWS • MUSIC • FASHION • RESOURCES • AND OTHER INTERESTING ST

Cherish Your Client
By Chris 51

I am gonna depart form my normal comedic, overlined, pop-infused antenna for a moment of solace and gratitude. I sat here at the Springfield Lutheran Church ready to enter my first funeral in more than a decade. Hell, it's my first church in more than a decade for that matter. Churches give me rashes, but I will endure the itchy discomfort to honor such a special person who touched my life.

Old Man Bill Snondrom was an icon around our stop. He was the 90-year-old kid with more life experience and wisdom oozing from his feet than most wear knew what to do with. But I looked that shit in. He was a fighter and a lover in more ways than one.

Born in 1920, back when America was barely a country, Bill survived what the others could. He was a Navy veteran who served in WWII and the Korean War. Yet in all of his military service, he never got a dreaded tattoo. As was a pilot to transport the wounded, yet still had no tattoos to show for it. He administered polio vaccinations to children in Africa. He tended with passion, Bill was one who had seen it all and was able to share something new to feel alive, or to get up living without it.

Bill walked into my shop at the age of 93, years young and immediately became the coolest man I had. The whole shop fell in love with him and he with the art. He came in biweekly with his social security savings, to put down deposits, until he had enough saved to start his next piece. Once charged him more than half price. I didn't have the heart. He never tipped me, and I would have never accepted it.

We began our friendship with a tattoo of a piece he once owned, on his shoulder. That artwork quickly grew into a whole native scene complete with teepees, a river, and even a warrior, which he loved so. The best part, though, was the shadow of a UFO behind some clouds on my old back seek to me he saw one in a fight, and I believed him. 1,000 percent. We talked about it often, and it was he became the "first magic that solidified our friendship. New tattoos per visit at my lovely daughter's receipting. He made me look good and. When his tears back was full, he told me he wasn't nearly done.

so we decided on starting a sleeve consisting of the passport stamps from his travels, which was extensive enough for probably two sleeves. He only got to do the first session on the sleeve.

Bill was late for my appointment. That never happened. In fact, he was always a good half-hour early because he was so excited. I knew right away something was wrong. My hope that hopes and immediately feared the worst. Bill would never miss an appointment. I called the sheriff to check on his place, even called his neighbor to look, but before I got a response, I almost knew I formed a lump in my throat so that of my eyes and his client waiting very serious. My office manager, Nina, was off to the printer. She would stationary that went in from one day prior. Everybody was quiet. I hoped I'd hear from him back to my own warehouse for some solitude. I was not alone. I cried.

William Snondrom had no idea of what it meant to love. Every time he mentioned his wife who passed years prior, he would cry in front of a room full of big, ugly, inktaking tattoo artists. He would cry, and cry proudly. I respected the shit out of him for that. We could all only wish we love so vividly.

Bill traveled the world through his stories about and rebellious adventures. Every time informed him of my next international contrast he would have a dollar wadded up to hand me, before. "Oh, you are going to be Philadelphia huh, well I was stationed there in my Navy days. Here's $5, have yourself ask anything then I did I went looked, at berated, not shit" town the street or that wheel because you will get mugged. I did way back in 1955, and I can tell it's worse now." Getting up from the tattoo table, Bill reached to his pocket, "Here, let me get you a long way outta there. Have fun." As he pulled out $10 to hand me. That was the last thing I'd ever said to me.

I will never forget Bill, nor will the many whose lives he touched by being himself. It makes me think of the rest of my clients, who are all some friends at this point. I need to take more time to appreciate them while they are here. They don't only have so much to teach but they can live as only their lives. I will never let another Bill slip away without them knowing how much I admire and appreciate them.

—Chris 51

SLINGING INK
TATTOOS IN THE NEWS • MUSIC • FASHION • RESOURCES • AND OTHER INTERESTING STUFF

Tat Talk

Sponsorships 101
By Chris 51

Work ethic? Where has it gone? Seems like work ethic has worked its way over to China. Is it because my fellow 30-something-year-old artists and I grew up doing construction, plumbing or other labor-intensive, hour-intensive jobs that we understand it takes hard work and sweat to succeed in this industry? Is it because most 20-something-year-olds today grew up on a steady diet of video gaming and Internet instruction to lack the intangible teachings of before school paper routes and after school, after football practice, after homework night jobs?

If I have one more young artist ask me for a sponsorship with one of my companies without a resume of accolades, list of references, or making me go through their Facebook pages to view their portfolio, I am going to go off. Okay, so I am going off! Class is in session.

Years ago, I became one of the first sponsorees of a popular ink company strictly through hard work and grueling promotional hours. Did I email the owner saying, "Hey, can you sponsor me?, you can view my work at this place; go ahead and take time out of your busy-ass schedule to go view my crap to do me a favor. Oh yeah, and can I get some free shit while you're at it?" No, I spent months putting together a portfolio explaining which colors I used in certain photos and why. I became an expert on the company's colors. Next, I printed every compliment that I received on my work about my colors from social networks and my responses explaining to the person who commented how it was using and suggesting they should try it. I included magazine interviews in which I gave the ink company shout-outs. I then wrote a long letter describing what I could do for the company and how much I believed in its product, never once asking for a single free item in return. I just thanked the company for making such a respectable product, and after I could be honored to hang its banner at my booth in conventions. Lastly, I mailed (yes, old-school by gasoline and white truck) all of this hard work to the owner. Within one week I got a call

and was offered a full sponsorship. This gave me motivation like ammunition. I started shooting off letters to companies that I believed in. More sponsorships followed with different companies, until I ultimately started some of my own. Now, I am the one who reads these letters.

Am I saying all of this to brag? Absolutely not. I am trying to help young, aspiring artists that actually have drive and motivation, because I see them out there and meet them in my travels. A lot of them deserve a sponsorship or endorsement opportunities; they just need to understand you cannot get one with text messages and emails. Your work doesn't just speak for itself anymore. You have to learn how to find an audience for it. You need to think outside the monitor.

Never ask for a sponsorship; rather, ask yourself what you can do for that company you want to sponsor you because that is what the decision-makers are asking themselves as they

pull hundreds of dollars worth of products off of the shelves to send you every month free or discounted. Earn the honor of a sponsorship, then learn to honor it by working hard to keep it.

Sponsorships are a gift of marketing genius that can benefit both parties involved. Owners understand this but are not only looking for the next big name, they want the soldiers that are working hardest in the trenches too, blowing up their company. You have to separate yourself from the lazy men's militia and give those generals of industry reason to recruit and promote you.

As brand names grow, star personas will grow with them at warp speed. Sponsorships are becoming more and more relevant in tattooing, and companies want consumers to associate their products with a popular face and name to live long and prosper. Even Spock would find the logic in that. If you don't agree with it, stay stubborn and get left behind as we all blast off.

Don't Cheapen What We Do

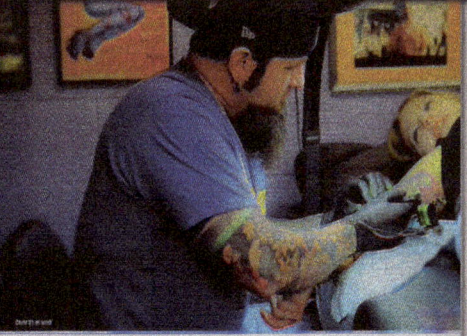

To con a classic Wholesale song, "Here We Go Again." OMG, remember the hot ginger slithering around on the car hood...holy sh-t. Okay, I'm getting off track. Here we go again, with another Chris 51 rant, but like usual and all PC Hammer references aside, I'm too legit to quit. Sorry about that visual.

I was on Craigslist the other day selling some awesome Star Wars stuff (so I could get some even awesomer Star Wars stuff) and I ran across an ad for a tattoo trade. That's right, a licensed tattoo artist from a local shop was doing some side trade for an X-box and all his home. I rather him not to his shop owner faster than a Kerry King guitar solo. If you want to trade your work for a toy that's perfectly fine, but don't take a scratchers approach and be shady about it. Check with your boss and offer to do it on your own time, like a day off or late night so it doesn't cut into the shop's walk-in availability or the building's rent money he is expecting. Don't be a d-chebag and cheapen what we do. Your skill is way more valuable than a quick classified ad of desperation.

I understand that the market is flooded with more shops than the radio is with Rihanna songs,

but that doesn't mean you have to undersell everybody either. Be a man and let your work determine the price you set, not the current market price. If you want to take nothing but flesh-seeking, heart-fetching bargain shoppers and never progress as an artist, then go ahead and lower them rock bottom prices. Advertise in your window for $20 fats and see how many lifelong clients you get and more importantly, where it gets you. Now I understand that apprentices need to do cheap tattoos to gain experience and there is no loss of respect in that, but don't cheapen what we do. Be the bigger man and call some local shops to set a common minimum price or call them out if you have to, just like another new Madonna record, this crap has got to stop!

Sure there are going to be arguments like; "Oh, Chris 51, what if I just opened my own shop and I need to do cheap tattoos to get business?" And sure, I might rebuttal with something like, and then I guess you aren't ready to open your own shop if you haven't been tattooing long enough to build a clientele or smart enough to promote yourself to acquire one. And some might say, well there is

key much competition I might snap back with your shop in such a or then work harder rather than feed it.

What happens if lowering his prices for movie that comes out and loses all respect to 9-pointers and doesn't reserved for relevant happens to you. You pay cheaper over what demand. Soon every getting his table sets here taken and step gets the shoves and your family for the roof raise and reputation want real art go. That own Oscar.

Unless you got in this industry to join make a quick buck and be cool, then there is no help for you anyway because you just don't understand what this is all about to begin with. —Chris 51

Other books by Chris 51.

Gemini Son (Paperback) 1993

Four Downs To A Pro Football Trivia Champion (Paperback) 2008

When Nature Calls (Hardback) 2014

Local native gets tattoo TV show

Chris Rohaley, better known as Chris 51, owns Area 51 Tattoo in Oregon

By Charles Runnells
crunnells@gannett.com

Chris Rohaley got his first tattoos in Southwest Florida. Now the Fort Myers native is a celebrated tattoo artist who's about to star in his own reality TV series.

Rohaley – better known as Chris 51 – owns Area 51 Tattoo in Springfield, Oregon. The new A&E TV show "Epic Ink" revolves around his tattoo shop, its geek-culture-loving artists and their realistic tattoos of fantasy/science fiction characters such as Harry Potter, Spock and Boba Fett.

"We're all a bunch of nerds," says Chris, 41, of Springfield. "And we're into Star Wars and comic books and all that stuff."

You can bet Chris's Fort Myers parents, Denis and Yvonne Rohaley, will be watching the show when it debuts Wednesday night. Most of Chris' family members still live in Southwest Florida.

"He's just a go-getter and we're very, very proud of him," says De-

See TATTOO » 3

Chris 51
Posted by Chris
July 2 · instagram ·

Thank you so much @funkoboss for the epic @popvinyl you made me. I love it. You are a true artist. #epicink #chris51 #area51tattoo

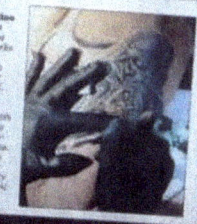

👍❤️ 2K   109 Comments 35 Shares

(Above) My favorite custom toy. This was made for me by Funko Boss, complete in my Star Trek Captain's uniform as seen in an Epic Ink episode.

The Register-Guard
Springfield, Oregon
WEDNESDAY, AUGUST 20, 2014

Hackers steal patients' data
Offices associated with McKenzie-Willamette Medical Center say victims of an attack from offshore

By Elone Alanisse
The Register-Guard

TV MAKES TATTOO INK A REALITY
First episode of a series featuring a Springfield artist airs today

HARD WORKING-MOTHER-FUCKIN ARTISTS

I'm certainly not the only hard-working motherfucker out there. It seems that when you are one, you subconsciously surround yourself with others who are too. It's that collective atmosphere that helps inspire you to do more and earn respect from the peers that you respect or emulate.

I have met several such artists in my career that have not only inspired me but helped shape my attitude and drive.

As a genuine artist, you naturally have that burning itch in your soul to create and keep creating. It never goes away. It's like a crazy stalking ex-girlfriend or a horrible case of genital herpes . . . only much more rewarding.

Before I sound like a total arrogant douche in the next lines, allow me to explain. I never look at other art and say, "Man, I want to do that." Art itself doesn't inspire me. What does inspire me is the time, dedication, and talent involved to create an artistic masterpiece. What inspires me is the sheer volume of work some artists have done in such a little time. These artists are the hard-working mother-fucking machines that I respect endlessly.

When I say that I pull no inspiration from other artists' artwork, I don't mean that disrespectfully. What I mean is that I just do what feels right in my mind only, and I purposely don't look too hard into other artists' styles and applications. I practice this because I want my art to be 100 percent me and influenced by nothing but life experience, the current world around me, or nostalgia.

When I say that art itself doesn't inspire me, I mean that I can't just look at an artist's painting and want to go paint. I am a slave to pop-culture nostalgia, so what inspires me is watching old Saturday-morning cartoons or collecting toys from my childhood. The vibrant shapes and colors do something to me way down deep in the adolescence of my soul. The creative juices must be released like a bad case of teenage blue balls.

I know a few artists that probably have similar practices and opinions. These are guys I have met through the comic con circuits who just pound the pavement and hit the studio all day and night, never giving up or slowing down. These are the same guys who I call my friends. They are the dudes I want the world to know about, if it doesn't already, because they deserve it. They are not only great artists but they are great people. Their moral makeup is as vibrant as their canvases.

Jermaine Rogers

Jermaine Rogers

Jermaine is a pioneer in the field of modern-rock poster art, designing work for hundreds of bands including Tool, Weezer, the Cure, David Bowie, the Deftones, and more. His artistic endeavors have been used by everyone from Verizon and Sony to Entertainment Weekly and even for labels on beer bottles. His work is on permanent display in the Rock & Roll Hall of Fame. To say he's a hard-working mother-fucking artist is a drastic understatement, and I respect the shit out of him.

Jermaine even helped mold the way for the vinyl toy collector's game. As early as 2003 he was designing figures destined to shape a whole new era of collecting and rebranding toy-culture phenomena. I'm talking ground-breaking shit that western artists had never seen. To date he has six major vinyl releases and countless other mini releases with leading companies like Kidrobot and Jamungo.

I have personally collected and idolized his art and style since the mid-1990s. I don't get inspired by many artists, as I have always just done my own thing artistically. Jermaine is the exception. His style is forever changing and progressing.

When Emilio, my set designer for *Epic Ink*, asked me for some art to hang on set, I immediately requested (demanded) that we first include work by Jermaine Rogers. I personally reached out to him via Facebook that very night and explained who I was and what I was doing.

To me he's a celebrity in the art field, so I was excited that he even answered my message. Like a little schoolgirl, I ran and told my wife right away when he said he'd be honored to contribute his work to my project. Before long we became friends, and we even started talking about tattooing him on an episode of the show. Unfortunately, our schedules never aligned to work that magical ink, but one day it will happen!

I have since become good friends with Jermaine and see him at comic cons from time to time. I still buy his work, even though he offers it to me for free, because you always have to support your favorite artists—and he's my favorite!

 @JermaineRogersArt

Keith Ciaramello

He will bust your balls, but he will also give you the shirt off his back. He's your typical opinionated New Yorker, but nothing of your typical tattoo artist. Keith has done it all in the industry and blazed new ground the entire way. He filmed a TV pilot before reality tattoo TV was a thing. He owned a pin-striping rat-rod business, made instructional DVDs, and ruled conventions while most of us were home discovering our little wieners.

Over the last twenty-three years, Keith Ciaramello has developed a reputation for vision, courage, and integrity and a commitment to the betterment of young artists. With a background in education and the arts, he possesses the rare ability to both DO and TEACH. His instructional approach breaks down complex concepts into practical information that can be immediately applied by artists on their creative projects. Keith's Tattoo Mentor Program has helped artists overcome struggles in art, marketing, and the business of tattooing.

Keith also hosts The Tattoo Podcast, which interviews the who's who of the tattoo industry. When not ruling the tattoo interweb waves, he's holding educational painting seminars and getting busy with his own brushes.
www.tattoosbykeith.com

Rob Prior

Rob is a fucking machine. He even paints like a machine, working with brushes in both hands simultaneously. I swear you've never seen anything like it. It's pure entertainment; in fact, he often paints live on stage during concerts with bands like HELLYEAH and Shinedown. He's not just ambidextrous— he's ambidangerous*, combining genres of movies, comics, and iconic pop-culture deities with ease. When he's not touring the country and painting live at comic cons, he's designing album covers and art for bands like Linkin Park, Shinedown, and Tech N9ne or creating licensed *Star Wars* movie artwork.

I've worked no fewer than fifty comic cons with Rob, and he never stops! He's always painting, promoting, doing event press, and even finding time to hit the hotel gym in between. He truly is a beast, and I respect the hell out of him for it.

I had the honor of working live on a Batman painting with him at the Heroes & Villains Fan Fest show in San Jose. I do art every day of my life, and even I was a little intimidated to be holding a brush next to this modern legend. Hope I didn't fuck up his painting too much—sorry Rob!

www.RobPrior.com

Shad Nowicki

I was strolling through a Wizard World Comic Con in Philly and got a giant artrection* (art erection). The cause of my awesome boner was Shad's booth. I knew nothing about this dude but instantly knew that we were long-lost brothers from a Hanna-Barbera mother!

He reminds me a lot of myself. Neither of us had any formal art training. We are just fueled by the power of cartoons and geek-culture, throwing any art composition "rules" to the wind without a care.

Shad has such a unique way of creating his art. He adds vintage materials such as comics, advertisements, and retro product packaging relating to the subject for his backgrounds. I definitely suggest following him for a daily dose of nostalgic smiles.

To say he's a hard-working motherfucker is a sick understatement. I wake up every day to see some insane new Super Friends or Star Wars painting he did through the night. I swear he paints while he sleeps. Shad creates art daily, whether it's just a sketch, a complete new pop masterpiece, or even a painting on the back of a damn pizza box. Add to that a busy comic con schedule and all his commission work, and he's easily earned my respect.

@Shadpaints

9

EPIC INK
(Take 2)

For once I got completely lucky. I should have pushed the envelope and played the lottery on the day I got the most important e-mail of my life.

I was on a layover on my way to *Star Wars* Celebration Germany when I got the e-mail from the Matador Production company rep. He stated that he had heard of my ink company and seen my work, all related to sci-fi themes. He asked if I would be interested in a TV show idea that he had about a geeky sci-fi-themed tattoo show. As you can imagine, my jaw dropped to the floor, and my boner burst out of my pants! I somehow knew in my heart that it was no hoax and got an instant gut feeling about my future with Matador. Funny thing is, Josh Bodwell got the same e-mail, and he texted me about it right away, knowing it was just our cup of proverbial tea. I said to him, "I got this, you trust me right? Don't worry I'm already on this, dude, I'm ready for this." That was the God's honest truth. I was more ready than even Matador was prepared for! As you read previously, I had the entire turnkey package ready to go!

I replied to the Matador rep, "No fuckin way, dude. A show about geeky sci-fi tattoos? I have the same idea except it expands to encompass all of the geeky genres, not just sci-fi." I further explained how I had an entire cast picked out (which I hadn't confirmed with any of them yet), a shop made just for filming, and even stories and plots prepared. He wanted to see everything I had prepared immediately. I quickly called my wife back home to get on my computer and e-mail me all the files that I had been so intently working on for six months. I had a four-hour layover, and by God, I was going to nail down this show in less than that! From my iPad in that uncomfortable airport chair, I sent Sam, the Matador rep, everything he would ever need to pitch a show and more. The cast bios and photos, storyboards, graphics, tattoo portfolios, resumes, shop photos and the essays on the cast's roles all got to him with time to spare. While I was awaiting his reply (if any), I contacted my cast individually. I told them about the outside chance of this possibility and asked if they would be interested if it came to glorious fruition. Josh said, "Of course;" Chris Jones bitched a little but was in; Jeff said, "Whatever you need, cuzzo, I am down;" and Heather replied with an enthusiastic, "DUH!"

(Above) With my Epic friends at Star Wars Celebration Germany, just one day after I returned the e-mail about using them as the cast in a TV show . We were already a tight crew long before the show would ever see the light of day.

"I was honored when Chris 51 called and asked me if I wanted to be on a show he might be making. I said yes immediately, then almost had a panic attack because the thought of being on TV was overwhelming!" recalls Heather.

Just before I boarded my last flight to Germany to geek out for the weekend, I got the reply. Sam was so impressed and enthused that he informed me his search was over, and he would take all my ideas to the powers that be for presentation.

"When Chris 51 showed up in Essen, Germany, the first thing I was excited and anxious to speak to him about was the 'cold call' e-mail we received. When Chris told me earlier that he had received the same e-mail I told him to e-mail them back, tell them we are talking together on this, and I'm down with whatever you guys cook up. If anyone could seal this deal I knew it was Chris 51," remembers Josh Bodwell.

So there you have it. I was so prepared for Sam's e-mail that I wasn't even giving him an option to say no. If this show was going to happen, there was no way that I wasn't going to be involved. Ah, the benefits of working hard, being prepared and being responsible. You must manifest your own destiny.

In the end, before I could ever send my first TV-show pitch via e-mail to any production companies, one got a hold of me instead. But, little did I know of what was to come. You cannot prepare for something you don't know exists in your world. My life would soon change for the better and worse.

But did I rest or hold my breath? Fuck no! I started writing storylines and plots between doing tattoos at the *Star Wars* Germany convention. I began making lists and notes of what to do to the shop to prepare it as soon as I returned. I was already preparing like I had the gig because in my mind I did!

By the time I got off the plane, I had an iPad full of ideas and to dos. I had a dozen hours of TV-production research under my belt just from the flight and was about to dive into a dream head first without checking the depth. And I didn't give a shit if I surfaced with stiches or leeches stuck to my balls; I was gonna swim for the stars and nothing was going to hold me back.

10

DO YOUR BUSINESS

Get all up in my business; I don't care, I got nothing to hide. And I'm confident that in the end my business experiences might actually help you with your own. And let's face it: if I didn't want you all up in my bidness, I wouldn't have written this book, right?

Allow me to preface with a reminder that I am an alpha male to the extreme. I don't like people bossing me around, and I think, actually I know, that I can do their job better than them, so who are they to give me orders? There's no worse feeling than the belittlement of knowing you are smarter and harder working than your superior.

I worked at a Pizza Hut as a college kid once, and we ran out of pizzas every night and had to borrow them from another store because the manager was too cheap to risk having waste. What he didn't understand was that he was losing customers to Domino's down the road because his delivery times got out of control. Rather than rushing out pizzas, we spent our late nights waiting on some unreliable college kid to drive across town and borrow pizza dough from their sister restaurant. I finally had enough, and proceeded to point out why business was declining and that common sense would tell him that the cost of an extra batch of dough far superseded that of paying an employee the wage and fuel to drive across town. I came in for my shift the next morning and saw that I was totally removed from future schedules. I guess he didn't like being called out by a nineteen-year-old . . . or the fact that I called him an idiot. I found out later that he was fired too. Karma, bitch!

The whole point is, if you don't follow your business dreams, you are going to live that Pizza-Hut life, and that's no life at all. That's just being sheep. Eat the sheep on a pizza—don't be the sheep. I must add, though, that I went on a date with this super-hot waitress from that Pizza Hut named Catarina Felix; no lie, her legal name was Felix the Cat. How cool is that? So in the end, you can always take away some good from any bad situation.

As the *Point Break* legend Bohdi would say, "Fear causes hesitation, and hesitation causes your worst fear to come true." If you fear starting your own business or taking a chance at your dream, then what will happen? Nothing! And nothing is the worst thing that can happen to somebody. Nothing gets you nowhere. Nothing will make you regret not facing fear for the rest of your boring life. Nothing is safe, and safe is taking orders from a moron boss at Pizza Hut.

Ask yourself: what is the worst that can happen? Failure. . . sure. But you can take pride in the effort and respect yourself for having the courage that ninety five percent of your peers don't. You invest in your education by learning from your mistakes and trying differently next time. You invest in yourself, and that's a safe bet. There's no shame in going back to delivering pizzas until you save and plot for your next goal.

The following subchapters will give you ideas and examples of how I conquered my employment demons, and hopefully they'll motivate you to face yours. Allow them to inspire or ignite you, or even piss you off enough to prove me wrong out of spite and do it your way. I don't care either way; just react and do something about your situation. Quit aiming for the corner bar each Friday and chase that gold bar!

PERSONABLALITY

It wasn't a real word before, but I just made it one. Damn right! It's the only way to describe this chapter. It's what you need to possess to get places in life. I didn't get to where I am on just talent; in fact, I probably have less natural artistic ability than many of my peers. It wasn't luck either, because all I've seemed to have is shit luck. It's about hard work and personality. It's about working hard on your persona. And it's about being personable with others (i.e, personablality!).

All of my long-time friends with successful careers have one thing in common. It's certainly not intelligence, or they wouldn't be hanging out with me. They didn't go to prestigious schools, and many never even graduated college. What they do have are personality and a great persona. They are personable with everyone they come across. They are likable. They are witty and funny. They are infectious to be around. Add all of that together and you get a lethal weapon in the workforce.

It doesn't matter how smart you are, or how good you are at a job; if you're an asshole, nobody wants to work next to you. Nobody does favors for douche bags and nobody recommends dickheads for advancement. People want to spend time working next to people they like, people who make their day happier and shorter so they can get home to their families or hobbies.

Yes, I got to where I am through hard work. I preach it and believe in it. But there are different categories of hard work. Working on your trade or skill set is just part of the job. You have to work equally as hard, if not harder, on yourself. YOUR PERSONABLALITY IS WHAT SELLS YOU.

I have always stressed the importance of this to my employees. From day one I explain to them that no matter how good your tattoo work becomes, people come back to you for your personality. It's the sad truth that you could be the best artist in the world, but that doesn't matter if you don't know how to carry yourself and impress others with your personality. People are attracted or repulsed by living, breathing people, way before they see the pages of a portfolio. Connections are immediately formed through eye contact, smiles, and trust. Clients may come into your business because of its reputation, but they stay or leave because of YOU!

I am the first to admit that there are a million artists more talented than me. I have no delusions of grandeur. But I am also confident enough to admit that I might be more talented than a million artists when it comes to customer service, business, and self-awareness. If you can't talk to clients and understand their needs, or put yourself in their shoes, then you haven't got a prayer. If you are so self-absorbed that you think your work will speak for itself, then you are delusional. You have to speak for your work, and you have to be funny, articulate, and captivating when you do so, or nobody will give a shit.

Like it or not, you are also a brand. Your persona is your best sales tool. It's your resume, reputation, portfolio, and appearance all wrapped into one fragile fucking bow. You have to treat it as such, or it can ruin you as fast as it makes you. Your brand is the only thing you have complete control over, but once it's labeled it's very hard to change it.

My brand started out as the "nice-guy people's artist." I always smiled and never showed anger or aggression. I always immediately replied to clients on social media and was a man of my word. I added entrepreneurialism to my repertoire by constantly trying new things and including my clients in them, asking their opinions and utilizing their suggestions. I gave away free products that I promoted to keep my clients involved in future projects and products. I found that what people want most from you is your time. Then again, they also like free shit (haha). Take the time to listen to them and to respond to them positively. Eventually this brand of mine secured a TV show, which suddenly put my brand in the national spotlight to be judged 10,000fold. I had to be even more careful and always conscious of where my brand was at every given moment so it didn't stray.

Even when my reputation and brand multiplied immeasurably, I still held strong to my roots that built the foundation of it so many years prior. I still respond to all social media as quickly and positively as I can. I still involve fans and clients in my projects and listen to their opinions and suggestions. It takes a lot more time now, but it has secured me the most loyal audience I could ever dream of. I feel like I have 50,000 friends, not fans! Now my brand has elevated to a geek ambassador, or as I like to say, "Artertainer," for uniting the worlds of tattooing, art, and entertainment.

I have even become a positive role model to younger aspiring artists and children searching for career paths. I get letters asking for advice, and I love responding. I have become a teacher and a motivator. People actually care about what I have to say, and you know why, because they know I care about what they have to say. No matter how busy I am or what I'm doing, I listen and I treat them as the equals they are. Those practices are the foundation to having both a good business and good life.

(Photos) Just a few of the Epic fans that I have met. Whether they became clients (top), laughed at me on TV (middle), or the Pitmaster at Cooper's who made me the best BBQ ever, I care about them all.

MARKET THAT MOTHERFUCKER

Marketing 101 is defunct. Welcome to Marketing 2017. This is outthinking and redefining the standard Marketing. This is privileged rich-kid-classroom lecture turned into real-life-survival-experience Marketing. This is "we are here to fuck shit up" Marketing.

You may have noticed that I so cleverly overuse and abuse pop-culture references more than Chris Brown, James Brown, and Bobby Brown do to women, but that's the genius of it. You must get in touch with your demographic down to the root levels of their true loves. Because like it or not, silly and inconsequential shit does matter. Movies, TV, comics, music, toys . . . all of it represents an important piece to our puzzled culture, and even the slightest recognition of it can spark fond memories in your client's mind. Nostalgia sells.

Comedy also sells. Alternative and controversial sell too. Depressing, un-unique, repetitious, and conservative do not anymore. What you need to do is shave your balls so they can see clearly and lead you towards the vagina of success. Time to get in touch with your balls (lol, I said touch your balls) and your clients (don't touch them). Time to use your time to bull's-eye your target demographic's interests and current trends.

I started a tattoo ink business from the ground up strictly out of spite. I was literally disgusted with the lack of artistic ingenuity and creativity involved in an industry that was solely aimed at selling their products to the exact demographic that is creative and artistic for a living. If I saw one more plain label next to the other plain labels from other boring brands with the same goddamn baby-blue, lime-green, yellow-ocher, and bright-red names, I was gonna freak out. I saw a need.

So I did something about it! I started my own company! I ran contests for tattoo artists to design graphics and included the very people I was selling to without them realizing they were being sold to. Not in a devious way, mind you, but in a family way. When somebody feels like they are a part of something they take pride in its growth and success. I enlisted the help of my graphic-guru friend Bill Rhine who was an amazing tattoo artist in his own right. He poured his heart into the company graphically and is responsible for bringing all of my ideas to life visually. I then sponsored some up-and-coming artists and gave them their own color to name and brand. When your soldiers have a voice in "their" product, they defend it until the end and promote it out of pride, not necessity. Suddenly you have free word-of-mouth social media advertising blowing up, and all you did was respect your customers and keep them on your level and involved. In just two years I became one of those big dogs, and had the fastest growing ink company in the business.

The success of my ink sales opened doors for manufacturing and marketing other products. I researched companies in Europe and China to make my own brand of tattoo needles. That quickly led to selling tattoo supplies. Before I knew it, I was in the packing and shipping business, spending my days tattooing and my nights boxing up orders to send around the country.

I then marketed my products all over the world, reaching to distributors in every corner of every country. I would offer huge discounts on their initial orders and provide custom, eye-popping graphics for their websites.

Everything begins with a unique product. If yours doesn't stand out from the crowd, it will get lost in it. Realize what makes your product different from the rest, and then market that motherfucker like there's no tomorrow.

COMEDIC INFLUENCE

Consumers are looking for something different today, anything that stands out from the boring norm. I asked myself, what makes people pick up a bottle of anything? Vivid colors and catchy graphics get it noticed, and laughter gets it into the cart. With so much misery in the real world, people like things that make them happy. A funny company is a happy company that they can trust.

I looked at the status quo and gave it a big middle finger! I took their traditional baby-blue ink and named it Smurfis Dermis (Smurf skin). I took that lime green and called it Granny Panty Smith (like a Granny Smith apple color, with a pair of old granny panties on the label). I turned yellow ocher into Crack Rock, and bright red became Baywatched. I mean, what else could refer to Baywatch than a beautiful pair of giant breasts in a "bright red" bikini on the label, right? If you can laugh at yourself and not take yourself too seriously, others will join in, and open their wallets with a smile. Why have just teal or aqua when you could brand it Mystery Van after the famous Scooby Doo dope ride? Everyone associates that color with that van,

and they get a chuckle out of it. What color do you think of when you hear the old 1980s' slogan, "Where's the beef?" I think of a bloody red piece of meat, and that's exactly the color I made to represent it. Some of my colors weren't even conceived until after I thought of their catchy names, then I had to engineer the matching description.

Comedy sells, and sells well. People love to laugh because there isn't much left to laugh about these days. So when you take a random and tedious task like buying hair gel or shampoo before you get home to cook, sleep, and repeat, you may want to consider adding some spice to that rack of bland monotony. If you simply see product names that make you chuckle, you are going to pick them up first. First impressions are everything in business because you rarely get a second look when the product or service next to you is the same price but looks cleaner, more vibrant, or more appetizing. Presentation is everything! I am sure I will say it again, but that's good, since it should be embedded in your head like a good Tay Tay song.

With products, looks matter! I thought about my products like a sexist pig would. Were they beautiful or appealing? Product presentation is innocent manipulation.

Sure, it takes a shitload of more time to design 51 individual labels, all customized to each bottle of ink color. Sure, it is more expensive and stressful. But it sells. And wait, aren't we doing this to make money? So you have some late nights at first and have to work overtime at your old job to start your dream a little later. But you know what a big splash is—it is the water that slapped the little splash in the face and drowned him. If you aren't going to come out big like a porn star, then stay a virgin.

I was in the art business, so I made sure to have the funni-

-est, flashiest, most vibrant, and most noticeable ARTISTIC labels on the market. And it worked. The traditional artists who turned haters at the big "fuck-you" monkey wrench I threw into the industry machine turned to supporters when I invited them to help design my next label. My name and reputation as an individual and owner skyrocketed. I used that to my advantage and personally answered every e-mail and phone call from my customers to once again maintain that respect level. Respect sells too!

PRESENTATION IS EVERYTHING

If you are going to cut costs by using cheap bottles or packaging, it will make even the best product appear cheap. I call it the wine-bottle theory. What wine do you always gravitate towards first? Yes, the fancy-shaped bottle with the bright killer artwork on it. Amazing how the right packaging can make even a mediocre product the right choice for the customer.

Every time I displayed my ink at trade shows, I made sure to have rows of it available on step shelves. I only had 51 colors to compete with other brands' hundreds, so I had to make mine appear grander than they really were. It's all an optical illusion, really; the more product you have out, the more choices customers think they have, even if it's a repetitive product in different size options. A little extra investment on a huge vivid banner, some table spotlights, and internet coupon flyers, and the return could multiply dramatically.

The same extra attention to detail is necessary in all avenues of presentation. Whenever I released a new color to the market, I didn't just show a picture of it and ask people to buy it. I made an artistic flyer that had a humorous detailed description of the color explaining what it was about, needed for, or named after, with a funny or risqué anecdote to seal the deal. I sent out free bottles to artists, and in exchange, they'd share the ad on social media. That's going the extra mile for your customers. It takes a lot of personal time, and that's exactly why they want your product, because it shows that you invest yourself and your time into every bottle. When you truly care about its quality and presentation, your supporters will too..

CONTROVERSY IS THE NEW LOTTERY TICKET

I had the first ink company to put profanity on the label. Everyone else called a peach a peach, but I named it Fuckin' Peachy. Which do you think sold better? I was the first to put a pair of women's scantily clad boobs on a label. I called one of my sets the Criminal Color Set because it featured colors like Bobby Brown and O.J. Call it bad taste; I call it truth—and profit. I was the first to put silhouettes of big black cocks on my

labels to describe the hardness or softness of my blackwash mixes. The four bottle set ranged from *Soft* to *Rager*! They sold to way more people than they pissed off, and that's exactly what I was after . . . well, maybe a little of each. I even went as far as creating an exclusive color, available only in the UK, called God Save The Green with a Sex-Pistols-esque reference of the Queen on it.

When Richard Sherman of the Seahawks tipped the ball away from Michael Crabtree in the playoffs to advance his team to the Super Bowl, he let everybody know it. He got cocky and proud and said he was the best and

Crabtree was mediocre. Guess what, he spoke the truth at that instance, and became on overnight sensation. He was chastised and he was loved—either way, he was known. And, he will be taking those comments to the bank to cash his next huge contract and endorsement deals. He had the balls to give his product (himself) a spark of controversy and uniqueness over the other products in the league, and it paid off. His sales and stock went through the roof. He's one of the smartest and most efficient self-marketing athletes I have ever seen.

The whole point is to get your shit noticed! Get it noticed for some controversy if you have to, just get it noticed. If you don't, then what happens? Nothing. And nothing is worse than nothing. Try and stay classy, but be different. Be the fuckin monkey-wrench thrower.

People are tired of conservatism. They want realism. Old timers are just that now—old timers. They have no money to spend anymore anyway. The Tattoo Age doesn't give a fuck and is proud to be anti-establishment. They want a service that is on their level and thinks like they do. Olive drab was grandma's color—yours is Electric Matrix green! So paint that shit over everything and have conviction while you do it. That will get you respect, and respect sells.

I know I talked a lot about one of my old companies, but shit, it's what I know and how I learned. Let me give you some examples of other business ventures and how to throw that monkey wrench in the status quo. Remember, if you don't try something new, what happens? Nothing. And nothing sucks balls. Even if you fail, you will be proud to say I tried it my way and I gave it my all, and I'll get them on the next venture.

SAY IT AND DISPLAY IT

It amazes me how much shit you discover about a new product or service only after you have bought it. Had I known that Joe's Generic Plumbing used the finest plastic fittings made with recycled material that kept waste out of my local landfill, adding to the green consciousness of my community, I would have chosen him in a heartbeat over the competition. Even if the fittings were a few bucks more. The bottom line is not always the bottom line. People want more today. They want to know that in this Tattoo Age of crime and greed, there is still an honest hand-shaking businessman out there they can rely on. Even if Joe's plastic fittings were the same damn ones that all the other plumbers used, Joe was the only one smart enough to appeal to his customer's personal side, not just his own business side. Joe did his research and found out that the fittings were actually partially post-consumer goods, so he could legally spew his sales pitch. On top of that, plumber Joe's work van had a killer paint job, and it was the only one washed clean daily. That translates to Joe taking his dirty shoes off before entering my house. Have I ever said presentation is everything? Hell, I would even put writing on my truck that says, "I have the cleanest truck in the business cause I'm the cleanest guy at the dirtiest job!" Bam!

RISQUÈ ISN'T ALWAYS TOO RISKY

Cupcakes. Imagine, if you will, two cupcake shops side by side. Both have bomb-ass deliciousness within. One is called Cupcake Heaven, with lace and doilies in the window, a two-foot wide antique sign hanging above the door, and an iron filigree table out front. The other is called The Orgasmic Cupcake, Debbie Does Cupcakes, or Cupcake Revolution. Big vinyl graphics in the window show a hot tattooed chick, of the classic strong-arm symbol Betty Blowtorch, popping out of a cupcake while holding up a cupcake. Under it reads, "Low-Calorie Diets not welcome, lol." Out front is an old church pew painted hot pink with dancing cupcakes all over it. Hmm, which one am I going to. One is boring and safe. The other is daring and alternative, and I bet their cupcake flavors and recipes are too. Again, PRESENTATION.

I would take it ten steps further and have a collection of

gaudily framed cupcake art, from photography to cupcake tattoos, strewn about everywhere. I would sell custom-made cupcake jewelry made by my partner. Offer cupcake shirts and hoodies, even make some crafts out of cupcake material I got at the local fabric store. White walls inside, fuck no. I'm going sea foam, pink, and purple. White walls are for doctor's offices and the other cupcake shop you are soon putting out of business. Truth is, your cupcakes don't even have to be as good as safe old Ethel's, but nobody will give a shit, because they want to hang out at the hip and hot cupcake spot.

EMBRACE YOUR POISON AS PASSION

Vapor Cigarette shop. Call it what you want, but your'e still a smoke shop. Embrace that shit. Put pictures of famous actors and rock stars smoking all up in there. Don't hide it; flaunt it. If you worry about politically correct when you are trying to sell a cancer-causing product disguised in a new and improved format, then you are worried about the wrong thing, homie.

Why call it Vapors Unlimited when you could hook people with just a name like Kick Your Ash, or Butts are for Staring Not Smoking. Risqué and controversial? Exactly. Noticeable and memorable? Absolutely. On the front window reads, "We smoke the completion," or "A pack a day is so yesterday." Why name your flavors the same titles in which they are purchased? You are the owner, the captain, the store god, so change that shit. Appeal to local interests, sports, activities, fame, etc. I would rather buy Death Valley Melted chocolate if I was at a shop in southern Cali than plain old chocolate. Or what about Packed Fudge—that is some funny shit that plays on some paranoid gay hysteria. If I owned a vape shop in Seattle, I would name a flavor Twelfth Man Green & Blue-berry in a second over just lame blueberry. Give them not only what they want but what you would want!

SOCIAL MEDIA QUICKSAND

Social media is awesome and has changed the entire landscape of small business advertising. There are definitely tricks and tips for advertising that route, which I will go into soon. But remember, nothing beats good old-fashioned hitting the streets with coupons, and cross promotion with neighboring local businesses. If your neighbors don't know you, you will sink faster than Lindsay Lohan on a relapse.

I would personally hand deliver a fresh cupcake to every owner on the street where I was opening my business. Furthermore, I would give neighboring business owners gift cards for their family and kids. Ask for a stack of their business cards, but don't ask for anything in return; remember, they are established and you need the help, not them. When they come in and try your orgasmic cupcake they will offer to take your cards, or you can gently offer them a stack of coupons (that you had already made, ready and waiting!) for their loyal customers and employees. Your respect and reputation in the neighborhood will blow up faster than a mob snitch's car.

Now you are ready for social media, but never stop hitting the streets. People like to see the legitimacy in people's eyes if they are gonna spend their money, and they will respect that the OWNER himself is out on the streets. It screams volumes of respect and hard work to other hard-working blue-collar folk.

The first friends I "unfriend" are the ones constantly shoving shit down my throat. There are ways to advertise like a motherfucker without looking like one. Be smart, use your head. What would make you get involved in a local business, or at least tell a friend to? Start by running a contest. Appeal to all local artists and designers to create your shop logo. It doesn't matter if you already have one picked out that you love—they don't have to know that. Word will spread; people will get involved. Most importantly, the buzz will begin. Keeping the buzz is the hardest and most important thing to do. Like a horny bee, that buzz must stay constant. Run your campaign between six to nine, prime time, so the customer base with the most potential can see it as they are settling on the couch or into bed for the night. This is when they really pay attention.

Okay, got your three-week logo contest done. Now on to a "name-that-local-flavor" or "I-need-a-popular-local-flavor" contest. Before you know it, hundreds of people are talking about your business without you uttering one word of advertising. They are even excited for you and support you. Why? Because they all feel involved. You brought the business to the people and offered them something, without asking for any business at all. You just had a solid month of free buzz that you would pay hundreds or thousands for on local radio, but with much better longevity in return.

Even though social media is an important and vital tool in marketing your business, it can become quicksand if it's the only ground you stand upon.

YOU ARE YOUR BUSINESS

Make no mistakes about it, like it or not, you are the face of your business. YOU are who everybody wants to see and who everybody wants to talk to. People feel privileged and respected when they can communicate directly with the head honcho. Everything you do and everything you wear reflects directly upon your business.

Personal appearance is the first round of the presentation fight. If you look sloppy, your service or food will look sloppy before you even turn a wrench or preheat an oven. If you are clean-shaven with styled hair and white teeth and wrinkle-free clothing, you are already ahead of the curve. Then kill them with kindness. Your product or service is a direct extension and representation of you and your persona. If people want to buy dirty shit from a sloppy asshole, they will go to the government, lol.

Employees are a whole other bloody round in the fight for independent business success. The employees you hire are a direct representation of you as well. They are a personal extension of you and your choices and your judgment.

If someone with tweeker teeth serves me a Danish, it becomes a dirty, nasty Danish. If someone uses profanity the whole time behind the counter, I won't ever bring my kids there, and if it's not inviting to my kids it's not inviting to me . . . or over half the local population. Get the picture? The picture needs to be painted as a pretty and inviting picture!

Nothing drives me crazier than a couple employees having a stupid convo when I'm in need of help. I refuse to let them finish, and I'm not polite when I interrupt them. I get all up in there and butt right in with authority. They are there to help me buy shit, which in turn is the only thing that will help pay them a salary. It is not me who's rude, it's them, and I have never had one say otherwise. It kinda makes them feel stupid, and that can be fun too. Then I look for the poor boss who is losing money and business with his or her shit-for-employees (or soon-to-be empoorees*), and I let that boss know. If you aren't going to take your job seriously or have some pride, then make way for somebody who will!

Manners and social skills are a defense you cannot survive the fight without. When you argue and yell at just one client or customer, you are arguing with their entire family and friends, who will hear about it. One pissed-off customer can become a dozen with one group text or dinner convo, and that shit will spread faster than some creamy Skippy.

Have manners. Manners matter. If yo momma didn't teach you any, then ask mine. If I didn't hold the door open for my mom, my dad would give me the look of death. If I chewed with my mouth open, I'd get it smacked . . . and I'm grateful for it. All a customer wants is a simple acknowledgement or door held open for them. Don't harass them, just let them know you are there for them when needed, and make eye contact. And if you hold the door open for them on their way out, I can promise you they will open it themselves when they return to buy your shit. Now they want to buy it because it's from you, because you are nice and polite, and they don't get that down the road at dickhead's shop. WalMart doesn't pay tens of thousands in yearly salary for sweet old-ass lady greeters to just stand there and acknowledge you for no reason!

FACE TO FACE

There's something to be said about the acts of doing things man-to-man and face-to-face. As I write this portion I'm on a plane on my way to do just that with the CEO of Wizard World comic con. Last week, I asked him for an hour of his undivided time, and he said we could have a phone call. I told him that I would rather fly to him to meet face-to-face (like a fuckin man). Not only does this show him my sincerity for my proposal and respect for his time, it shows him that I will make the sacrifices it takes to get what I need and work hard the right way to do it. Is this trip gonna hurt me financially? Absolutely. I had to reschedule a couple thousand dollars' worth of appointments and will probably be late on a bill or two. Between the short-notice plane ticket and hotel, I'm even more in the hole. But don't think for one second that I won't make it worth every penny. You see, I know myself. My infectious, optimistic personality; energetic charisma; and absolute confidence will show in person, but not over a phone call. I need to sell my proposal by selling myself, in person.

This little two-day trip is way bigger than a one-hour meeting. It shows the CEO and his company how serious I am about my craft and my relationship with them. Even if I fly home with no concrete answers or plans, you never know what impact this trip will have on future dealings with this company. People remember people! They remember smiles, handshakes, and looks in eyes that cannot lie. When new projects or opportunities present themselves, who will they remember and call on to be involved with them: the guy on the cell phone or the guy who spent thousands of his own dollars to communicate his commitment?

Are all these strategies foolproof? Absolutely not. I have been known to act a fool from time to time, but I learn from my mistakes. Are these strategies realistic and needed to make a splash in today's private business sector? Abso-fuckin-lutely!

Having your own business and being your own boss is the ultimate freedom. You will put in way more hours than you ever did punching a clock. But, there is no better feeling than accomplishing something each day and personally benefitting from it both monetarily and emotionally.

This chapter is dedicated to Hans Gruber, genius businessman lost too soon to the horrible tragedy at Nakatomi Tower in 1988.

10-B

EVERY BOSS IS AN ASSHOLE

If you're a small business owner or the boss, then guess what . . . you are an asshole. Yup, that's the way it will play out every time.

No employee will ever own up to his or her shortcomings, laziness, or wrongdoings, so they need someone to blame. Guess who that will be every time? No piece of shit is ever going to take personal responsibility because it is much easier to lay blame. Even if it is the most amicable split in the history of firings or layoffs, eventually gossip and trash-talking will take form.

I fired a tattoo artist one time for misspelling his third tattoo. He pissed off my clientele and made the shop look retarded. Then he ran his cowardly trap to everyone in town that he got fired just because I was an asshole. Imagine that, the boss who was nice enough to give him three chances after fucking up customers' tattoos for the rest of their lives, and I am the asshole. But somebody like that is never going to say, "Oh yeah, I just kept fucking up and pissing people off cause I am a retard, so he fired me after doing stupid shit for almost a whole year." It is laughable. And, you have to learn how to laugh it off, because things like this are inevitable and it will eat away at you if you don't.

Another time I fired a guy because he kept cheating on his wife with his clients at the shop. Morally I just couldn't take it anymore; it hurt my heart every time I saw her. He would brag about it and I even caught him, yet kept giving him chances to change. All the other employees had to lie and cover for him, which put everyone in a very uncomfortable position. He couldn't believe he was fired, like it was appalling to him. Mr. Man-whore then ran his mouth all over town that I was an asshole, of course. Isn't that funny—he was the one cheating on his wife for a few years' stretch with dozens of women, yet I was the asshole? The way some people justify their actions baffles me. When they look outside of their world for a second to examine their lives do they not see what they do wrong? That's the problem; they are incapable of looking at themselves from an outside perspective.

You cannot let people like this bring you down or get inside your head. You fired them for a reason. Why let someone who has nothing going for them bother you when you have so many more important things and people to worry about and focus on? Who are they to judge when they have nothing in life except the loss of what you gave them.

"Horrible Bosses" Acrylic and Oil on wood. By Chris 51, 2014

The Evolution of K-9 Anthropomorphism

Pink With Envy

11

MY 1990s

I still hadn't outgrown my love of cartoons. Hanna-Barbera classics will always be my first love, but new gems were starting to glisten that also helped light the future of my culture and modern pop-culture addiction. The *Teenage Mutant Ninja Turtles* were amazing in every way. Since I was a jock in high school now, and into this thing I liked called girls, I regrettably hid my love for the turtles and toys from all my friends. But I still have my original figures to prove my love, along with one of the best mint-on-card collections of TMNT around! And that is a scientific fact proven by me and science. I can post pics if you'd like. With new prime-time scheduling of shows like *Beavis and Butt-Head, Southpark, Space Ghost Coast to Coast*, and the everlasting influence of everything *Simpsons*, there was never a better time to fall even more in love with animation infiltration. Toy lines began to dominate the very shows they represented. Color-infused plastic figures became a necessity; you couldn't fully embrace an imaginary television character without its tangible and fully poseable counterpart.

Hair metal gave way to grunge, and I fully embraced the culture. Nirvana, Soundgarden, and Alice In Chains ruled my world . . . and my wardrobe (haha). Rap gave way to gangsta rap, which gave way to hip-hop. I feel very fortunate that I got to experience all those major shifts in the music world. I lived it and loved it all.

My grades slipped a little in high school cause I focused more on girls, football, baseball, and wrestling. At about a 3.4 GPA I was a good student, but I spent more time learning how to cheat the system than studying. I found clever ways to get out of schoolwork, and my charm and pleasant rapport with teachers saved me from any detentions. My parents didn't mind too much because I was still a good kid and didn't drink, smoke, or get into any real serious trouble. I did, however, excel in one thing: architecture. I received the Outstanding Architecture Student of the Year award my senior year, and my teacher said I deserved it my sophomore and junior years, but it was only allowed to go to seniors. (Check out that virgin nerd to the right.) With this passion as fuel, I applied and got accepted to both the University of Oregon's and University of Florida's architectural schools. However, I was too eager to start real life and too inspired and driven to be tied down to school for another four to six years.

SHELDON HIGH SCHOOL
Awards Ceremony
May 30th, 1991

As soon as I graduated high school and turned eighteen I was out! I moved a couple hours north to Portland to attend ITT Tech. I thought it was an easy out from a full-length college, and I could still get my foot in a door, then let my work ethic and lovable talent for wit and bullshit get me the rest of the way. I had no lacking in confidence. Turned out that school sucked balls and the recruiter promised all kinds of shit that they didn't do. I dropped out after a year and moved home, head hung low. I tried my brain at community college. Hated it too.

One day, I was driving home from class when my car hydroplaned on a rainy I-5, spinning me in a 360-degree whip in high traffic. Almost crashing, I came to a sudden epiphany in the middle of the road; I didn't belong in this town and trapped in this life anymore. Fuck this shit, it isn't me. There was a different path in life I had to follow, and I couldn't do that until I was happy. At that moment, sitting sideways on the highway with oncoming traffic bearing down on me, I decided to move back to my early childhood home of Florida to start a new life. That's it; it hit me, and it was all the motivation that I needed. I moved two weeks later. I never fucked around after I made a decision. I never looked back.

My good friend Nate Hopkins soon followed me there, and we bought a house together

(Above) The beginning of my grunge era. Why I was picnic table surfing I have no idea.
(Right) My friend Nate and I in our first house together. It was a grungy party house...but it was all ours!

by age nineteen. We didn't fuck around either. We formed a metal band called Alcatraz Swim Team and partied like rock stars for a couple years. Practicing in our bedroom morphed into having the whole band over all the time, which in turn led to a shitload of partying. We got so sick of the spilled beer smell that we tore out all the carpet for ease of cleaning the concrete floors underneath.

Beer turned into hard liquor and pot, and that turned into acting like fools. We target practiced with rifles in the backyard one night, and the police were called, of course. This was before some bad apples ruined the whole fuckin orchard with school shootings, so the po-po just chalked it up to some idiot-kid antics and we narrowly escaped arrest. Among many other spontaneous adventures, we even stole a hot tub that was displayed for sale at the end of the street. How the hell we three drunk friends carried that big heavy thing is still a mystery to me. One night we used the front drainage ditch to jump our Spree scooter to see who could wreck the best. It is no mystery that the scooter ended up in the canal behind our house by sunrise. Through many girls and kegs, it's a wonder we ever made it out of that house alive . . . and that the house is still standing.

When I wasn't partying at night, I tried to write songs during the day. My lyrics quickly turned into poems, and I fell in love with the art form. I quit our band to focus on writing a poetry book. The band thought I was crazy, but I knew what had to be done to make me happy and quench that insatiable thirst for artistic expression that I couldn't find playing an instrument. I began trading the parties for quiet nights writing alone at Barnes & Noble. Writing and focusing on a creative project pulled me from a spiral of self-destruction and aimless existence. I self-published my first book called *Gemini Son* a few months later.

I was already looking for more fulfillments to life, right during my legal drinking age. I thought that answer was marriage. I thought wrong. I was twenty-two and already bored of the single party scene. I knew there was more out there in the vast world, something more meaningful. I met a wholesome girl (way too wholesome, looking back) who was trustworthy, and figured it was worth the risk to change my life. What I didn't know is that although I was ready to change my relationship status, I was not ready to change careers or see the bigger picture. I was too young and didn't really know what I wanted yet.

What a four-year, practically sexless marriage will teach a young man though, is that there is a lot more in life to explore than the confinements of suburban daily routine and status quo. One day I returned home from a trip to see my best friend Joe Ricken in Oregon and I immediately decided that my current life wasn't for me anymore. The freedom and renewed life I felt in one weekend was all it took. I filed for divorce a few days later and lost my house, car, my savings, some friends, and a lot more, but regained what was left of my youth and energy. It sparked the focus and motivation I needed to become an adult and a risk-taking businessman. It was heartless and she was blindsided, but in the end, it was the right thing to do. My heart was long gone.

I wasn't doing her any favors anyway, and I hold nothing against her. She is way better off without my loveless lack of attention, and I wish her the best.

As the decade lengthened, my back-pain tolerance shortened. I was in constant agony. The years of pain caught up to me, and I was starting to have trouble even walking normally. I had to have major reconstructive back surgery. They called it Spondyloslisthesis, a severe curvature of the spine when vertebrae start slipping forward onto the bone below. The doctors fused my bottom two vertebrae to my tailbone to strengthen my back and then removed bone from my hip to shore up the construction there. I was given a fifty-fifty chance of walking, and was told that I would definitely never be able to play sports again. My soul was crushed. I was cut down in my prime.

My days of physical labor were over. I had no choice but to

give secondary education another try. I went to a vocational school, wearing a full back brace. I fought through the pain. At first, I couldn't even walk unassisted from a car to my classroom. By the time I got my degree a year later, I was jogging three miles a day! Nothing is more satisfying than proving doctors wrong and proving yourself right. Once you've conquered your own pain and fear, you can accomplish anything in life. I am living proof.

I got my degree and quickly landed a job as an electrical engineer. I was taking that real-world plunge headfirst. I sweet talked my way into a good position, thanks to a deadly combination of aggressive attitude and confidence. I lied like a presidential candidate on my resume and application, but knew that I was smart enough to back it all up. Before I knew it, I was designing complete electrical systems for multi-million-dollar high-rise condominiums along the beaches. I had no idea what I was doing when I started, but I worked hard and learned on my own, and was never afraid to ask questions. I had a great job and bright future, but the only problem was I hated every minute of it. It wasn't me. I was not a nine-to-five suit-and-tie guy getting fat in a cubicle. It screamed at my soul. It corroded every ounce of my life force. The second I realized that I was meant for something different, I gave notice. I don't fuck around. All that education from two stints in two colleges and awards in high school, and it lasted me eleven months in a cubicle before I was passenger number one aboard the crazy train. I happily threw it all away, much to the chagrin of my parents, who thought I was out of my mind . . . again.

Although I accomplished a lot in the nineties compared to most twenty-year-olds, I still found myself searching for myself. Answers would soon come through heartache and what I like to call heartwork.*

12

THE ART OF COLLECTING

If you haven't action-figured it out by now, you probably never will. I am a geek—and very proud of it! What goes hand in hand with being a geek? Being a collector. Maybe like me, you're into action figures. Or maybe you're all about Legos, stamps, coins, or Hot Wheels. Doesn't matter what you are into, it's just being passionate about something in life that helps you escape from life. Jocks can even be geeks, collecting autographs and football cards from their favorite athletes. You will get no judgment from me—just ridicule if you don't stand up proudly for your geekery and geek-laden collections.

There are a few main types of collectors: those in it for the future financial gain, for the thrill of the hunt, for the passion, and for an escape from reality.

I am a conundrum of sorts, combining bits of several collector types with the love of toys as art. I could care less what they are worth one day. Of course, the thrill of the hunt is what makes the treasure so special. I am definitely passionate about vintage toys because they remind me of happy childhood moments too. Collecting helps me escape the reality of grown-up stress. But above all, I love the art of the packaging and the careful poses of the action figure, which you can rarely duplicate. The vibrant artwork on the box or the goofy kid with a bowl haircut playing with the toys in a dream-scene of snowy Hoth-like conditions or the vast dunes of a Tatooine sandbox; this is why I leave my toys mint in box. They are wall decorations that speak volumes more than most paintings, and bring smiles, memories, and emotion to everyone who sees them.

Let's explore my collection just for a moment. If you don't care, just skip the next page, though you geeks will like this. For the inexperienced layman, I am a vintage MOC or MIB action-figure collector. MOC stands for Mint On Card and MIB stands for Mint In Box (or Men In Black, depending upon how you look at it, and both are awesome). This all means that I am into the collection for three things: the nostalgia of vintage, the

toy I had or wanted when I was a kid, and the artwork on the box and the condition it comes in. All are equally important to vintage MOC or MIB collectors. I am driven by the nostalgia way more than the value though, and that's why my collection is awesome! I daresay that I have one of the top vintage TMNT-MOC collections on my side of the country. I have a huge early 1990s' collection including almost every *Simpsons, Star Trek,* and *Star Wars* figure ever made, along with short (but arousing) complete runs like *Bucky O'Hare, Exosquad, Captain Power, Captain Planet, Cadillacs and Dinosaurs, Pirates of Dark Water, Jurassic Park, The Real Ghostbusters, Biker Mice from Mars, Starting Lineup,* and lots more. My pride and joy, though, are my 1980s' carded figures. I am constantly adding to my solid collection of *Star Wars, He-Man, ThunderCats, G.I. Joe, Transformers, SilverHawks,* WWF Wrestlers (by LJN), *Eagle Force, Dino-Riders, Voltron, Robotech, Bionic Six,* and more.

I am a vintage football-card collector, probably amassing over 100,000 stars and rookies from the 1960s to the 1980s (the only years that really matter in sports-card collecting).

They have lost tons of value, but I don't give a rat's ass. They are my serenity. When I need some childhood nostalgia, I look through box after box of old cards and remember where, when, and how I saw or know those particular players. It brings a smile to my face. When I need to clear my mind and relax, I do the same thing. It makes the stressful world around me disappear. When my son cried in his crib at night, I would rock him to sleep showing him old cards and reciting the statistics on the back of them. Once every few years I throw a giant wrench in the whole thing and rearrange them, either alphabetically, chronologically, or by team. It's exhilarating and therapeutic, and it keeps your mind sharp and your statistical trivia knowledge impeccable!

Collecting toys has kept me out of trouble and away from many of the evils of the world. I always collected football cards, while I knew some friends who collected needle tracks. Collecting Legos inspired me to want to design houses, and led me to school for architecture and engineering. Collecting comics turned me into an artist, which in turn led me directly to who I am today.

"Who's Toes are Frozen?" Chris 51 original photo art

13

EPIC INK
(Take 3)

Hurry up and wait! That is the common theme in Hollywood. I planned my whole life around this TV show, and it was taking so fucking long!

My staff at the tattoo shop were not the happiest that the possibility of the show would cramp their routine, so the bitch fest started. They couldn't see the bigger picture of how the show's popularity would benefit us all. Small-town mind, small-town attitude. To set an example for morale, my business partner (at the time) and I decided to let two of our artists go. We could no longer take their whining and complaining, let alone their infidelity and drug use. It was time for change. While I was away working for a weekend, the staff talked my partner into opening a new shop with them rather than getting fired. He did just that, betraying me and abandoning our joint decisions in the process. He blamed me for everything to try and save face with the disgruntled employees who would now become his new staff. Needless to say, that shifty motherfucker is no longer my partner. Never really was, because I had to do everything myself. He was a simple-minded idiot anyway and really just slowed me down by riding high on my accomplishments, never creating any of his own. So in the end it was such a blessing in disguise.

Get to the point, 51! Anyway, the point of this story is that I just got word of the show, and suddenly my thriving, money-generating tattoo shop was diminished to a staff of two . . . my wife and I! I now had to pay $5,000 per month overhead by myself and keep a full travel convention schedule I had already committed to.

For months I worked double time. I took out loans from my parents and sold off cherished collectibles all in a far-fetched hope to get that damn TV show that I knew would change my life. Katie all but quit her nursing job to run the shop so I could just focus on tattooing. I sold my shares of my Formula 51 Ink company to my ex-wife and same ex-partner for a mere $30,000. It was worth ten times that, but who the hell wants to work with both the people who betrayed them in life? It wasn't worth it to me anymore, not to mention that the $30,000 would now help keep me afloat while waiting for the TV show.

I had to work through the hardest situations too. Disgruntled ex-employees tried to sabotage the shop and show, stooping as low as calling construction companies doing work in my shop (getting it even more show ready) to say I didn't pay my bills and shit. Feeble, malicious attempts at my stature in the community didn't work because I already had an honorable name from being a part of the local small-business collective for the last decade, long before these butt-hurt ex-employees were around. They talked trash around town, only to diminish their own reputation in the end. They tried to bury me, but I stood tall. I took the high road and never slithered to their level. It definitely took its toll on me emotionally though. I was very close to throwing in the quitter's towel on several occasions. The ONLY thing that kept Katie and I going was the hope of the TV show.

Hanging on by a thread, and now bankrupt, I finally got some encouraging news. The Syfy channel wanted us! They paid for a good producer and crew to come film a sizzle. A "sizzle" is a term for a very short pilot pitch to showcase what our show could be like, sort of a highlight reel to attract network executives. We filmed for a couple weeks and life was back to normal. We got regular updates about how our sizzle was moving up the chain of command. It then made it to focus groups. Focus groups are groups of different demographics of people who are shown the show, and their reactions and comments are collected to see if the project can be a viable source of revenue for the network. We passed that test too. Finally, it went before the big boss who stamps the approval papers.

It was one of the most disappointing days of my life when I heard the news. I was told that the network, even though they loved the show, got a brand-new executive who wanted nothing to do with tattoo programming. So that was it!? All of this hard work, and with the snap of a finger we were out.

Now, how was I to close my shop and survive? I wasn't giving up on my show, but there was no way it was happening at this location. I had tapped out every loan and favor that I could to keep my doors open. My days off were already being spent fulfilling tattoo-trade obligations to contractors who had helped me get the shop ready for filming. I was in the hole, at the bottom with no shovel of hope.

Three days later, my producer Jerry Carita, who's one of my best friends in the world, called me. "Sit down, Chris," he said. He explained to me that A&E got wind of our project and wanted to snatch it up.

All I ever wanted was a pilot. I just wanted a chance to prove what we could do in one full-length episode, and I was confident we could make it work, and make them fall in love with us and our message. But A&E didn't want a pilot. A&E wanted to sign us to a full ten-episode season! They saw something in us that I saw all along. Holy shitballs! All I was hoping for was one episode, and now we had ten. That is unheard of in a situation with an unproven cast in a new and unproven themed reality show. My energy and excitement were renewed. I was not only out of my hole, I was reaching for the stars.

"*Epic Ink* almost didn't happen at all, and then when it did, it had to happen crazy fast! We had developed it with Chris 51 for another channel, and they passed on the project. Then A&E suddenly had a hole in their lineup, so we told them we could deliver *Epic Ink* in time to fill it. They said yes," explains my executive producer, Jerry Carita.

Hurry up and wait! It continued. Promises and schedules came and went. Months passed. Luckily I found two guys to hire at the shop. Kyler Shinn and Casey Baker literally helped make this all possible. The three of us generated just enough income to keep the shop doors open just a little longer. They saw the bigger picture and were supportive and helpful until the end. I promised them things would get better if they just stuck it out. The hardship and experience of it all brought us close together like brothers.

"If I didn't know any better, I would say that Chris and I were separated at birth. We share the same love for many things, from the beautiful voice of Fred Durst to our obsessive collecting of toys," confesses Kyler. "He has taught me everything there is to know about tattooing and has helped me excel in this industry. I never had the thought that one day I would get the chance to tattoo alongside some of the greats, but he has given me that chance, and I am grateful for it. He's my mentor, but first and foremost he is my brother. I am so happy he is in my life, and I'm so happy I stuck it out at Area 51 with him."

He and Casey can actually be seen in the background on many episodes, and have since become my best friends. "I was living in North Dakota at the time when Chris 51 told me about the possibility of a TV show he filmed a sizzle for. He sent me a copy of the sizzle reel so I could see what it was all about," admits Casey. "Not only

Casey Baker, Kyler Shinn and myself.

was the show about geeky, fun tattoos, it had some of the best artists involved. Then he offered me a job because he was having trouble making ends meet alone. I couldn't pass it up. I moved out to Oregon to join him and crashed on his couch for a month."

The day it finally felt real was when A&E flew out an executive to wine and dine us and fill our head with possibilities of grandeur. After that dinner, I knew that the network wouldn't waste the time and money on us like that if it wasn't a legitimate deal.

Over the next couple months, we were busy trying to understand Hollywood contracts and attorneys. We were carefully given rules and responsibilities to adhere to. They owned our asses completely—but why not, it was us that needed them more than they needed us. That's just how it goes on a first-season show.

After more than six months of back and forth, hopes and dreams realized and then crushed, we were on an official schedule. Jerry flew in early to coordinate things with me.

Next came my interior designer, Emilio, who I personally helped get the shop ready over a span of many long, late nights together. Since we didn't have any legal releases to use copyright décor such as *Star Wars* or TMNT, we had to get creative. How do you keep the geek-culture theme when you aren't able to use any comic-book stuff or movie props? My entire shop had to be packed up in a couple days. I called in favors to all of my artist friends for original art and prints to hang up, promising them promotion through the show. Their work would be seen by millions of viewers. Luckily some of my good friends eagerly helped my cause. My favorite artist of all time, Jermaine Rogers (who I was still fanboy-ing over), sent me a bunch of stuff just on my word. Joe Corroney, Brian Rood, Steve Anderson, Emek, and Alan Forbes all stepped up too, and really helped. I will forever be grateful to them for that.

Emilio and I then literally got dirty. We did some landscaping outside, hung lights and fixtures, built new furniture, and went shopping crazy. A&E gave us a $5,000 budget to get the shop to where we needed, which was nowhere close to what we needed. But, Emilio is great at what he does, and he found sales and deals and made it work. I called in a lot of freebies, and traded work for more. We had the shop ready in just a few days because we were on a tight schedule now and crunch time was nearing. The production company promised a completion date to get the show finished in time for a prime-time spot, and we all had to deliver.

While I was busy getting the décor and feel of the shop done with Emilio, the lighting and sound guys came in. They installed tens of thousands of dollars' worth of high-end lighting to give the shop a certain feel. Patrick Cummings, our genius lead cameraman, came in to work with them just to get it right and achieve his vision. He wanted a very vibrant and oversaturated look to give the shop that larger-than-life comic-book page feel. Unfortunately, I never got to keep all that expensive lighting.

Next, the line producer (who handles the budget and expenses) came in with more help. They got the offices in the rear ready, and the whole back of the shop started to transform into a working film studio and operations center.

It was really happening. The producers were moving into their local apartments and settling in for the long haul. Catering companies were being lined up. Chairs, tables, and supplies by the dozens started stacking against the walls for things to come.

One by one, more producers, editors, sound guys, techs, and cameramen came into town. They each did their separate jobs perfectly but worked together like a well-oiled Autobot at the same time.

On the following page is a letter that Emilio Fields, the Epic Ink Production Designer, wrote me when I asked him for a simple quote about his experience working on the show.

I wish we could have shot Area 51 Tattoo as it was when I first walked in, chockfull of the selectively curated art and memorabilia that drives Chris 51 and his creativity, but in Television where almost every item that appears on set has to be cleared and approved - especially when it comes to iconic imagery and characters - that just wasn't feasible. Fortunately, Chris instantly felt my commitment to keeping the shop's identity intact within those confines, and took a very hands-on approach to help me see the re-staging through, from reaching out to his artist friends for custom contributions, to staying up until the wee hours of the morning with me until every last item was in place. Ultimately, that clearance set-back turned out to be a true blessing, because that time I got to spend with Chris is what nurtured my deep respect for him as an artist, far beyond the limits of the tattoo needle, and garnered me a life-long friend whose personality I got to experience and explore through every inch of his shop and his stuff!

After all, I still have the text where Chris told me that we were "more in synch than Justin Timberlake!"

To this day, I remain in the loop of those generous and supportive artists that Chris introduced me to, soliciting the likes of Jermaine Rogers and Steve Anderson, along with Josh Bodwell and Chris himself, for artistic contributions to some of the other TV shows and films I have since designed.

There's no question that "reality television" often distorts the reality it is supposed be documenting; but when it comes to "Epic Ink", the fun, engaging, quirky, lovable, and talented group of dedicated friends you saw on the show, from their off-center humor, to their ridiculous antics, to the core sense of family that unites them, is very much real.

Love you!
E.

Jerry, who also worked on *Comic Book Men* with Kevin Smith, had another project deadline to finish first, so we got a new showrunner, Sarah, before we even started. A showrunner is the term used for the big boss producer in charge of everyone else. Sarah didn't have the geek knowledge that Jerry did, but she did have experience with tattoo reality TV, having made a season of *LA Ink*. This would be a way easier task for her because we were all much more behaved than Kat Von D (haha). Jerry would still edit all the videos and make the final product in the studio in NY, so we were in good hands all around. "I worked mostly in post, and we had another executive producer in the field. But I had helped develop the series with Chris 51, and so we stayed close during production. Holy mother of God is he a pain in the ass . . . but in the best way possible," laughs Jerry. "I'm a pain in the ass too though, and we were in lock. Chris and I were in agreement on everything we wanted to do, from the tattoos to the fun field trips."

With everything and everyone in place, all snuggled into Area 51 Tattoo in the rainy little logging town of Springfield, Oregon, it was time to get to work and make TV history. It was time to change our lives . . . and change they did!

14

INSIDE THE HUDDLE

Call me a jock, just don't call me a stupid jock. It actually takes a very intelligent jock to write a book, lead a team to a championship, or brand themselves right into a stable post-career business.

I like to think that I am among the one percent with passion for both pop-culture and sports. Most geeks are not and never were into sports. In fact, I hear most geeks knock sports and often put down something they have never tried to play or understand. How is that judgment different from the grief geeks get for being the nerds they are? I am here to take a stand and say that you can be both a jock and geek and enjoy both.

Sports made me who I am today! Plain and simple, without sports I would not have the friends I still love and trust today. Without sports, I would not know the pride of victory and the

work ethic of fighting to overcome all obstacles, both mentally and physically. Sports teach you to perform under pressure and in public, which in turn parlay into handling work-related stress and developing proper social skills. Battling on that field taught me confidence and leadership, which made me successful in the workplace. Hurting on that field taught me toughness, inside and out, and how to handle shit like a real man. I quickly learned that quitting is not an option on the field; therefore, it isn't an option off the field. All of these things, and so many more, are not lessons that you can learn in a classroom or from a textbook. They are lessons learned on the dirt and grass, on the court and the track.

Watching, talking, and attending sports are what bonded my family. To this day, no matter what problems my brother Kevin and I have, we can always find common ground through peacefully talking football.

I truly believe that those who dis sports have never really given them a fair chance. You don't have to be the best athlete to learn from the game. You don't have to win to obtain victory either!

There is a virus growing in youth sports today. It's called the participation award. Since when do kids get rewarded for being average or get the same reward as those kids who tried twice as hard or who practiced outside instead of playing video games inside? It sickens me. What are we teaching our children? We are saying it's okay to slack off and screw around in practice because they are going to get equal playing time and treated the same. How does this benefit them in life? And trust me, the lessons you learn in

youth sports live with you throughout life. The whole point of sports is to teach you that hard work, pain, and sacrifice are what it takes to succeed and receive rewards. It's the same in life. There are no participation awards in adulthood. It's playing through opposition and competition that teaches invaluable characteristics. Uptight parents have ruined this, and they are usually the parents of those lazy slacker kids. So they whine about junior not playing enough without putting in the time at his practices to see that he is a distraction to the kids who are working the hardest. He's the fat kid playing video games and eating candy all day, while the star quarterback kid is out throwing at targets after school and sweating.

Those with natural talent are going to do well regardless, but it's the lump of kids lost somewhere in the middle of the sidelines and the bench who I worry about. Those are the kids who need focus and direction. Those are the children who can rise above their predisposition with just a little push and motivation. How do you get motivation in youth sports when the playing field is equal and fair? There is no fair in sports, and there is no fair in life; both are what you make of the hand you're dealt.

Screw the participation award and not singling out players who deserve the MVP trophy. They need to be singled out

(Photos) The toys pictured throughout this chapter are Starting Lineup by Kenner, and are mine that I kept from my childhood. I included them because they remind me of both the sports I played and the imagination required to play with them. The toys themselves also helped form bonds with siblings and friends through trading and hunting for them.

and crowned as positive examples of what other kids should aspire to be next season. If you don't understand the value of losing and learning from it, then you are missing the whole point of it all. Winning and losing brings teams together and builds strong bonds.

I won't apologize for going off there. I see this shit firsthand having three children in sports, and it drives me crazy. I go to every practice and game to make sure that my children are being the best version of themselves. They don't *have* to play sports forever, but as long as they do, they are going to try their hardest, and they will never quit. If I let them quit, I am quitting on them as a parent.

(Photo) I cried after taking this picture. I waited my whole life to meet the man who inspired me to be more and do more despite my average size and ability. That influence carried into my adulthood and helped mold the man I was to become. I was lucky to have Steve Largent as a positive role model in my life, and I thank him from the bottom of my heart for being gracious, classy, and humble.

15

THOSE LIFE-CHANGING MOMENTS

Sometimes those life-changing moments can take years to register, and other times, you realize their impact right away. Whether it's in small increments or large doses, our progression in life is determined by recognizing all those life-altering moments and acting upon them accordingly. You only get so many in your life, so it's critical that you not only learn from them, but enjoy them. Savor those moments.

I have been fortunate enough to have had several of those life-changing moments. They have sculpted me and made me appreciate everything that I put into creating them. And believe me, you can absolutely create your own life-altering moments. Your destiny can positively be what you manifest. You just have to give maximum overdrive effort to your opportunities without hesitation.

The following are just a few of my moments. They range from the obvious to the subtle. Whether they relate to work, my love life, a passionate hobby, or a charitable project, they are all important to the chemistry of my persona.

I can only hope that one of my little stories might help you recognize some of your own moments and help you appreciate who you are and what you've done in your life.

I had one such moment while working in England in 2010. I was tattooing at the South Hampton convention and had the pleasure of doing a large piece that I just knew could be unique and maybe even spectacular if I truly gave it my all and more. I refrained from  several invitations to drink and party with all my peers the night before, and instead went back to the hotel to redraw my tattoo over and over until it was perfect. I got a good night's sleep and was the first artist at the show the next morning. I didn't take a break all day and ended up being the last artist to finish. First in—last out. It paid off. I captured the most coveted Best In Show award for the weekend, beating out some amazing artists, even a couple that I looked up to. I instantly earned the respect of all my peers. It was my first award of that kind, and the feeling of pride I got on that stage while accepting it has rarely been duplicated.

I knew right away that the moment had changed my life. I had a new confidence in my abilities as an artist and a renewed fervor for the craft itself. But, what I later realized was the absolute proof of the axiom, hard work pays off. I worked harder and longer than everyone else, and I came out on top, even though I may not have been as skilled as them. It showed me that hard work could beat talent that doesn't work as hard. I proved to myself that if I was willing to put in the effort and make the sacrifices, I could accomplish anything. It is a lesson that I live by every day of my life and has helped me get to where I am.

I had another major life-changing moment in 2015 when I married my soul mate, Katie. Las Vegas was the perfect setting. We were there to work a Wizard World Comic Con, and all of my closest friends would be there tattooing at our show, so it was the perfect time. We planned ahead to do a *Star Wars*-themed ceremony at a little chapel on the strip; you know, class it all up and shit! Everyone brought his or her *Star Wars* apparel, and my best man Rob Smead even wore a Boba Fett helmet. Coincidentally, Rob married his soul mate that same weekend there, so the whole crew attended that too. It was flawless.

That wedding was my third, something I said that I would never do. But, when you find the one you were meant for, there is no fighting fate. I will always cherish that day with all my friends there, but even more because I married my best friend. We never fight, and we are always loving. We are a team. It's us vs. the world, and there's nobody else I'd rather have in my corner!

I honestly feel like I robbed heaven of an angel when I scored Katie.

After doing a celebrity Q&A at the Hard Rock Cafe in St. Louis, I quickly became friends with the manager who was a fan of *Epic Ink*. She asked if I could maybe do an art exhibit there when I came back to town. I was honored to oblige, of course, and it gave me a great idea. Why don't I do an art piece for Hard Rock as a limited print to sell in person at the cafe and donate 100 percent of the proceeds to their favorite local charity? I didn't care if I made any money on it, and it would go a long way in the community. The added bonus was that since I wasn't making a profit, I didn't really have to worry about legal releases for using *The Simpsons'* theme that I had in mind. Anyone who would try and sue an artist for making a non-derogatory print solely for charity would be shooting themselves in their own foot. Could you imagine the negative press that would receive?

This project was a huge deal for me, and I worked extremely hard on it. It was a proud moment because not only did I get to give something back to a children's charity through my art, but the Hard Rock Cafe, one of the biggest restaurant chains in the world, wanted and endorsed my artwork.

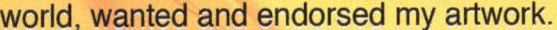

On a different kind of artistical* (made up word) front, I began to mess around with painting just before I became a father. I tried acrylics, watercolors, and oils on all surfaces. I discovered that what I loved most was using old kitchen cabinet doors I found at the local recycling yard. They were cheap at two dollars each and had the smoothest surface for my style of cartoonisms* (another made up word). Once I applied some Kilz spray primer to them any paint would stick, so I could use a combo of acrylic, oils, and markers. I tried a couple dozen paintings and was relatively happy with them, but nothing truly clicked until this painting. Having never had a formal education in art, I tried hard to study all the "rules" and even attended a couple painting classes. But in the wise words of Yoda, I had to "unlearn what I had learned" to really succeed.

With this painting (*next page*) I said "fuck it," and just did what I wanted, regardless of what anyone thought or what any book said. Turns out, that is just what I needed to do to free my mind.

This piece has now sold over 5,000 prints and has been copied multiple times. Looking back, I don't think it's my best work, but it represented a moment that defined my focus and resolve as an artist. Its immediate success allowed me to shed all doubt and break away from any artistic boundaries I may have had. It provided me limitless confidence and reminded me to never care what any critic or any rules tell me about what I can or cannot do in art. It made painting my biggest passion. If I had my little way, I'd just paint every day. If I had my little way, I'd also eat peaches every day.

It may seem ridiculous and trivial to some, but in my world, when the Seattle Seahawks won the Super Bowl, it was definitely a life-changing moment.

It was probably the first haphazard monetary risk of my life that had no chance of financial return. It was solely an emotional investment. Other than buying a house or car, spending almost $4,000 on a football game ticket is flat-out risky, not to mention somewhat retarded. But, when you and your entire family live and love over a sports team, their championship becomes as important as any other event in life. It's not a shame to spend your hard-earned money on something you love. And, when your wife supports it because she knows it's been a life-long dream of yours, well then, you'd be a fool not to jump at the chance.

I waited my whole life to see my team make it to the championship. I missed it live the first time they went in 2006 because I was a broke, young tattooer trying to find his place in life. I told myself then that if the Seahawks ever made it again, I would be there live, no matter the cost. I did just that. I begged and borrowed to afford a single ticket. Crashed on a buddy's couch and froze my ass off at the game. It was worth every penny.

When the final whistle blew for victory, I cried like a baby. It was the biggest defeat in Super Bowl history, and I witnessed my team serve it! Tears of joy froze in my bearded face. I couldn't move, not because my ass was frozen to my seat, but because I was in a trance of sheer joy and wonderment. A dream had come true for me that night, one that I had been envisioning since I was a little boy. I made it happen and I was there, fulfilling a promise made to myself long ago. That game changed my life.

16

MY 2000s

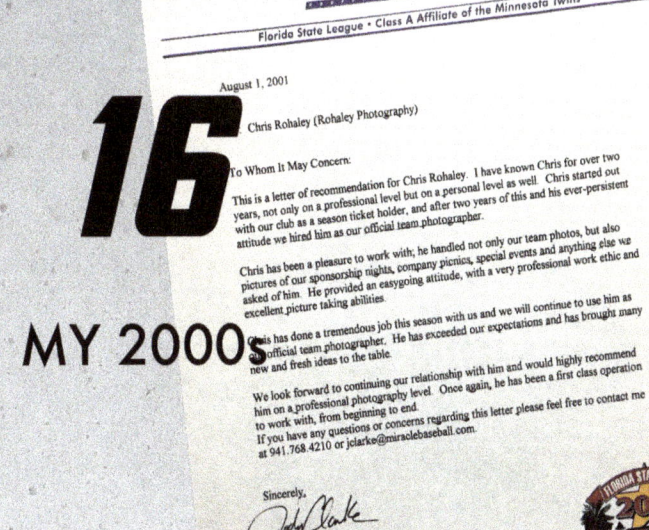

I have four loves in life. Art, sports, music, and pop-culture. I was going to succeed at one of them or die trying. This chapter is a lesson in never quitting.

My entrepreneurial ways found me again, this time in the form of baseball. I was a huge fan of the game and attended all the local minor league Fort Myers Miracle games at the turn of the decade. After befriending a stadium worker in 1999, I convinced him that I could do a much better job than their current washed-up old-man photographer. I told him that since I was young I could hang and bond with the players and get the kind of pictures nobody else could. I was so cocky . . . but I was right. (More in Chapter 26.)

Before long, my pictures were turning into baseball cards for Upper Deck and Just Minors card companies and sporting the pages of magazines. Another nearby team, the Port Charlotte Rangers, caught wind and wanted me to take pictures too. I was in my own field of dreams. It wasn't enough though. Soon the grind of plumbing all day in the heat for my dad to support my baseball photography dreams proved fruitless. Then the infamous Major League Baseball strike hit hard at home, and a lot of the guys I respected turned greedy, and the guys who really wanted to play got shafted. I saw the ugly side of the sport from inside the dugout and locker room, and it salted my passion for the game. I saw how money ruined players' lives. After witnessing that, I wanted nothing more to do with pro baseball. With the swing of a bat, I was done with it forever. Retired in my sports photography prime. I have been to only a couple major league baseball games since, and I take my family to occasional minor league or independent league games only for a fun night out and to see the guys who are driven by passion, not just money.

 Why not try another sport? I was taking a piss in a sports bar one afternoon and saw a sign above the urinal for semi-pro football open tryouts. Ever since I broke my thumb my senior year in high-school football, I had been completely unfulfilled in the sport. Although it had been a decade since I touched a football, I knew I was not only stronger and faster than my younger self but much more driven. After a few weeks of hard training, I trained myself right into a double hernia. It was the worst pain of my life, dropping me to my knees several times per day. Surgery a week before tryouts put an abrupt end to my football career, or so I thought. The coach called me the day after the first practice and asked why I didn't show up. I explained and he replied with, "Can you still run and tackle?" I said I don't know, but I was willing to try. I went to practice that night and gave it my all. With my stitches bleeding, I managed to make it through. I could barely walk the next day, but I sure as hell was gonna sprint at practice. I endured the pain. I wasn't going to give up on this one chance to reclaim some kind of lost glory. I never wanted to be the dude who asks himself, "What if?"

 I was way too slow for receiver, so they put me at backup tight end. I was too short to do any damage there, so I suggested I try linebacker, which I tried briefly in high school. By this time, weeks had passed and positions were all but set—

but I would ride the bench before I quit! I still hit with all my might, and I hit hard. I knew where to hit because I was a student of the game. If I was going to be a backup, I was gonna be the best backup on the fuckin team. I am proud to say that out of almost ninety tryouts, I was one of forty to make the team, stitches still in my abdomen and all.

During the first game, our starting middle linebacker, and captain of the defense, broke his femur. He was done for the year, and probably his career. I was thrown into not only the starting position but also the new captain's spot, in addition to playing backup tight end. I took charge and played my guts out, literally. I lasted a couple more games until I tried making a crazy tackle and tore my subscapularis tendon in my shoulder. I waited on surgery until the end of the year, and against doctors' orders, still suited up with a sling on my arm and all. I told the coach I was ready at anytime and would play one armed if I had too, but luckily he was wiser than me and didn't risk my injury further.

My semi-pro career for the Florida Stingrays lasted three glorious games, and a lifetime of pain residue, but the memories are much stronger than the pain will ever be. Like the greatest movie quote of all time from *The Replacements* goes, "Pain heals, chicks dig scars, glory lasts forever." I became my own version of my idol Steve Largent; I was too small, too slow and injured, but I succeeded against all odds stacked against me. I played injured and drug free. I take great pride in

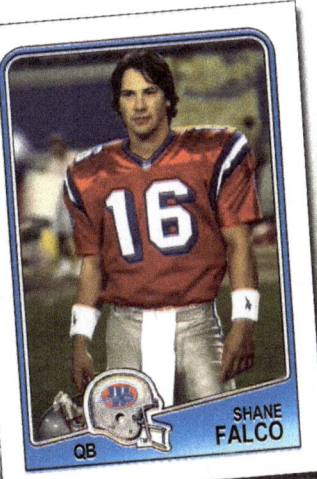

that, and looking back, I wouldn't change a thing . . . except maybe letting a teammate get that last tackle, lol. I still had to support my team, so I came out of my sports photography retirement to be their official team photographer and started a game program called the Stingray Stinger, in which I discovered my love for writing. You see, even out of devastating career-ending injury can come something good if you don't give up and stay the course following your passion.

One of the proudest moments of my life. These are the only pictures in existence of me playing semi-pro ball.

My burning desires to find my place in life and in business didn't die with the baseball and football dreams. It was time to try yet another of my four loves, music (again). Playing in bands never panned out, so instead of a bass guitar, why not try my hands at owning a music store?

I hit every flea market, garage sale, auction, and pawnshop available for six months. After working all day as a plumber, I would hit the streets by evenings and weekends to collect inventory. When I was finally ready, I was confronted with the toughest job I would ever face: telling my father I was quitting the family plumbing business to open a record store. The very business that I helped him build and run for the last decade was no longer for me. The one that I was supposed to carry on when he retired. Needless to say, when the time came, he was very disappointed. To put it mildly, he had a few choice words and strong opinions on the matter. He later understood though. Plumbing just wasn't for me, and I would never reach my potential digging ditches and laying pipe. I was meant for more, and I think he knew that.

Above) *My plumbing crew (foremen only). I am second from the left and my brother is on the far right. At one point I was responsible for thirty-six employees in the field. My best friend Nate (tall ugly one to the right of me) bought the business when my dad passed away, and it is still going strong! My dad would have wanted it that way.*

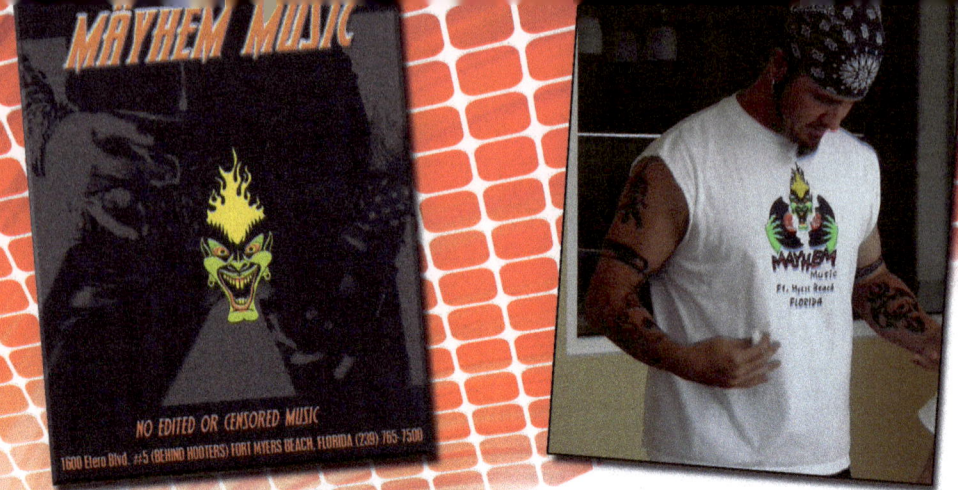

Mayhem Music was initially born on Fort Myers Beach, Florida. I opened a little independent store and never looked back. It was the first time that I had felt absolute freedom in my life. I felt like I could do anything I set my mind to.

The store started off great. I was located behind a Hooters and dated half of their staff. It was the epitome of a dingy metal-punk-rock independent music store. You literally wanted to raise up the international metal sign when you walked in. I catered only to rock and hip-hop. I even had a sign on the wall that said, "If you want classical, easy listening, or jazz go to Walmart cause you won't find that shit here!" The front door read, "If you want edited and censored music, don't bother coming in cause you won't find that shit here!" It was my little local slice of paradise. I was broke, but I was living the dream. I started to find myself and my purpose. I learned about business, branding, marketing, and advertising all on my own through trial and error. I managed some local bands, sponsored local concerts, and held album release parties. I wrote new-record reviews for the

local beach newspaper and did cross-promotion with lots of nearby businesses. I was happy . . .

Then, this little thing called Napster hit the Internet and I was fucked . . . and not in the good way by the Hooters' girls. I turned to selling concert tees, chain wallets, and the like, and then Hot Topic really blew up. I couldn't win. My childhood best friend, Joe Ricken, convinced me to move back to Oregon and give the music biz a shot there with him. It produced the same non-profitable outcome a year later but opened the idea to something strange and new that would forever change my life and become my destiny.

I was willing to try anything to keep my music store dreams alive. One day, I got a new tattoo to join several others I had been collecting on my body. Back then nobody had sleeves, so my arms were quickly becoming something of a rarity. The tattoo needle sparked an idea. Why not tattoo in my music store?! Nobody tattooed then—not on TV and barely in my town. It was a taboo thing hardly seen anywhere in society other than on bikers or rockers. My store was totally metal, so why not; it would be a perfect fit. I could still sell records and hire a tattoo artist to work in the back, and then I could maybe even get free ink!

It was a revolutionary idea at the wrong time. You see, back then, the only people to answer my "tattooer wanted" ads were tweekers or ex-cons, the kind of untrustworthy sludge I didn't want around the only thing I owned in life. So finally, I adopted the truth, "If you want something done right, you gotta do it yourself." I closed the store with the intention to quickly open it back up with myself as the tattoo artist and some college kid as the record seller. Then a new problem presented itself: nobody would teach me. I got laughed out of two shops in town and had no kind of portfolio to back up my confidence. My art resume wasn't one that I could easily lie on. It was a trying time that tested my faith in myself. I didn't quit though. No tattooed assholes were gonna hold me back! Finally, I found a shop that didn't care about my experience. They just wanted money, but it got my foot in the proverbial tattoo door.

I had what you would call a traditional apprenticeship—or

apprenticeshit* as I like to call it. I scrubbed toilets and cleaned ashtrays for months before I was allowed to tattoo. I learned most everything from the apprentice before me who learned from the apprentice before him. This led to a vast knowledge of incomplete half assery. But, the moment I made that first line on that first tattoo, I swear I heard a choir of angels sing. Cherubs floated around me, and purpose and meaning filled my soul. THIS IS WHAT I WAS MEANT TO DO! Do you know what the most exhilarating and mind-altering feeling in the world is? It is that moment you discover what you were meant to do in this life. It is more euphoric than any drug. After all these years, trials, and endeavors, I finally found myself. And thanks to my friend Fudgy (Troy Olson) who trusted me with giving him my first tattoo that would forever change my life.

Needless to say, I worked my fuckin ass off. I sold my pickup truck to afford the apprenticeshit, so I literally rode my bike across town through rain, sleet, and snow to conquer my new world. I played in a new band on the side, worked as a bouncer at the local dance club on weekends, and did construction with a buddy during my days off to get by. I did whatever I

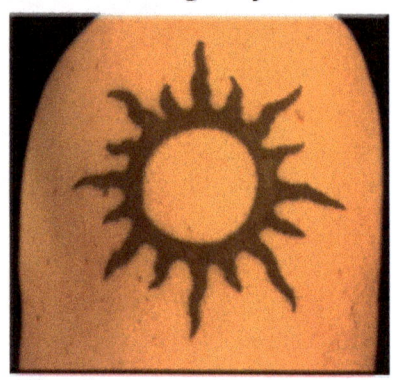
The first tattoo that I ever did

needed to do; nothing was going to stop me. I was so confident in my self-obtained knowledge that I packed all of my shit from the tattoo shop the day I went to take the state exams. I knew I wasn't coming back. They looked at me like I was crazy, but trust me, I mirrored the look back. They were the crazy ones to think that I would stay and do shit their way. Unbeknownst to them, I already had my business license, tax ID number, and small building for lease. That was the level of confidence I was playing with. I got a 100 percent on one exam and 94 percent on the other. I was off. The music store dreams died the day I put my first line of ink into skin, and I was boldly going into new territory—and gladly. Area 51 Tattoo was born that day, and has grown to be one of the most famous tattoo shops in America since.

So, after being an electrical engineer, semi-pro football player, official minor league baseball-card photographer, licensed plumber, carpenter, rock 'n' roller, music store owner, three-time homeowner, bouncer, college dropout, college refinisher, and book writer all before age thirty, I finally found my calling . . . not due to lack of trying.

After thirty, I started honing my skills in life. I gave every passion everything I had and chose my battles more carefully.

I found more solace in writing. Art in words was a perfect balance to my art in skin. I published and created a book-based trivia game on football called Four Downs to a Pro Football Trivia Champion. I started writing letters, stories, and opinions to tattoo magazines on current issues and unique insider perspectives. Before I knew it, I had my own monthly column in the nation's top-selling tattoo magazine, Tattoo. I picked up another regular column in Tattoo Spirit, Germany's leading magazine, where I interviewed other famous artists. I gained yet another monthly spread in the online UK publication, Under the Skin.

Eventually, I stopped all three to focus on another book project. I wanted to do something different in the industry. All the current tattoo books were on skulls, portraits, and American traditional fare. So, I went the opposite direction and focused on flowers and nature. *When Nature Calls* was the first book of its kind that gave every artist a page to themselves for their art, tattoos, selfies, and bios. My friend Bill Rhine did the layout, and I did the collecting, marketing, and writing. It was a grueling adventure, which has since been surpassed, but I am very proud of the accomplishment nonetheless.

Through all my accomplishments, nothing would compare to what happened to me in 2009. I became a father—and then truly became a man. Nothing else before mattered anymore, and only one thing would ever matter again.

By the time I reached forty, I had added plenty more to my life's resume. I had created a tattoo ink company from the ground up that became a leader in the industry. I had three books under my belt with more on the way. I had amassed over 800 tattoos published in books and magazines. I'd been employed as a writer for three separate magazines. I had traveled the world to tattoo, from China to Brazil, to Europe, to the Philippines, to New Zealand, and to most destinations in between. I was creating a TV show that would soon change my whole world. And most importantly, I became a father.

17

EPIC INK
(Take 4)

AN EPIC ADVENTURE

At first I hated the name. *Epic Ink*. The cast wanted to call it THAT ONE TATTOO SHOW, which was basically the ultimate homage to us not taking ourselves seriously. I soon found out that we had absolutely ZERO control over the naming. The network has a whole dedicated team of employees whose sole purpose is finding the perfect show name through testing, algorithms, and research. We soon came to accept and even love the name because in the end, it truly did describe the kind of tattoos we were doing compared to any other show of the same genre.

We refused to let the producers and staff call us "the talent" when it all started. In the business, that's the proper term for the actors or stars. That just sounded weird and pretentious to us; I mean, for fuck sake, we were just some ugly tattoo artists. We quickly settled on "space friends" as our designation. From that day on, they never called us "the talent," or talented (hahaha), again.

Filming *Epic Ink* was the most fun, tiresome, and rewarding thing I have ever done in my professional career. We filmed sixteen-hour days, six days a week, for almost three straight months. It was like tattoo boot camp. Almost every tattoo we did was an all-day event, anywhere from six to twelve hours long. We would start early in the morning and go all day and night, and we had to stay high energy. After maintaining that vigorous schedule, I can see why so many Hollywood stars turn to drugs for aid in keeping up their energy and stamina. Not that I approve or ever would do them, I can just understand the reasoning.

We all missed our families. Everyone was homesick. We were all as broke as MC Hammer circa 1996. Despite all that, we grew to love one another even more than in the beginning, and we were Too Legit to Quit. We left behind being best friends and became family. When you spend that much time in such tight quarters with a bunch of people, only one of two things can happen: you learn to love one another, or you grow to hate each other. Luckily for us, we all became closer, even the production crew.

Did I mention that we were all completely broke? We weren't allowed to charge for tattoos (which was totally ludicrous). We were paid the minimum actor's wage of $1,000 per week. When you are used to making that in a day, and have enormous overhead, it is quite an adjustment. So we basically took about a 75 percent pay cut to make the show. I laugh my ass off when people accuse me

(Top) *Josh & Heather taking a beverage break from summer filming.* **(Above)** *Chris Jones' first of dozens of takes as a yard gnome in the baking sun.*

of being rich because I was on TV. Throw in the added bonus of not being able to have my shop open to the public for three months for regular business, and the sacrifice begins to unveil itself. Thank God my employees Casey Baker and Kyler Shinn understood enough to fight through this low-income chaos with me, cause we were all in this together for the long haul now. Casey Baker explains, "it was pretty insane to me at the time, not knowing when I could even walk somewhere in the building, and trying to get my few clients in and out of my station without interfering with the filming. There were many times that I had to stop tattooing because my (coil) machines were too loud when they were filming near my station. While it was definitely hard to work around the camera crew, it did draw in plenty of attention, which helped me and the shop get by financially during that time. As frustrating as it could be working around cameras and sound crew, having to tattoo in different locations, and not knowing what days we would be closed to the public or what days I could even work, it was so worth the struggles. To get to see those friends work on something they all believed in so much made it all worth it."

(Above) Upstairs at Area 51 Tattoo was where we did all of our interviews and photo shoots. These were usually held late at night, after tattooing and filming skits all day. It was about 120 degrees up there in the summer without AC, so we would have to stop between each take and wipe sweat from our faces.

Sometimes we would be out at the river or park doing skits by 9:00 a.m. This was after we tattooed until 1:00 a.m. the previous night. Then we would tape our shenanigans over and over and later reconvene at the shop to do an all-day and all-night tattoo. After tattooing eight to nine hours, you were completely exhausted but nowhere near done. Now it was time to be high energy again and do post-tattoo interviews and OTFs (on-the-fly interviews). When we were finally done, we would get eight hours to figure out how to sleep, eat, and draw for the next day's tattoo that a million people were going to see and judge. Then wash, rinse, and repeat. To say it was like tattooer's boot camp is no exaggeration.

Even though it was an assload of grueling hard work, we always found the time to commit total fuckery and have fun! For every scene that was used, there were a half dozen before that they had to reshoot because we were either screwing around, laughing like immature school children, or not paying attention. Nobody seemed to mind on the crew because we usually involved them in the chaos or pranks. Before long, they

were doing the same back to us. As you can see in the pictures below, our producers even initiated some of the Epic debauchery...and we loved it!

(Below) I bring all the boys to my yard. My Executive Producer Jerry Carita gets frisky on my milkshake along with my wife Katie, during a diner skit we were filming. And yes I kept the props!

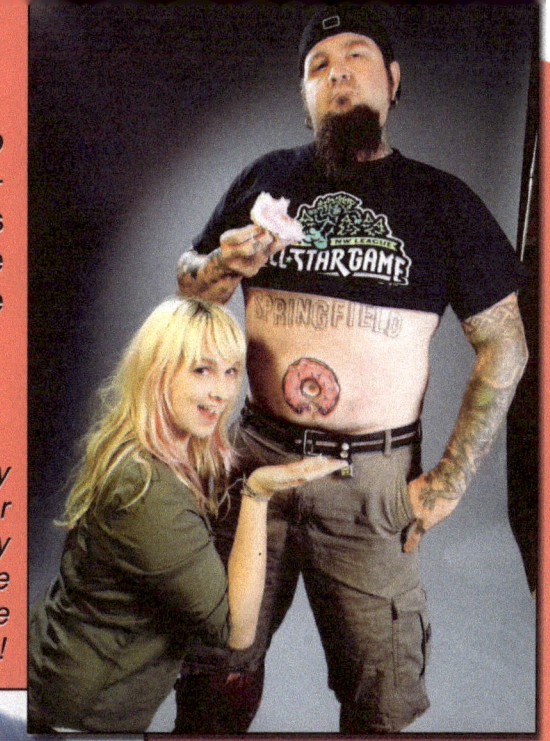

(Above) Our Show Runner boss Sara gets an extreme closeup of my finished donut tattoo during photo shoots.

(Below) Sara interrupts our dancing in front of VooDoo Doughnuts scene to show us the Thriller dance, which she was actually an expert at.

THE EPIC POSTER

The show poster was a topic of major importance to Josh Bodwell and me, and we stayed up many nights talking about it. Our concern was that if the show was going to be called *Epic Ink* it needed an Epic-type movie poster to fit the title. Something you would see representing *Star Wars* or *Lord of the Rings*. We wanted an over-the-top geek wow factor, especially since all the other tattoo shows just had the cliché tough-guy-with-folded-arms poses.

We decided together on Steve Anderson, an artist out of my own state of Oregon who was a licensed *Star Wars, X-Files*, and *LOTR* artist. Josh and I had met him at some comic cons and we had a good rapport. We loved his style.

Here came the tricky part. While Josh made contact with Steve, I had to convince the network to pay to have a professional do our art. They wanted to keep it in house. I was getting nowhere fast through many phone calls. I decided to go straight to the top and talk to our executive in charge. Over an hour-long phone conversation, I convinced him to let us try and give Steve a chance. I even offered to cover the costs out of my own salary they were paying me (luckily, they didn't take me up on that). Wouldn't you know, they fucking loved Steve's art. They loved it so much they made it into a billboard on Sunset Boulevard in Hollywood and plastered it all over bus terminals in New York City.

"When asked to do the *Epic Ink* show poster for A&E, I was thrilled to do something that was serious, yet something I could have a lot of fun with and go a little crazy on," explains Steve Anderson. "The fact that Chris 51 and Josh were already friends of mine and were the top in their field was just icing on the cake."

(Pictured) I'm with the man himself, Steve Anderson, who lives in Portland and drops by every time we work at a comic con there.

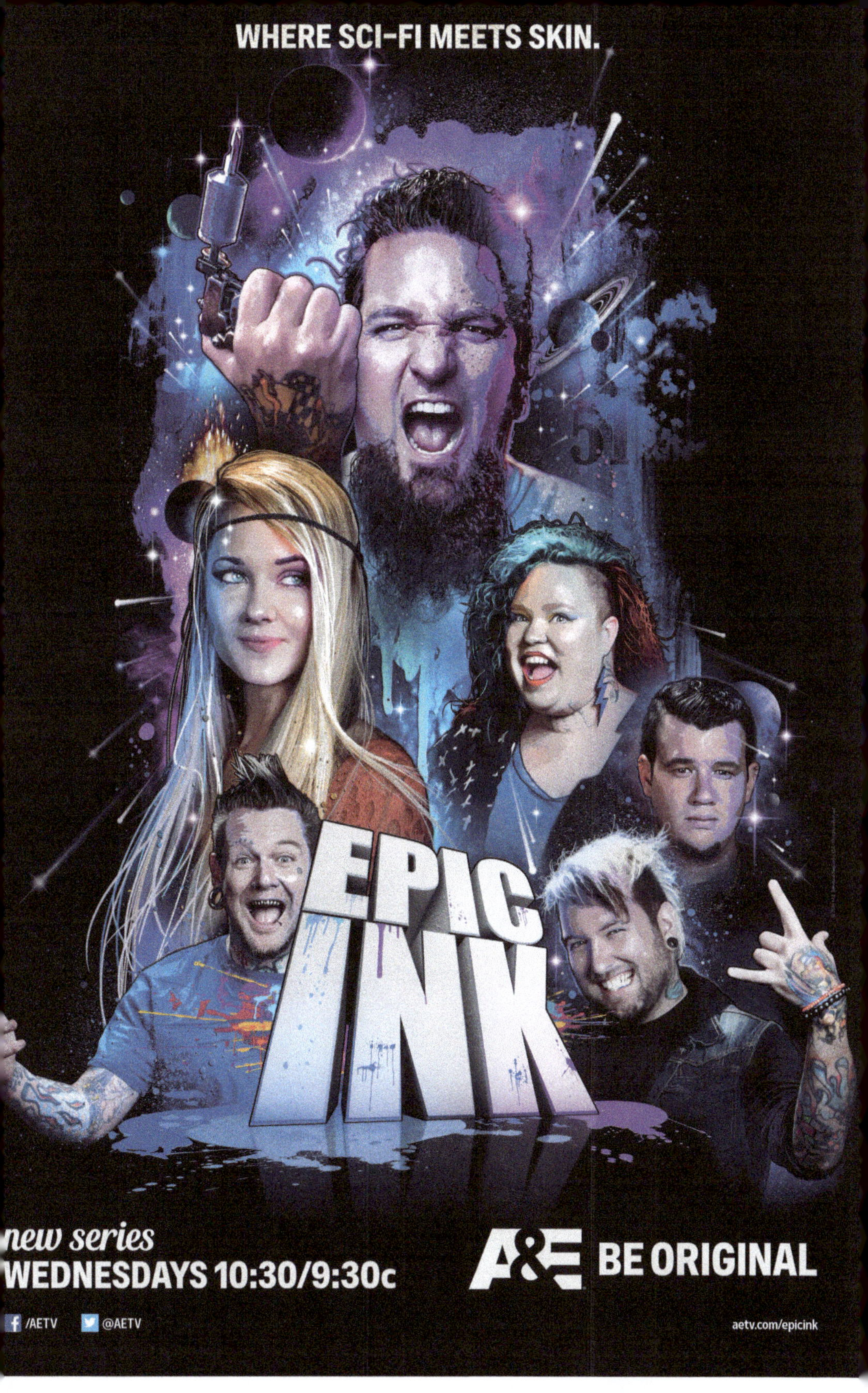

WHERE SCI-FI MEETS SKIN.
EPIC INK
new series
WEDNESDAYS 10:30/9:30c
A&E BE ORIGINAL
/AETV
@AETV
aetv.com/epicink

THE BILLBOARD

Can you believe my ugly mug was on giant billboards in Hollywood and New York? I can't either. I still can't believe it. In my wildest dreams, I never thought I would see my face on something so . . . well, Epic!

A&E flew Heather and me out to LA to do some press on a morning show. We heard about the billboard and walked Sunset Boulevard the day before to find it. We were very disappointed when it was nowhere to be seen, but it was almost one of those too-good-to-be-true moments anyway, so I wasn't really holding my breath to begin with.

The next morning, we had to get up at 6:00 a.m. to make the morning show in time. Heather yelled "HOLY SHIT" as our limo rolled right under our own giant faces. We made the driver turn around and backtrack so we could get out and take pictures. They must have installed it overnight. I wish that I could have soaked the moment up a little more, but we were already pushing tardy with our interview, and the nerves were

starting to kick in. We made it just in time to see Rick Springfield exiting the studio. Of course, I fanboyed out and got a selfie. Now the nerves were even higher because we had to follow a rock star's act. We did our thing and did it well. I find that the key to nerves is laughter. Once I made the show hosts laugh, my nerves disappeared and the hosts let loose a little and lightened up. I use that trick to this day. We drove back by the Billboard on the way home. I still can't believe it.

A&E spared no expense in the promotion department. Some of these posters could be found around New York City  in bus stops and subway stations. My NYC friends were constantly finding them around town and sending me pictures like this one. It is still hard for me to grasp the magnitude of what lengths everyone went to to ensure the show's success. And to think our quarter-million-dollar-per-episode show with a multi-million-dollar advertising campaign all started from a geeky idea I had and stories I wrote late nights on my computer while stuffing my face with milk and Oreos. Crazy! If it can happen to me, it can happen to anybody. You just have to dream big and work even bigger!

New York   Los Angeles

DON'T HATE

18

THE HATE SCALE

I have come to realize that haters are a necessary evil. They manifest only to solidify that you are doing something big or successful! If you have them, then you are doing something right. Keep collecting those haters because the lovers will soon outweigh them. I call it the hate scale. You need counterbalance for any old scale to even out properly. The more hate you acquire, the more success you are probably piling up on the other end. It is a measure of contrast. Haters (a.k.a. jealous douche bags) hate for one reason: they don't have or don't like what you have. Period. The only way they can make their miserable lazy asses feel better is to bash on you or try and ruin your moment. Don't let them!

Giving into hate leads to the dark side (pun intended). Nothing drives haters crazier than denying them your response. Don't give them ammunition to fuel their fire. Imagine how furious they are when you ignore them. They will try harder the next time, and the next, until in the end they have made their negative personalities crystal clear to everyone around them. When their smoke blows over, nobody will believe what they are spewing anyway, realizing they are miserable pricks. Some haters will even leave the dark side to join you at that point. I know this because it has happened to me.

I am not saying ignoring haters is easy. Actually, it is among the hardest things that I have ever had to do. Human nature is to defend yourself against the lies and aggression. It takes every ounce of self-control, and then some more that you will have to borrow from friends and loved ones.

When my ex-partner (and ex-friend) left my tattoo shop with all five of my employees it almost sank me. He convinced them of some lies about things he thought I had done without any proof, all heresy. In the end he was proven wrong, of course, but since the damage was done, he had to hold onto that hate because it was the only thing he had left. It must have been so miserable to be him, knowing what he had done, and losing not only his best friend, but his meal ticket and easy ride in the process. He ran his mouth all over town and turned his small posse of

lackeys against me. They went as far as creating fake social media accounts to harass me—without the balls to do it to my face. It got so bad that my own friends started defending me, and I had to stop looking at my own accounts to avoid the awful and hurtful things posted.

Ultimately my ex-partner dug his own grave as his own employees and friends came to me secretly apologizing and confessing what a hateful and bitter person he had become. They finally understood what I went through. I never had to say a word; I just waited it out and karma reared its beautiful head. The funny thing is, he had the ear of a few locals who I didn't give two shits about, and I had a voice on an international platform to retaliate and really ruin him, but I chose the high road and didn't want to stoop to his level. All that did was gain me more respect in the community.

That same year I was simultaneously working on *Epic Ink*, and it was clear it wasn't loved by tattoo artists alike. The tattoo industry already hated tattoo reality television because of the pompous and wrongful reputation that past shows have given our craft. Even though it was totally positive, drama free, real, and respectful, they wouldn't even give it a chance because they were so soured from previous forays into the Hollywood scene. Again my social media flooded with hate.

What was even more shit on top of the steaming hate pile, we got

blamed for the cancellation of the network's previous tattoo show. Because we took over the show's time spot, their fans immediately assumed we had intentionally planned to replace it. Even the star of that other tattoo show publicly bashed us thinking we had something to do with a billion-dollar network's programming schedule. How idiotic do you have to be to think that? There are teams of researchers and focus groups around the globe whose sole purpose is to study these things and decide which programs stay and go, then those decisions have to be approved by a board. I guess he thought instead that I secretly sat on that board and told them to get rid of his show and use mine, which they knew nothing about, risking five million dollars in the process, bwahaha. In the end, he made a fool of himself and has done nothing more with his career (and lots of his fans came over to enjoy our show anyway). We killed him with kindness and gave him no ammunition for rebuttal. The quality of the show's work spoke for itself.

Somehow, we (*Epic Ink*) also got blamed for the cancellation of *Longmire* on A&E. How fans correlated a tattoo reality show replacing a high-budget original drama tanking in ratings is beyond my comprehension. I guess they needed someone to blame, and we were the new tattooed hooligans on the block, with a predisposed reputation for real-life trash and violence. (See posts on last chapter page)

Threats, personal emotional attacks, lies, and rumors almost got the best of me. I am a proud man and it is very difficult to resist defending myself publicly. But I couldn't, because I am also the kind of stubborn man that wouldn't stop arguing until it was too late, and I damaged both my reputation and my new television opportunities.

Thank God for my wife's brilliance and sympathy. She talked me through it all and helped me see a lot of situations in a different light. She saw the impact that reacting to the hate could have on the bigger picture of our lives and held me back from making some poor decisions.

Josh Bodwell is also as wise as a seasoned Jedi with such matters. He calmed me down numerous times and knew just how to reach me on my level. I can't thank him enough for that.

Probably the biggest inspiration to me through my year of hate was my good friend Dan Chandler, lead vocalist of the rock band Evans Blue. Dan replaced an established singer in his new band, one that already had a couple hits and a big fan base. Logic told me he had probably gone through an equal or worse share of hatred in his tenure with Evans Blue. He sent me a text one day (more like a novel), and I must have read it a hundred times. It was sensitive and understanding. Dan explained to me how he got through his tough times with haters by realizing what they really were, jealous and miserable people. He went on to convince me that my time and energy spent on them wasn't worth it because I had way more going on in my life, and way more to live for than they ever would. I read that letter every time I wanted to strike back or lash out.

In the end, through the help of my wife, Josh, and Dan, I learned to redirect the haters' hate. I taught myself to turn that energy and time spent on retaliating and worrying into something positive. If you add up all the time and effort it takes to give a shit about negative people who have no business judging you to

SO MUCH HATE!

begin with, then it makes you realize you could use it to create something wonderful instead . . . like a new TV show that impacts people's lives for the better. So I did that and more—much more.

I actually get mad at myself now for ever caring about what those hating fools thought of me. What a waste of valuable time. And to think of what these people who judged me have done with their own lives is laughable. Think about that. Is someone hating on your job who doesn't even have a job? Is someone hating on your tattoos whom you could tattoo circles around with your eyes closed? Most people who are bashing you don't have their shit together anywhere close to yours, so fuck em. They are as important as the gum on the bottom of your shoe (as my wife would say—love that woman).

Haters = gum on the bottom of your shoe. They are annoying, dirty, and hard to get rid of, but eventually they go away and are forgotten and flavorless.

The Masters of the Universe toys pictured in this chapter are made by Mattel and from my personal childhood collection.

Beverly Hurst Such high level of thinking on this show? Just what we all need to see--someone get a doughnut on his belly--not. Give it a break! This is not worth whatever the network paid to produce it. If some want to watch it fine as long as we get our choice of programming. Giving us a diet of this is just not fair. I want great story telling and superb acting. There should be room for both. Sure what I want costs more, but there is money to be made with diversity. #LongLiveLongmire. #WEWANTLONGMIRE.

Although we received waaaay more love than hate, here are some examples of how cruel and uneducated haters can be. These aren't even the personal attacks, just the Longmire ones.

 Colin Covey SAVE LONGMIRE!
Like · Reply · September 1, 2014 at 10:46am

 Timothy Harrison Trashy TV Don't watch it.
Like · Reply · September 1, 2014 at 2:12am

 Romney Cox Hit them where it hurts! Tell the advertisers on this network. Everyone send messages, post, post, post on the walls of the advertisers.
Like · Reply · August 31, 2014 at 6:45am

 Alan Tomich How about, "Out with the crap, and back to Longmire."
Like · Reply · 1 · August 28, 2014 at 6:18pm

 John Bruce We don't need a show about tatoos!!
Like · Reply · August 30, 2014 at 9:01pm

 Donna Whitman Dodd Another stupid show but yet you cancel Longmire. Dumb asses
Like · Reply · 1 · August 28, 2014 at 6:17pm

 Donna Magee Who gives a rat's booty? You cancelled the best s[how on] television for more "reality" crap.
Like · Reply · August 30, 2014 at 12:29pm · Edited

 Rollin Morgan A&E will suffer the wrath is Longmire is messed with.
Like · Reply · 1 · August 28, 2014 at 5:11pm

 Toni Pimentel LONGMIRE!!!!!!!!!!!!!!!!!!!!!!11
Like · Reply · August 29, 2014 at 8:50am

 Kathy Reese Feel like I lost a family member.
Like · Reply · August 29, 2014 at 7:32am

 Judith Stearns Crim Longmire is the best show on TV and these idiots are keeping all the crap and not renewing this. A huge mistake.

 Kent-Judy Baker Really? Another tattoo show? Another reality show? Your network, without Glades, without Longmire, really does suck.
Like · Reply · August 29, 2014 at 6:29am

Meghan Hoffman I don't even have tattoos and even I know this show is stupid. I really liked watching Kat Von D, tattoo.. I've always thought she was very talented and her show was entertaining.

 Laura Flynn SAVE LONGMIRE! #SaveLongmire
Like · Reply · August 29, 2014 at 6:05am

 Cynthia Leigh Nau Blakesley Dumb ass move canceling LONGMIRE! Only show worth watching on this idiot network.
Like · Reply · August 28, 2014 at 9:53pm

 Dawn Fromel The only show worth watching on A&E...guess I will no longer be watching that channel, but whoever is smart enough to pick up Longmire, a great show. A&E =FAIL
Like · Reply · August 28, 2014 at 7:42pm

 Bernadette Mixon
I can see why you took Longmire off for this trash with his fat belly and stupid tattoo. Yea great job A&E. Do what AMC did and get rid of unscripted shows.
19 hours ago · Like · 👍 1 · Reply

 Jeff Blalock Exactly what we needed another stupid tattoo show.
Like · Reply · August 28, 2014 at 9:06pm

Mary Q Turner YOU CANCELED LONGMIRE!?!?! WHAT IS WRONG WITH YOU PEOPLE??? You have just lost a LOT of viewers - this is the most, absolutely, insane thing you have done since DD.....Goodbye A & E!!!!!!!!!!!!!
Like · Reply · August 28, 2014 at 5:40pm

 FiftyOne Household
Does it make you feel better to put people down? I'll have you know he is the kindest man I've ever known. Shame on you.
Just now · Like

Bobbi Toth Yeah, cancel Longmire on A&E, but keep crap like this on the a[ir]. Good call, A&E....not! smh Hopefully, there will be a smarter network out the[re] that will snap it up.

 Lisa Fitch A&E doesn't deserve a GREAT show like Longmire. They deserve crappy shows like this one, Epic Ink! A&E you can go suck it! #LongLiveLongmire!
Like · Reply · 2 · October 21, 2014 at 7:09am

 Shelia Ireland In a word.....Longmire. Bring it back.
Like · Reply · 2 · October 20, 2014 at 7:48pm

Shane Turgeon Hey Longmire people, we get it. You're upset that your show got canceled.

But your group is deliberately trolling this page in an effort to raise attention to a show that's been canceled through no fault of the of Epic Ink cast or producers and in doing so, you're disrespecting the hard work that this amazing group of individuals has put into trying to make this show succeed. They have just as much heart and soul invested in their product as do the Longmire team and your constant trolling of Epic Ink related posts is incredibly disrespectful. Just because you don't like it, doesn't make it bad. Guess what? Other people DO like this show and have every right to enjoy a program that's fun, light hearted and looking at a subject that's INCREDIBLY popular right now.

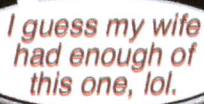

I guess my wife had enough of this one, lol.

Kind, intelligent response from Shane. Thank you.

19

COATTAILS

I have long coattails. They stretch for miles and wind through lots of others' careers. I leave them long for people to ride on because I am a giving person. I steamroll through my endeavors, and I always include my friends, who always reap the rewards. Whether it is through art projects, press, TV shows, promotion, or conventions, I share the spotlight and accolades out of love, without looking for what kind of monetary gain I will get.

But what I cannot tolerate is ungratefulness and nonappreciation for those coattails. If you ride on them, fuckin acknowledge it once in a while. Learn to say thank you and they will forever flow behind me. Do I need regular recognition? Abso-fuckin-lutely! I am not afraid to admit it. Is it a character flaw? Maybe, but it is also a small price to pay to have me in your corner working, pushing, and fighting for you, and a price that should be paid naturally without hesitation. If I am not getting paid for my hard work, I better get some damn thank-yous for it every now and then. Boy, you sound like a bitter, little bitch, 51 . . . damn straight. I am so tired of doing, doing, doing for others and getting disloyalty and dishonor in return.

My ex-partner was a pill-popping head case. I hired him anyway because I saw potential in him if he could clean up. I helped him get sober. When his tattoos improved, I sent his work to magazines to help him get recognized and build his brand. When his anxiety disabled him from tattooing, I let him take over my tattoo-schooling program so he could support his family. He was literally deadweight, but I kept him on because he had become my friend. When my ink company blew up, I gave him a portion of it, so he could help me make ink. He started out doing great, but by the end didn't help much, preferring to cage fight or laze about, so I had to make most of the ink myself, while doing every other duty required. I still kept him on out of loyalty. When the drugs resurfaced and his family life was in turmoil, I let him move in with me . . . several times. His whole career and reputation in the tattoo industry was constructed on the foundations that I laid for him. After all this, he betrayed me and stole my entire crew. I wish that I'd had the cold heart to push him off of my coattails long before he could have hurt me.

Then there was this time I hired a couple who wanted out of their town. I took the risk, not really knowing them, which was retarded in retrospect. That was my first mistake. I reminded them two months prior to their move to file the necessary taxes to make them eligible for the Oregon tattoo license laws. I even traded my accountant some tattoo work so he would help them get all the proper documents. I trusted that they were responsible adults and didn't think I would need to babysit them. That was my second mistake. When they arrived, I discovered that they had done nothing to prepare for their employment with me. I discovered more pill-popping mental cases who didn't have the wherewithal to do anything for themselves. Yet I still tried to help. I promoted them. I even took the risk of letting them tattoo in my shop while unlicensed, after hours, just so they could make ends meet. I let them live with me rent free for two months while they tried to get their shit together. I tried to pull some strings and get them fast-tracked in a local tattoo school to get their license requirements, but they were "too good and too seasoned" to attend a so-called school with amateurs. They pissed off the school instructor so much that he called me threatening to come shoot up my tattoo shop if they were ever employed there. That was the final straw. I asked them to leave and even rented them a U-Haul and gave them $500 in gas money as to harbor no hard feelings. Then they road my coattails down the road to their next failure.

After they finally left, I found my guest room in shambles, with wine stains and dog piss all over my new carpet. Months following their departure I ended up having to do over $1,500 in tattoos for which they secretly took deposits, not only never telling me, but never giving the shop its percentage initially owed.

After all I did for this couple, they still publicly talk shit, like it was my fault they didn't make it out west. Of course, I was to blame for their failure because my coattails stretched only so far.

Why do I ever still bother then? Another character flaw. Sometimes you want to just believe that people can redeem themselves after all you have done for them. So you keep doing. You say to yourself: there is no way that they aren't going to say thank you or have my back this time after doing another thing for them. I can tell you this—my back is very strong from always having to back it myself!

Be careful once you put on the coattail jacket, because you will be the selfish asshole when you take it off. It's funny how quickly people forget all that you have done for them when you stop doing it. I'm not sure if it's resentment because they realize they just can't do on their own what they did when you were helping them, or if it is just jealousy. Either way, it happens so frequently that your shell hardens more each time and you no longer want to lend a helping hand. Your coattails become a jacket of thick-ass skin.

On the other hand, don't be a selfish dick either. Let people join in your success. It's a lonely toast with one glass of champagne. Just make sure that you trust them and that they are worth supporting. Try taking off the coattail jacket sometime and see if those people stick around. It might get cold out there in real-life land for them. Then you will know if they are your true friends and there for you, not just for what you can give or help them get.

20

THE KLINGONS WERE RIGHT

When did people start forgetting about pride, honor, loyalty, and respect? All the traits that make a Klingon's name revered throughout time and space have seemed to remain in their galaxy, alien to us.

I think that I was born or destined to be a Klingon. With the exception of the Klingon culture's violent tendencies, I truly admire the traits it is built upon and how it defines importance of character.

It's not just that some people purposely undermine these most important values that baffles me; it's that some people don't even understand what they are in the first place. Generations today aren't taught respect or honor through computers, and their parents aren't around enough to notice their lack of integrity. The only act of loyalty I regularly see is to money.

I am loyal to a fault. Like a Klingon warrior, I would rather die defending my captain or comrades than live by betraying them. I would go to war for my family and true friends. But when war comes to your Kronos (Klingon home world), how many true Klingons do you know? Who will have your back, or who will put a d'k tahg (knife) in yours? Loyalty war has made me stick to one truth: if your friends aren't there for you through all the good and the blood, then they are no longer your friends. Period.

Get rid of those p'tach (Klingon expletive).

I always hear this term uttered as an excuse: "But deep down they are good people." FUCK THAT. If you have to go deep down to find the good in someone, then you hold too tightly to a shovel of desperation. Not everyone is a good person inside, and the sooner you accept that, the happier you can be. Reread this paragraph because I can't stress it enough. Some people are just evil, vindictive, and selfish, and there should be no room in your life for them.

Respect is everything. When someone disrespects you, he is shitting on who you are and what you are made of, so why is that person still allowed to be in your life? They don't deserve you.

Respect your elders . . . unless they are assholes. Just because someone is old or has been doing something for a long time doesn't mean you have to give them respect. Maybe your appreciation, but not automatic respect. An asshole is an asshole regardless of age. Respect has to be shown before it is given. A Klingon would kill you for disrespecting him. I will just never acknowledge you again, so it's like you're dead to me anyway.

Pride. If you take pride in everything you do, then you will be the best you can be and nobody can take that away from you. Be proud of who you are. You are the only one like you—alive, unique, and beautiful. When you take pride in who you are and have no fear in how you look, it takes away all ammunition from those who aim to harm you. Eventually they realize that all of their bullets of ridicule can't scratch you and it's a fruitless endeavor. They will move onto bullying an easier target. Stand strong in your beliefs and have pride in your stance, no matter what anyone thinks, because that is who you are. People without pride are weak.

Honor is a lost art. So many people use it only when it serves their best interest. To have honor is to hold true to all loyalty, respect, and pride and do it in a morally just manner . . . with manners! It is probably the hardest trait for most to master. Without honor, anything you do becomes vain and selfish. Doing something great is rewarding, but doing something great while keeping your honor is untouchable. People can take away your money and glory, but they can never touch your honor.

I have had lots of friends over the years . . . or maybe I should say that I thought I had lots of friends. Once one of them loses one of these predescribed traits then they are banished from my life. Needless to say, I have plenty of enemies out there (ex-friends) because they simply cannot understand or accept this philosophy, and maybe that is because they let people walk all over them and have no pride, honor, or respect for themselves.

Don't ever discount Star Trek innuendos and philosophies. The Vulcan minds behind the iconic universe were far ahead of their time. They imagined a diversified society driven by peace and exploration, not money or war. Intelligence and moral fortitude is the basis behind every episode. We could all learn a lot from its creators. Live long and prosper!

21

EPIC INK
(Take 5)

EPIC INK CLIENT CASTING

As with any reality show, the proper casting of clients is as important as the cast themselves. No matter how good the tattoos were on *Epic Ink*, a boring client would make for a boring show. A depressing or rude client would have changed the whole message we were trying to convey, and the entire landscape would have been ruined.

There was an entire casting agency at work to find the perfect clients with the perfect artwork wishes to fit our brand. The only problem was, the agency had no clue what it was that we were truly after. This is not a bash on their job performance, because they did outstanding work within

---

CALLING ALL SELF-PROCLAIMED GEEKS WHO WANNA GET INKED!!!

Ever thought about getting a hyper realistic tattoo that appears three-dimensional? Maybe an image of your spine down your back or the Terminator's forearm where flesh used to be? Into the softer look and want a huge Hawaiian nature-scape on your shoulder? Are you the biggest My Little Pony, Back to the Future or other retro-pop culture fan and have always wanted some ink to prove it? Should Star Wars or Battlestar Galactica be your middle name?

If any of these things ring true, then a new national TV show is looking for YOU!! We want any and all unapologetic pop culture obsessed nerds who would LOVE to get a tattoo done by the dope staff of **AREA 51** to tell us their story!

Area 51 is home to some of the hottest tattoo artists specializing in creating sick life-like tats, so if this is right up your alley, please send the following information ASAP to **GeekyInkCasting@gmail.com**:

*Name, Age, Location & Contact info (phone & email)

*3 **RECENT** photos of yourself (include a full-length)

*Must provide your own travel to the shop in Springfield, OR

*MUST be at least 18 years old

(This flyer was plastered all over social media.)

the parameters they were given and were used to. The thing is, it takes a geek to know and understand a geek. And, it takes a smart geek to see a fraud just wanting a free tattoo and fifteen minutes of personal TV-appearance fame.

It could not have been an easy job to sift through the hundreds or thousands of submissions to be a client on our show. The agency had to take everything that was customary to casting reality-TV guests and throw it out the proverbial window. No sob stories. No memorials. No political or religious tales. No vulgar, dramatic, or hostile personalities allowed. This program required the reprogramming of the status quo. We needed geeks. But not just geeks—passionate, funny, unique geeks. Not an easy task for the unacquainted.

The first thing you see when you enter Area 51 Tattoo is a sign that reads, "Geeks Always Welcome." It's a motto I live by. I don't care about your race, creed, looks, or wealth; if you're a geek you are my kind of people!

The agents tried their best to line up the ultimate clients with the ultimate backstories. Through rounds of Skype interviews, they were fed bullshit lines by people who'd say anything to pass to the next level. Ultimately, it was up to us to decide if we wanted to tattoo the artwork or not. We made that perfectly clear from the start. We WOULD NOT tattoo stupid shit that we didn't want to just to make a more compelling show. In the end, we knew the tattoos would speak the loudest volume so they had to be the perfect subjects, not just a part of a perfect story.

    I came in one of the first mornings to find tattoo reference pictures pinned under each cast member's name on a giant board in the producer's office. You bet I was the first one there to snoop at what was going on. And why not, it was my shop and my show. What I saw just wouldn't do! The producers had clients who wanted American traditional style art paired with an artist who strictly does photo-realism, They had a realistic portrait client scheduled with an illustrative artist. This may look good on paper, but when it comes to permanently marking someone's skin it is imperative to find the correct artistic match. You must pair the type of art with the proper artist who performs that exact style. They had fairies and text and all kinds of shit they thought would work for our subject matter. Needless to say, I called a private meeting right away with a couple producers. From that point on I would decide which client would go with which artist, and which art wouldn't even be considered. I knew my cast, my friends, so I knew what they'd be best at and what they'd most love to do. I rearranged that whole board to a more suitable scenario and would continually meet with the producers about it every day to keep it that way. New Chris 51 ancient philosophy: "happy artist do happy tattoo…make happy show much better!"

Still, my efforts weren't always enough. Since I couldn't control who was allowed, (through casting) I wasn't always able to make the correct cuts in time for tattooing. Easily, over half the shit that got advanced to us was undoable, and we turned it down. We turned away more than what came in to fill the filming schedule. It wasn't that we couldn't tattoo what they wanted, because believe me, we are a confident and proficient bunch and can tattoo the shit out of almost anything we put our skills to. It's that the art either wasn't geeky enough to fit the whole concept of the program, or it was something that we didn't want to be known for and have to tattoo the rest of our lives. For example, a girl wanted a bunch of fairies playing around a tree. I didn't want to tattoo stupid fucking fairies for the rest of my life, so I turned it down. I knew that millions of people would be watching, and although I could crush a fairy, I didn't feel like repeating the early 2000s' Amy Brown era of my career that I worked so hard to move past! Since I had nothing else approved on the schedule that day, I compromised and talked the client into doing a realistic, colorful tree with one little elf-like mystical creature (not a fairy) poking his head out. Therein I found somewhat of a geek factor, and it pleased both sides.

One tattoo I did eventually came around to bite me in the ass. I tattooed a giant octopus on a woman. I loved it and it was a blast. It looked like a giant kraken or something from an

old sci-fi story, and I got to freehand almost the whole thing on her. I was so excited to do it that I didn't think ahead about the repercussions of it. I have since done no less than fifty octopi because of that one episode. I am so sick of tattooing octopi and wouldn't care if I ever did another one for the rest of my life. In fact, unless it's for a good friend, I won't. A true artist doesn't like repetition and the feeling of forced motivation. Call it snobby or eccentric, I don't give a shit. I just know that I didn't work so hard in my career and make a TV show from nothing just to tattoo shit that I have no motivation or inspiration to do. You must understand that an artist's work is a direct extension of how he feels and what he loves.

Since we turned down over half of the clients that the agency provided, we were left with a huge gap in our costly and timely filming budget. We were on a very tight schedule, and network demands wouldn't allow for us to individually seek out our own clients. ENTER KATIE! My fiancé (now wife), Katie, was our savior. She went out on her own around town, searching and scouring for the perfect, willing clients. She hit up the MAC-makeup counter at the mall, alternative stores, and restaurants, and anywhere and everywhere she could think of that might harbor the right demographic for our needs. She approached her friends and former shop clients who she felt had the personalities to succeed in the role. She did a marvelous job and ended up personally casting almost half of who ended up on air. I think the whole cast would agree that she should have just done it from the start. Again, this is not a knock on the casting agency; Katie just knows exactly who we are and knew what we needed, and has experience in both the

(Right) Katie and I at SDCC. She saved Epic Ink with her casting skills.

tattoo and geek industries.

Art wasn't the only problem with casting. One dude was simply just too fat. No offense intended, but he was just too big to fit on our specially designed tattoo chairs, which we had to use for the sponsors that provided them (which I got for free from a letter I wrote, but more on that later). I don't know what excuse the producers used to tell him why he had to go, especially after his art was approved and he came all the way for filming, but I'm glad I didn't have to do it.

Then again, sometimes the planets aligned and we got the perfect client with the perfect tattoo idea, with the perfect look, and with a great story. But when they showed up, it was a whole different story.

We had one such client. She wanted a Gremlins tattoo. She was bubbly and somewhat cute. Everything seemed great. But once she sat in the chair, she turned into a complaining, take-everything-for-granted, ungrateful bitch. She didn't want to stick around for interviews after and complained when she didn't get free food, after getting a free $1,000 tattoo and getting on TV. I personally told her to do the fucking interview because that was part of the deal . . . the free deal, mind you! Without the interview, all of our time and budget would be wasted, because it cost us a small fortune to film her all-day segment. Reality TV doesn't work without the reality, which are the interviews. Without the clients talking about their experience it's just a silent and boring fucking time-lapse fucking bitch. How many people would have killed to be in her spot and get that wonderful tattoo from Heather? I honestly don't know how my editing producer, Jerry, pieced enough good

footage of her together to make it even work. He is a genius is all I can gather, because she was impossible and didn't deserve to be seen. But, we had few other options because of the casting problems, and the fact that we were actually allowed to use a cool, iconically geeky *Gremlins* tattoo. We were having such trouble getting permission to use actual pop-culture characters and references that we didn't want to waste this chance to use such a well-known one. (More on legal releases to use popular trademarked characters later).

Thankfully there were some successful casting outcomes too. There was the crazy dude who wanted ram horns tattooed on the sides of his head! He walked into Area 51 two weeks before filming started with his unique idea. I just happened to be at the counter to help him and suggested that he come back in a couple weeks when he noticed the chaos of filming going on. I knew it was a crazy enough idea that the producers would love it, so I casted him on the spot. I told him that not only might he be able to get it for free, but he could also be on TV and have that cherished memory on film for the rest of his life. He walked in one morning and was filmed soon after. Heather killed that tattoo, and it remains yet another definition of what *Epic Ink* was all about: doing things our way. The crazy way, the geeky way. The Epic way!

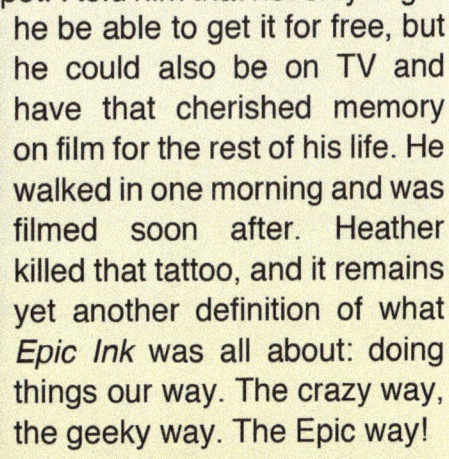

I've told you about a few clients, now I'd like to tell you a little more about my amazing cast of professional geeks.

HEATHER MARANDA

Heather Maranda loves the penis (haha) . . . especially in art form! She is a master at drawing dicks. I'm not talking like Jose Canseco- or Kanye West-type dicks; I'm talking about real cocks. Well, I guess that's the same thing (lol), but she does draw a good schlong. She makes the most incredible caricatures of people in the pecker form that you have ever seen. On *Epic Ink*, every time you saw her drawing in the background, I guarantee you it was of somebody as a dick. They even had to blur out the drawing once. The drawings were so spot-on and funny that even the cameramen and producers started wanting themselves as "dicks." She would add trouser trouts to every picture of the cast hanging up in the back production area and on storyboards, and started getting daily requests for dickatures. I have kept them all as magnificent mementos. She never drew one of me though, maybe cause I am just a dick anyway, who knows . . .

Heather always kept filming fun and free of anything resembling couth. What you see on camera is what I got to be a part of every day—nothing but high-energy, ruthless fun and fuckery. She livens up any room she walks into and puts a smile on every face, whether it wants to turn a frown upside down or not. She never holds back; in fact, we never really knew what was going to come out of her mouth next.

JOSH BODWELL

Josh is exactly how he appears on camera in *Epic Ink*: smart, laid-back, funny, humble, sweet, kind, quirky, nerdy, and lovable.

Funny thing is, I met Josh on a train in England, not in America or at a comic con like destiny would suggest. And I do believe that meeting him was destiny. We were both on the train and he noticed my suitcase with tattoo and *Star Wars* stickers on it. He asked, "You headed to the tattoo convention?" With my reply, he continued, "You American?" After another answer, he saw my stickers and asked, "You a *Star Wars* fan?" I followed with, "Did we just become best friends?" I did indeed leave the UK with one of my best new American friends ever. I honestly can't even remember a single tattoo I did there because all my memories of that weekend are occupied with Josh Bodwell sweet nothings.

Back to the point at hand. Josh is one of the most genuine persons I have ever met. He is calm and chill and has a way of making you feel the same way when he is around. I don't think he has a mean or evil bone in his body, and I don't think I have ever even seen him yell or get really pissed off. He is Switzerland to most problems and has a democratic nature of putting things in proper perspective.

Josh was THE most integral cast member at helping the show and my dream succeed. I asked his advice daily, and he was always right with his suggestions—we probably used every one he came up with! He was always there at a moment's notice to vent to and had a way of showing me a different and positive side to each situation. He was a rock, and he rocked!

To this day we still work on new projects together, I still seek his advice, and he is still one of my best friends.

CHRIS JONES

The "other" Chris on the show. Probably the way more talented one (haha). He was already at the top of his game long before the show ever came to fruition, so he didn't really care about the accolades associated with TV from the start. "I was never really interested in being on TV or being famous. I just saw it (Epic Ink) as an opportunity to spend time with my best friends and do cool shit. And, that's exactly what we did every day!" states Chris.

I knew the second I met Chris that he was destined for big things. I was a judge for a tattoo competition in Liverpool in which he entered an Iron Man piece (done by Josh Bodwell of course.) When he showed the piece on his thigh, he pulled his undies up enough to purposely expose his ball bag to the crowd. Unbeknownst to me, I was already bent over in my chair behind him preparing to view his tattoo when he turned around and suddenly I had a face full of Jones's nuts! Now that's an introduction I will never forget. Even Chris's obscure and incomprehensible Welsh accent didn't sway us from becoming friends at hyperspeed after that night.

He had the skills, the looks, and the personality to crush whatever he wanted. As soon as I got word about the possibility of the TV show, I knew I needed him involved right away. It took some convincing, but he couldn't resist my charm . . . and nagging!

He may seem like a diva at times, but it's only because he is so loyal to his principles and will not budge for anybody or anything. I respect the shit out of him for that.

Chris is the real deal. He is as talented as any legendary tattoo artist that I have ever seen. What he can do on the skin baffles me. But it's what he does with his heart that will always keep me closest to him. He truly cares about his friends and would do anything for them. Even my kids all love him because they can just tell he's a kind man, and the kind of man that truly loves his friends and would do anything for them.

. . . And he's one sexy bitch!

JEFF WORTHAM

When I casted Jeff I had known him only a short time. But in that time, I grew to love his personality, humor, and wit. I knew from the start that this guy needed to be on TV. His demeanor is infectious, and you can't help but be entertained by him. I pulled him out of his industrial garage shop and put him on the big screen, and introduced the world to him.

I honestly didn't care nearly as much about his art skills; in fact, they weren't quite up to par with the rest of the cast. But, that didn't matter. I just knew he was a piece to the puzzle working right. I initially slated him as the young artist with the smooth street background. His skills turned out solid enough, though, that the producers and I decided to just have him as an equal part of the cast, not just the young unproven artist.

When I first met Jeff at Megacon in Orlando, he was working in a booth next to me and wouldn't shut up. I was actually getting annoyed and gave my wife an eye-rolling look of impatience. She then whispered in my ear to just listen to what he was saying and how he was engaging customers, that he was actually very funny. A social wiz. A short time later I was tattooing a cousin of mine, and Jeff overheard. Without even knowing me, Jeff loudly interrupted by saying how ironic it was that I was working on her because he just discovered he was my long-lost cousin. We had a laugh and have called each other "cuzzo" ever since.

Jeff is a natural at marketing. He's savvy, inventive, and talented in many different art forms. He is very slick.

He permanently relocated to Area 51 Tattoo after the show, but it turned out that Oregon wasn't the right fit for him, neither was working full time at Area 51, or along side other employees. Unfortunately, we aren't close since he left, but I wish him the best.

22

SPONSORSHIPS, ENDORSEMENTS, AND GETTING FREE SHIT

Sponsorships and endorsements for tattoo artists work in much the same way as with other professions. In NASCAR, for example, companies pay to put their logos on the race cars and provide the car team with free products. This practice is an integral part of how companies advertise. Average Joe Public sees auto-part brands, supplies, gas and oil brands, and energy drink graphics on a car, then that product recognition is embedded in his head when he goes out to shop. And, if his favorite driver is drinking a certain energy drink and always winning the checkered flag, well then, he might think there is a correlation there. Although the money isn't as plentiful in the tattoo industry as it is in the stock car circuit, the formula is similar.

Popular veteran artists want free shit! And, for the most part, if they know how to properly market themselves, they deserve it. If they can help sell tattoo ink, supplies, or aftercare by posting about it on social media, wearing its logos, or doing press and interviews with sponsored product placement, then they are truly helping a company sell their products. Younger artists who look up to those high-profile veterans want to emulate them, so they buy what they are promoting. Maybe if they use the same products, they can reach the same level of expertise. Maybe if they excel by using those products, then one day they too can be sponsored. It's all a symbiotic circle of marketing, and companies that don't see that don't belong in the industry.

Although sponsorships are commonplace today, it wasn't an easy path for those of us who helped pave the road to getting them. I wasn't the first tattoo artist to get sponsorships or endorsements in general, but I was the first with some big companies. I've even introduced the idea to many companies since, and have taught seminars around the world on the very subject.

Over a decade ago, the concept of tattoo supply or aftercare companies sponsoring tattoo artists was rare, almost absurd. The very idea of professional companies putting their advertising and promotion in the hands of a bunch of anti-conforming hooligans didn't make much business sense . . . or cents. The popularity of industry magazines was reaching an all-time high, and MySpace was brewing in its infancy, so giving away free products really wasn't justified yet.

In the early- and mid-2000s I had been sending out pictures of my work to magazines. This was before any of them accepted e-mail submissions, and to get noticed, you had to print your shit at Walgreens and seal it in a padded envelope with a letter and some stickers. But, get noticed it did, and the publications started adding up. I went crazy and sent my work all over the world. My tattoos were landing on pages everywhere from South America and Mexico, to Scandinavia and Taiwan (some pictured below). After having hundreds of tattoos in print, my name started to get noticed, and I started sub-

mitting unique stories about my shop, career, and experiences that I thought might intrigue editors. Intrigued they were. Tattoos in print started turning into interviews in print. Then magazines started asking me for insider stories about the industry, places I've worked, and products I've used. The more I answered questions about the ink or machines I used, the more my entrepreneurial spirit started taking flight. MySpace became more relevant, and on my replies to complimentary comments on my work I started endorsing brands. What did all this add up to? A revelation: I was selling products for these companies.

There was no "boosting ads" back then, only buying magazine ads. Companies relied heavily on word of mouth, the original social media. All of a sudden, a few other artists and I started giving companies a new voice and platform for promotion. I realized that I needed to bring this promotion to the attention of company owners, and maybe my loyalty would be realized, and rewarded.

I started with Eternal Ink, a relatively new company with a strong reputation for quality that was taking the ink game by storm. I printed off every comment I made on MySpace in which I named the brand or particular color the brand made. I highlighted those words. I tore out pages from my magazine interviews and highlighted where I mentioned them yet again. After a few weeks of dedication to the project, I had amassed a one-inch-thick stack of a company owner's wet dream on paper. This shit was better than porn to an advertising-minded boss. I researched the owner's name and any info I could find on his personality or interests. I handwrote a letter explaining how much I loved his product. I further boasted about how proud I was to be asked so frequently about it, meaning my work was really standing out. I said that I would continue to stand by his product and defend it with loyalty, and asked if I could be put on some kind of mailer or e-mail when new stuff came out so I could be the first to buy it. I NEVER ASKED FOR ONE SINGLE FREE ITEM. That was key, and that was smart. I wanted to show no ulterior motives, just integrity and thankfulness. It wasn't common to get sponsorships or free product, so asking for one of those wasn't yet a viable option for me. Plus, I had a lot left to prove in the industry. I'd known of Eternal sponsoring only two other artists, Dan Henk and Myke Chambers. There was no way I could join the ranks of those veterans. I had to get creative, so I thought about what I would want to hear if I were in the owner's shoes.

Apparently, I said all the right things, and what he wanted to hear. Weeks passed and nothing. I had almost chalked it up to a lesson learned when I got a call from the owner. He said that my giant envelope and my dedication impressed him. He'd never seen anything like it and wished more artists approached him in that fashion. He offered me a full sponsorship on the spot and said that as long as I kept up that good work, I would never pay for ink again. I was in! I got off the bench and was ready to tear up the game. I was the third or fourth sponsored artist the company ever had, and my punk ass joined the big dogs. Before I knew it, Eternal Ink started promoting me, and my name grew because of it. Hundreds of magazine publications turned into a thousand. I was getting personal invites to tattoo conventions and comped free booths at them. All my new-found glory stemmed from some research, hard work, and a personal letter.

The spark had been lit and now the fire was out of control. I fevered for more, like a rabid fucking dog! I didn't even care as much about the free products. I saw the bigger picture. I wanted the endorsement and the promotion to help grow my name, my brand.

I evaluated the other products, and Tattoo Goo was next on my radar. They were huge at the time but had zero promotion outside of magazine ads. I could help with that, and I would do it for free! I called the owner, and because of the new-found legitimacy of my name in the biz, he actually listened. Again, I expressed my gratitude for his products and explained what I had to offer a business. His response was a little different. He knew nothing of sponsorships; I felt that even the idea sounded a little ludicrous to him. But I didn't give up. I wouldn't let him off that call until he understood what a sponsorship meant, and what my intentions were. I had to literally educate him on what it meant to sponsor an artist. The point I made was to trade his product for my promotion in the industry, which would equal to very cheap advertising directly to the demographic he was trying to reach. I was in the trenches at conventions and after-parties, in magazines and places abroad. I was the guy who could sell his shit without being an annoying salesman. I offered product placement in interviews and on booth tables at shows. I think I finally opened his eyes when he offered to send me as many cases as I wanted! Of course, I didn't take advantage of his graciousness, so I only accepted a few. I was way more interested in putting his logo on my website and convention banner! I was Tattoo Goo's first sponsored artist because I created the position for them.

Months went by and I chased more sponsorships. If opportunities didn't come to me, I made my own. I was a sponsor whore, but I didn't give a shit. I was like the NASCAR racer of tattooing with different stickers and logos plastered all over my brand. But it still wasn't enough. It was time to take this game into extra innings. No, fuck that—it was time to change the game again. I wanted more than a sponsorship; I wanted to endorse shit! I wanted to be that guy wearing the sexy butt jeans on the pages, not just having the

Levi's tag on my homepage.

Enter CAM Supply, my next target. I hit them in the bull's-eye! I look back now and can't believe the arrogant balls I had at the time, but this is what I did. It all started because I was sick of their horrible catalog covers. Seriously, how did a giant supply company, probably the biggest (at the time), put such little effort into their covers for catalogs that were hundreds of pages, selling tens of thousands in products? They had some homemade-looking models bearing the worst scratcher ink I had ever seen, and this was supposed to entice shops to buy from them. Issue after issue, it was like a running joke in our shop; how much worse could the tattoos on the covers get? Then the new issue would come and it would top the last. I couldn't take it anymore. I had to say something, not only as a consumer and professional, but as one businessman to another, whether they listened or not.

I had a marvelous idea. I called on my professional photographer friend, Bob Williams. I got my hottest female clients involved, because we all know sex sells, and if you don't believe that EVERYONE would rather pick up a magazine with a hot chick on it than a half-naked dude, then you are kidding yourself. I rented Bob for the day and sent the girls to his studio to shoot all of their tattoos in sexy, yet classy poses with real backdrops, something the catalog didn't yet understand.

Then I wrote a letter. Not just any letter, mind you, but a fuckin awesome letter. To start, I told them exactly what supplies I used and why I supported them, and then I laid into them (professionally). Again, I didn't ask for anything; I merely presented a problem and offered a FREE solution. But I didn't just offer it, I gave it to them. I sent them hard copy samples for tactile proof. Holding eight-by-ten-inch color photographs of hot, tattooed models is much more appealing and real than any still photos on a computer screen. Maybe they would throw it on their desk to be seen all week, or somebody else in the office would take notice and comment on it.

I proceeded to tell the owner that he was free to use them however he liked and that I wanted nothing in return except credits. I even included a standard release form so that he owned the rights to them. That showed ingenuity and intelligence, and it must have turned him on even more than the hot pictures, because I soon got a call. He used the pictures for four of the next five catalog covers, and all of a sudden, our relationship blew up! He admired my candor and work ethic. I think since I was the first tattoo artist to really just try and help him without asking for anything in return, he trusted me. Although I had some ulterior motives to help boost my own career, I was not greedy or selfish in this mission. Soon, my picture and work were appearing on the back cover, too. He eventually stopped using my work on the catalogs because he was overwhelmed with jealous artists bitching and whining that they couldn't be involved. But, that was fine by me because we were already working on bigger and better things. He wanted me to endorse his company's line of aftercare and gloves. That was huge in my industry; it had never been done before. I told him to send me some cases because I had a great idea for my photographer to blow his mind.

(Left) Some of my CAM covers by Bob Williams (Above) Advertisement on back of Chinese magazines

We set up a poker table in my tattoo shop after hours. I envisioned using the tin, disc-shaped aftercare products like they were poker chips. We went to the bank and took out every penny we had and haphazardly laid all the cash on the table. I put on a suit and tie and got all dapper-like and started throwing those "chips" around the table. We got a hot model to stand behind me and sip on a fake cocktail. I am pretty sure the CAM owner loved it, considering it became a full-page ad in half the tattoo magazines on bookstore shelves. He even made it into a poster for his warehouse and liked that so much he mass-produced the poster to hand out to attendees at his own tattoo convention in China! 10,000 of those things were made with my ugly mug on them, all because I followed some ideas and spent a few hundred bucks of my own money to invest in a much bigger picture. I never asked him for a dime to take the pictures. (See poster on next page)

I later made life-size thrones out of glove boxes and put some girls behind me sitting like the glove king. It was very cocky and bold, but that's what works in an advertisement. You want it to get noticed. I could care less if people said, "Who is this asshole," as long as they remembered what gloves that asshole was pushing. Those pictures ended up in dozens of magazines too, including some back covers. That was my first foray into product endorsement, and I am proud to say that I made that shit happen myself.

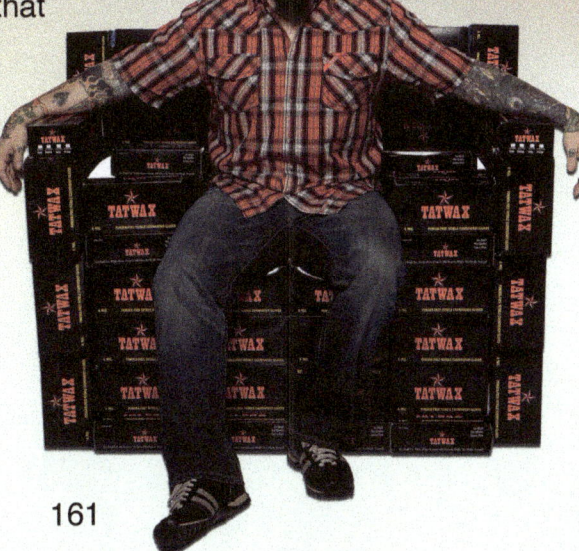

Eventually, the owner sent me to China, all expenses paid, in trade for speaking and educating Asian artists at the symposium before his convention. It was one of the best experiences of my life and opened my eyes to a whole new incredible culture. I gained so much respect for the Chinese and their relentless work ethic when I saw it all firsthand. The best part of the trip, though, was meeting and traveling with James Mullin. It's strange running into someone halfway around the world whom you have so much in common with and just so happen to live within driving distance of back home. "We were the only two American artists there so we ended up hanging together, and have been great friends since," says James. He has become one of the best artists I know, and has since tattooed both me my wife twice. He's also the cornerstone of my GeeksterInk Legends tour. "For the past few years we have been on a tour across the country tattooing at comic cons. It's been an amazing time getting to tattoo nerdy shit together. Chris 51 is a true geek at heart, so I think that's why we get along so good!" says James. After all that came of my CAM Supply escapades, meeting James is what I am most grateful for.

Once again, like most big things in my career, this all began with a single handwritten letter. It was a risky move to start a professional relationship with hate mail (haha), and I don't know if this was good advice, but the flip side is that if you don't try then what happens . . . nothing! And as I always say, nothing is the worst thing that can happen to anybody!

James and I speaking at a Chinese tattoo symposium. He made me do all the talking, which I had no problem with of course, lol.

Artists often ask me how to get their work published and get themselves noticed. I always answer; hard work, frequent work, research, and a lot of professional nagging!

I didn't just simply get on magazine covers. It took years of submitting work and forming relationships with editors and staff writers. It took getting over 700 tattoos published before my first cover.

I also paid for all the photoshoots myself and never asked anything of the magazine doing me the favor. I made it easy, painless, and CHEAP for them.

KIDROBOT

I have collected and cherished toys all my life. I bet every true geek has imagined the dream job of designing the very toys or video games he or she plays with. We all want that job; we are all waiting for that call.

I got that call! *Epic Ink* had been airing only a few weeks at the time. I was driving my children to a little, local fairy-tale amusement park called the Enchanted Forest. Enchanted cannot begin to describe my feeling when I answered the phone to: "Hello, this is Bob Africa, owner of Kidrobot toys." He continued with, "I was randomly flipping through the channels last night when I couldn't sleep, and I caught a glimpse of my (Kidrobot) toys in the background of your show. I wanted to just reach out and thank you personally for promoting and collecting my toys and displaying them on your show." That's right, he thanked me. The Kidrobot creator called me just to say thanks. I was floored. After I hung up, my wheels immediately began spinning about like they do. I would have to hold back my excitement and carefully plan out how I could turn this one phone call into a future dream endeavor for myself.

By that night, I had written several drafts of letters expressing how flattered I was that Bob called and how much I truly do love and collect his toys. I expressed my interest in continuing to promote them on a larger scale through all of my popular, new social media platforms from the show. I didn't ask for shit! I just wanted to be a part of something special and promote a product that was not only badass, but had an owner who took the time to reach out to me.

Within weeks, Kidrobot's marketing guy, Steve Elms, reached out to me per Bob's request. He started sharing my work that I tagged Kidrobot in, and I continued sharing theirs. I took a personal interest in their products and designers. I cared. I wasn't in it for the money. My goal was to design a toy of my own one day, because how many people (or hooligan-looking tattooers) can say that they have done that!?

Soon, I started my GeeksterInk Legends Tattoo Tour of comic cons. I asked Steve if Kidrobot would be interested in sponsoring my tour. Again, not for money . . . I wanted toys (haha). They could help me with promotion and my overall branding by the affiliation alone, and I could give them product placement and apparel promo in all my future shows, videos, and media. I explained how I could hand out small toys as trivia prizes to fans at my *Epic Ink* panels, and maybe turn on a new demographic to their products. My artists on tour started getting involved too, and put Kidrobot logos on their banners and cards, wore their T-shirts, and donned toy Dunnys and Labbits in their booths. The hashtags and exposure multiplied within a new fan community, and both our companies were on the way to a great business relationship.

Word spread of my love for Kidrobot on the tour, and I even began doing tattoos on their fans. (Pictured example.)

Months later, another dream call came. Steve reached out to invite me and my wife for an all-expenses-paid trip to the big one, San Diego Comic Con, as a thank-you and an opportunity to work with Kidrobot! They not only wanted me to do autograph signings in their booth, they also wanted me to design an exclusive Kidrobot limited print to give away to fans at the event. Needless to say, my boner didn't dissipate for like a week.

I got right to work as to not disappoint. I had one month to do this, but two other comic cons in between to plan for and work at. I sat down at the computer and was faced with a huge dilemma: how the fuck do I design a screen print?

They wanted me to design an original (non-character-infringing) four-color print. So here lay 51 damn problems. One, I am a tattooer who uses as many colors as I can to make my art, so limiting myself to only four went against everything I'd taught myself over the years. Two, screen prints are flat with no smooth multi-color blending for shapes, and no shadows and highlights for depth, so I was in deep because I'd never worked like that before. Three, my art consists of taking one pop-culture character and fucking with it to mash-up with another character, and here I couldn't use any popular characters.

Four, they wanted it done digitally, and I am a fuckin oil painter. I had no idea how to create art on a computer other than with some basic Photoshop skills. Five, I was designing a print to go along with a few other artists', one of whom was world-renowned screen printer Frank Kozik, the god-damn Godfather of the art! I was out of my league, out of my realm, and out of my fucking mind to think I could compete. I was gonna embarrass myself and lose all credibility with Kidrobot. Worst of all, I would never get my chance to design a toy, which I knew I could do well! Luckily, I am a confident (borderline-cocky) motherfucker. I tried and tried on that damn computer,

Above) *My first attempt at designing the SDCC exclusive screen print for KidRobot. I wanted to portray the decline of modern nutritional civilization & obesity through their classic Labbit toy theme.*

I came up with not one but two ideas, and submitted them with an explanation to try and cover my ass from a possible disaster. I told Steve that I was sorry if they didn't live up to my (or his) standard. I honestly expressed how much I struggled, and gave him my list of excuses (in a more professional tone, of course). I poured my heart out about how much the opportunity meant to me. Steve replied that he had no idea I was struggling, and he totally understood. Feeling like he had

Above) *My second attempt at designing the SDCC exclusive screen print for KidRobot. I kept this one way looser and more my speed, mashing up some KidRobot Dunny toy shapes with the classic Hungry Hungry Hippos game we all played as a kid. I ended up using it for an exclusive Wizard World print.*

handcuffed my true talent, he went on to actually apologize for tying my hands on this project. He asked if I could have a painting done in time, which the company could give away to one lucky fan as an even bigger promotion. I totally lied and said that I could easily do it, even though I knew that my thick oils would take weeks to dry, and I had only one week to get it done. Since my art was a giveaway, I was also free to paint whatever the hell I wanted, which freed up a hundred ideas in my melon. With a lot of oil and quick-dry hardener, and the use of a blow dryer to speed up the process, I miraculously got the painting done in time.

Why So Krusty" was a three-way mash-up of *Batman's* Joker, *Simpson's* Krusty the Clown, and Kidrobot's own Dunny toy. I poured my heart and soul into it. I wanted to blow their minds and wow the fans. I didn't want Steve to regret giving me this opportunity.

Not only did everyone at Kidrobot and all the SDCC fans love it, it went viral and paid off. A few days after the show, I got an e-mail from Steve saying that a lot of fans who had seen my  painting at the show or online had been inquiring about whether it would be available as an actual toy. All the hard work and not giving into overwhelming adversity and mental struggle led to actual talk about making my creation in to a real toy.

Dreams do come true if you work hard enough for them. Never give up, never surrender (okay, that one I stole from the movie *Galaxy Quest*).

Above) Signing cards and toys at SDCC for Kidrobot.
(left) The winner of my painting got even luckier when *Supernatural* star Mark Sheppard (Crowley) stopped by to check out the painting. Mark is a big Kidrobot fan!

WHY SO KRUSTY?

23

GEEKSTERINK LEGENDS TOUR

I refused to let all of the hard work I did to make *Epic Ink* quietly fade into reality TV oblivion. I poured too much of my heart and soul into that show to not get the most out of it. My fifteen minutes of reality TV show fame weren't nearly enough. Fuck that! I wanted more! I wanted to milk it dry—not for the money, but for the true love of what I was doing and who I'd become. I was the happiest version of me. I never wanted to stop living the geek life now. I never wanted to stop being a role model and inspiration to children and young artists. I needed to find a way to keep the TV show alive, the fans entertained, my mind motivated, my heart beating, and the geek flag waving proudly. My life had become a real-life comic con. That's the taproot of the GeeksterInk Legends. I was about to build the biggest tattoo tour in the world, and I had no idea how my life was destined to change again.

Tattooing at comic cons isn't a new thing; it has just never really reached the potential that it should. There's another comic con-tattoo-tour outfit out there, but they are a minor-league operation. They've been doing it for years but are stagnant and unprogressive.

You know by this point in the book that I like to keep things positive. I am naturally a very peaceful and happy person. I always prefer to take the highest road possible overtop the hardships and injustice I've faced. BUT, sometimes there is an individual or two who simply doesn't deserve that kind of respect.

I started tattooing on one of those minor-league tours years back. It was run by an ego-centric, self-centered asshat. Let's call him... Joffrey. Through his tour, I found my love for tattooing at comic cons, but failed to

(Above) It's never easy tattooing the thick hide of a predator.
(Left) Kyler and I like ghostbusting at cons when not tattooing.

see the point of continuing to work with the very type of person and personality that I was trying to get away from, and rid my life of, within the tattoo convention circuit. It was more of the same bullshit, just on a cooler playing field. This tour promoter thought he had all the answers and wouldn't listen to any criticism to help make his brand better, so everyone just sucked it up and kissed his ass in fear of losing their spot on the geek train. Except me.

That drama goes against every grain of my geek fiber. The whole point of truly being a geek is to get along and bond over your fanhood and passions, not to be belittled or to feel disdain for anyone around you. True geeks are accepting and welcoming to any character who has character. It was time for Joffrey's communistic-styled monopoly to end. It was time to take his small, stale day-old gas station donut tour and turn it into the sweet Krispy Kreme worldwide powerhouse that it could be. And I was the guy with the big balls and confidence to do it—and do it the right way. Do it with heart. Do it to unite the geeks and artists toward a purpose bigger than just work and fun, but for friendship, love, and respect.

My good friend Joe Pomparelli, owner of the GeeksterInk social app, was actually the one who planted the seed in my head. He was treated like shit by the same asshat tour promoter when he offered to help cover his event free of charge, just to get some material for his geeky tattoo app. We quickly became friends after a weekend at C2E2 con in Chicago, and met again a couple months later at a press junket I was doing in LA for *Epic Ink*. He leaned over to me (at a table full of TV production executives for my show) and whispered, "Dude, we should just do our own tattoo comic con tour, one that's actually fun. Your show is all about that very thing, and you have the fans that would come visit you in different cities." And that was all it took. GeeksterInk Legends was born from a

(Above) Joe Pomparelli and myself at one of our first shows.

whisper over cocktails and french fries, and a lot of mutual disdain for the status quo. We began planning later that night, and intensely over the next few months.

"My GeeksterInk app was about two years old when I met Chris 51. We had been talking via social media for a while, but didn't actually meet until I ran into him at C2E2 con in Chicago. We hit it off right away over our mutual love for all things pop-culture," says business partner, Joe Pomparelli. "A short time later he invited me to his fancy Beverly Hills hotel that his network put him up in just to talk geeky stuff. It wasn't long before we both confessed our mutual man crush on Brad Pitt, and then things really took a turn. That's when I knew that Chris and I were destined to work together. Before I left that evening, we had talked about starting our own comic con tour where we would bring in the best artists who specialized in and were known for doing geeky tattoos. That night, GeeksterInk Legends was born."

We knew we could easily do it bigger and better than other tours; that part wouldn't be hard. We'd do it with better artists at better conventions, and we'd do more conventions, and do them with our massive promotional platforms under the banners of *Epic Ink* TV and the GeeksterInk app. We would combine forces to change the game. And we didn't just change it—we invented a whole new game. We took what was then a ten-cent cup of stale diner coffee and turned it into Starbucks.

Needless to say, we easily secured a shitload of haters right away. Joffrey ran his mouth to his artists, tour vendors, and whoever he thought might care, but not many people listened to him anyway because they knew he liked to just hear himself talk a lot. He even went as far as trying to sabotage my new TV show by attempting to stop certain celebs from appearing on it and getting a comic con facility to refuse me access. He felt threatened, and rightfully so, I guess, because none of his antics ended up working for him. The GeeksterInk Legends did our thing and left that minor-league operation far behind, never looking back.

First thing we did was get on board with Wizard World, the world's largest comic con tour. They did twenty-six shows the year we signed on. We wanted to be the best, so we joined the biggest. I immediately went out and reeled in six to seven companies to sponsor the tour in the first couple weeks. I reached out to all my friends who were not only great geek artists, but great people at heart too. I recruited only the best and most professional tattooers, careful to not invite anyone from the minor leagues. The GeeksterInk Legends tour is proud to feature the top pop-culture tattoo artists in the world. It's an all-star geek team that drives one another to excel and represent the culture and each other in a classy and elite fashion.

We approached the tour as an attraction and spectacle, not just some dark corner pavilion of oddities. Our booths formed an island in the middle of each show floor, for a 360-degree

Photo by Angie Bergeron

fan-viewing position. We worked our asses off, and it didn't go unnoticed. We did more shows to bigger crowds and with more press in our first year than other tour companies did in a lifetime.

Before long, the-powers-that-be at Wizard World started hearing of my love for their shows and saw the press I was doing. They soon started lining up three to four morning shows, as well as celebrity parties, on-stage Q&As, live news reports, and more for me to attend at every stop we made. I became their unofficial celebrity (I use that term very loosely) spokes-geek-person. This would soon lead to even bigger and better things. At the time of writing this, I have done over seventy-five live and studio TV interviews in support of comic cons and my GeeksterInk tour.

I was "that reality TV tattoo guy" in the green room always taking advantage of the bountiful cookie tray. I also took advantage of my close access to the other celebrities to form

(Top) Early AM press in Vegas with Hercules himself, Kevin Sorbo. *(Left)* I always have fun giving conservative newscasters a hard time. In Sacramento I was asking if I could tattoo her live on the spot!

relationships and friendships. Your professional peers begin to trust and respect you when they see you week in and week out working on the same playing field as them. They let down their guards and begin visiting you at your booth, and they become interested in the buzz of the tattoos. The GeeksterInk Legends booth was becoming the place for stars to visit. Several celebrities still make regular appearances to check on the work that the Legends are doing. Bruce Campbell, Danny Trejo, Jason David Frank, Lou "The Hulk" Ferrigno, and many others are always dipping in and out of the booths to see the amazing work being done, often of their own likeness. Some of them even send their fans over to the GeeksterInk Legends booth to get the autograph they just signed permanently tattooed, and they are excited to see it when the fans return later to show them.

Josh Bodwell tattoos Daredevil star Elden Henson at GL booth.

"Being on tour with Chris 51 and the rest of the Legends since the beginning has allowed me to learn from the best geek artists in the industry. When you are constantly surrounded by the best of the best, you have to soak it up. I've been able to create friendships with amazing artists from around the world, which constantly drives me to try harder, not out of any sense of competition, but in a true common interest of all things pop-culture. Chris 51 has worked hard to build an Epic tattoo tour where everyone's geekery and fandom is welcomed and truly without limits. I feel extremely fortunate to

have been adopted by Chris 51 and the GeeksterInk family, and that's what we are: a family," says GeeksterInk original artist, Brandon Sommers.

Our hard work and reputation paid off yet again in the fall of 2016. I got an invite from a giant, up-and-coming comic con tour company called Heroes & Villains Fan Fest. Turns out that they were very unhappy with their current tattoo-tour promoter (guess who?) and wanted a change. They had heard about me and GeeksterInk through some celebrities, artists, and vendors, and our friends at the Celeb Photo Ops. They flew me out to San Jose to check out their show, and I fell in love, not only with the con but with the staff as well. These were good-hearted people, and geeky fans themselves. I immediately felt at home. A few days later they invited my tour to join theirs. Then I learned that they also owned the Walker Stalker tour, and they wanted us to join forces for all of their shows on both tour circuits! I was flattered and honored to do so. I am sure when that other tattoo-tour promoter gets wind of it, I will be the one who's blamed for "stealing" his shows. But I know the truth, and in the end, I really don't give a shit. If you are repeatedly an asshole, only driven by ego and putting out subpar work without progression, you can't expect to grow with a company that is opposite of that standard.

As of 2017, the GeeksterInk Legends tour has over twenty shows planned. Between working a couple Wizard World shows, every single show date with our new partners at Fan Fest/Walker Stalker, the Rose City Comic Con in Portland, and the massive Salt Lake Comic Con, the Legends of geekery have taken the comic con world by storm. And we have done so strictly by having the best artists, and by being the most professional and genuinely nice people we can be. We shattered the stigma of "nice guys finishing last." Watch for us at a city near you, and come geek out with the Legends.

(Above) A Tony Sklepic Hulk tattoo impresses Lou Ferrigno.

COMIC CON MEMORIES

The Sacramento Kings were kind enough to welcome Sean Patrick Flanery (*Boondock Saints*) and myself to town in style. They made us personalized jerseys and their dance team presented them to us on the red carpet, in full sexy *Batman* cosplay.

Turns out that *The Walking Dead's* Abraham (Michael Cudlitz) was a fan of *Epic Ink*. He asked the comic con staff for an introduction a couple years back. Little did he know, I was a way bigger fan of his work than he could ever be of mine. We have since become friends, and see each other often on the comic con tour circuits.

(Top) Tom Payne (Walking Dead's Jesus) giving the Legends a blessing at Chicago Walker Stalker 2017. Also in pic is Charlie Benante from Anthrax and Ming Chen from AMC's Comic Book Men.
(Bottom) Legends Angie, Brad, Joseph, myself, Jeff, Drewski, my wife Katie and Josh with the most legendary tattooed-boxer, Iron Mike Tyson.
Photos courtesy of Celeb Photo Ops

(Above) GL Rick Meggison teaching legendary villain actor, Danny Trejo how to tattoo at Wizard World, Nashville.

24

EUGENE COMIC CON

Creating my own comic con tour gave me an itch, an irritating itch to actually make my own comic con. Like a horrible case of crabs, it would only get worse until I did something about it (or at least, I assumed so. I've never had crabs). Let me clarify that I never once thought I could do it better than the Wizard Worlds or other shows that I worked at. I just had such a true love for them that I wanted my own community to experience what brought so much joy and fun to my life.

Luckily for me, Royce Myers walked into my tattoo shop one day. Royce was a local University of Oregon campus police officer, who like me, was just a huge geek with a true love and passion for everything pop-culture. He had been a fanboy, vendor, and aficionado of comic cons in the past, but had never attempted to put on one of his own. Royce actually recruited me as a local "celebrity" to appear at Eucon, his own comic con, and to possibly put on a tattooing display there. "I got a hold of Chris after I had seen *Epic Ink* on television and knew I had to have him at the show as a guest, then it quickly transformed from there," states Royce. I can promise you that Royce had no idea the floodgate he was about to open when he wanted me involved. Our quick meeting turned into dozens of hours of plotting and dreaming about bringing the best possible convention to our community. He had tons of great ideas, but not the experience that I had at living the convention life. I also had the celebrity connections, local pull, and social media influence he needed to complete the geek puzzle. He seemed like a stand-up dude and I liked his moral agenda. He wasn't driven by money, but by passion, the same attribute that fuels my life.

I turned down his invitation to "just" appear. I wanted more and he needed more! I said, "Not only will I be there, but I want to be your partner and help you make this the best damn show this city will ever see. If I am going to attach my name and reputation to this, we are gonna do it right, go big, and take risks!" Furthermore, I told him that I didn't want a single penny. I then warned him of my controlling nature and love for the spotlight, and we decided that I would be the "face" of the show, doing all the press and handling the celebrities, the photo-op area and tattoo area. Since I invited my damn self right on in, I wanted him to know I would work my ass off and that he could trust me to have no ulterior motives. Luckily for me, he unequivocally trusted me, and more.

I planned and ran a third of the facility myself, everything from setting up drapes and tables, to deciding how much line space each celebrity needed. Royce and his crew ran the other two-thirds. I designed the T-shirts and lots of the social media graphics while his promotional skills were applied to TV and radio advertising. He was like a Jedi business master, doing everything behind the scenes to make the event successful. I was very impressed, and very proud to be his wingman.

The morning of the show, I led the crew of celebrities to our local hospital. Royce and I thought it would be a great gesture to give a little time and happiness back to the community that was about to come out and support us. While Royce was going out of his mind at the convention center getting everything ready for the chaos, I was picking up Jason David Frank (the Green Power Ranger). We met wrestling icon Hacksaw Jim Duggan, Ghostbuster Ernie Hudson, and TV's Freak Show sweetheart Naomi Grossman at the sick children's wing. The cast had no "characters" to turn on for this assignment. They were naturally the most genuinely humble and caring group of celebrities I have ever met. Going from room to room, we would take turns signing pictures and giving out merch to the kids. It is such an amazing feeling to walk into a room with a sad child and announce; "Hi, Joey. My name is Chris 51, and I have a tattoo TV show here in our city, and I brought some cool people to cheer you up. A real-life Ghostbuster, wrestling superstar, Power Ranger, and beautiful TV star are all here just to say hi to you and hope you get better soon." Jaws dropped, parents cried, and my heart felt happy and grateful.

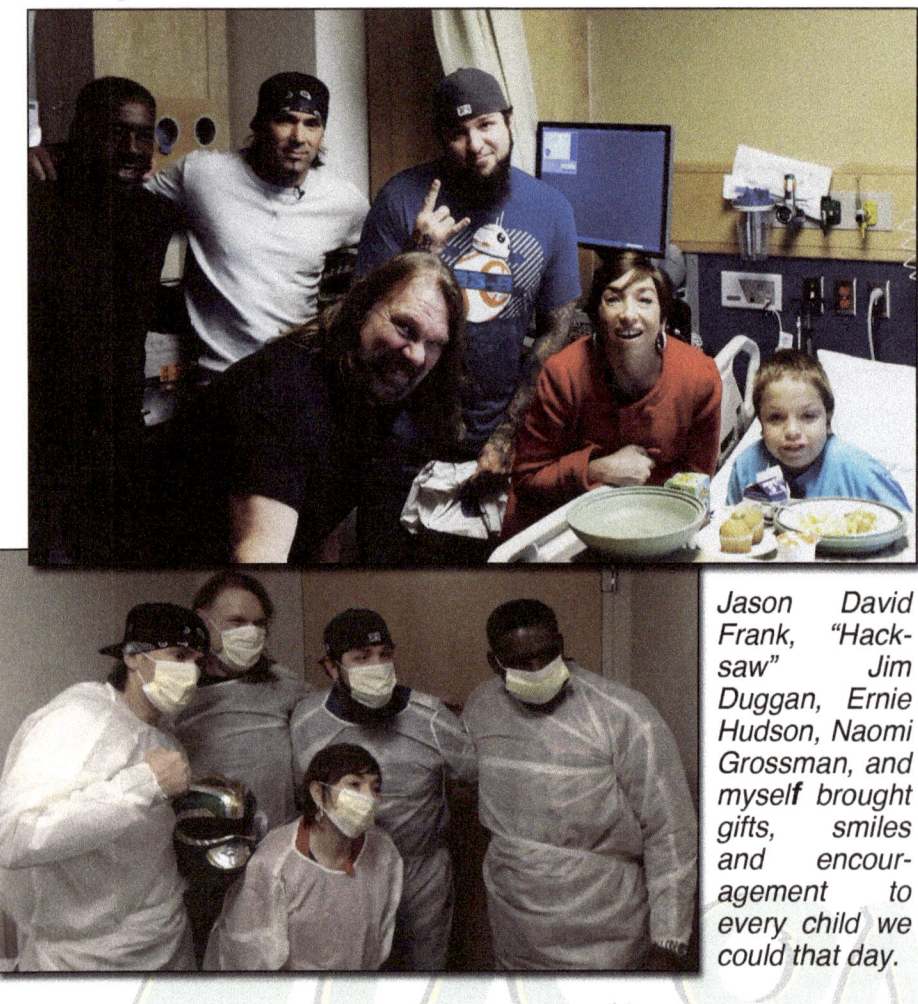

Jason David Frank, "Hacksaw" Jim Duggan, Ernie Hudson, Naomi Grossman, and myself brought gifts, smiles and encouragement to every child we could that day.

When I returned to the convention center, I couldn't believe my eyes. We had a problem—a good problem! The line was hundreds, maybe thousands deep, stretching down the parking lot and wrapping around the building. Royce asked me to just handle the fire marshal and facility manager because they were freaking out. It was time to get my ass right to work and put out fires.

The facility boss wanted to shut us down. He explained that he had never had a crowd like this in all the decades he'd been running the joint. I had to remind him that this was a "good" problem for us all to have and that we could all benefit from it. I literally had to take charge and shut him down! I looked him in the eye and said, "Dude chill! Listen, I am your man. You tell me what you need, and I will personally get it done right now. Trust me." Before I knew it, I was single-handedly shouting and moving a line of 1,000 fans deep across the parking lot to other areas. I was moving vendor displays around the floor per the fire marshal's commands. I rearranged police officers to different locations and walked the line outside to put wristbands on fans to speed up the entry process. My morning was a blur, and I needed to be the Flash. Everyone involved did everything they needed to, no matter how hard and tiring, and as a team, we pulled it off. We were all superheroes for a common goal. It is an awesome feeling when you see a team of strangers pull together and work their asses off to make greatness happen. The weekend ended with an attendance of almost 10,000, shattering records for the facility.

"You have to be fucking crazy to want to produce a comic con. Once you get going, there's a lot of excitement, and you start getting a vision of what you want it to be. Then it becomes this mixed bag of stress, determination, fun, and fear. You lose sleep over it, you obsess over it, and it occupies your every thought. You can't wait for the day you get to open the doors, and you are also completely terrified by the thought of it. You have no idea what's going to happen," says Royce Myers.

The biggest craze of the con, though, was the crowd around the Green Ranger! My good friend Jason David Frank took a huge risk on coming to a first-year, untested show. I hosted a panel with Jason, and I was happy to tell the standing-room-only crowd of his fans about the kind of character he had, not just the kind of character he played on TV. He single-handedly helped make

the inaugural Eucon a huge success. I can't thank him enough!

Enter 2016. Eucon round two was a fight from the start. It was a battle to get celebrities signed. Maybe we just had great luck on year one, or maybe it was because it was during a holiday weekend, and lots of big names were already long-booked for our slot on the calendar. Regardless, as soon as we would be ready to sign somebody, they would back out, have to go start filming a new project, or get offered more from another con. I called my long-time friend Butch Patrick (aka Eddie Munster), and he was gracious enough to come free of charge as a friendly favor to me.

We secured a combo of Ruth Connell from *Supernatural* and David Anders from *iZombie* and *Heroes* because we worked with their agent the year before and built a solid connection. *Star Trek's* Deep Roy and WWE Hall-of-Famer Greg "The Hammer" Valentine rounded out the small list. My friends Michael Cudlitz (*The Walking Dead*), Lou Ferrigno (Hulk), and Jason David Frank all wanted to come but already had prior obligations. Since we committed so much more money to renting out the entire convention center this go around, and added rent for an extra day, it was very difficult to front money for more big-name guests. When you dish out $35,000 just to rent a building, your wallet takes a hefty blow. Trying to sign celebrities at $10,000 (or more) a punch, you get beaten up very quickly. Nevertheless, our guests were amazing and as accommodating as could be. They had fun and said that they loved the show, and our community.

(Above) *Star Wars'* actor Deep Roy was a hilarious atraction, as seen here crawling under Chewie.

I expanded our live tattoo area to include twelve of the country's top geek-culture artists. Heather Maranda and Josh Bodwell anchored the lineup. Casey Baker and Kyler Shinn represented the local Area 51 Tattoo. Joe Riley of TV's *Tattoo Titans* came, followed by popular industry stars like James Mullin, Kevin Becvar, and more. The fans loved the interactive attraction, especially many children who had never experienced a tattoo being performed live before.

(Top) Mr. Eddie Munster and I at our panel.
(Left) Even the tattoo artist crew had to get in on a David Anders photo.
(Below) Deep Roy being his jolly self at my expense.
Photos Courtesy of **Life Slice Photography**.

Back to the Future's DeLorean and *Supernatural's* Baby were added for car buffs and photo opportunities. We tried to make the whole experience well-rounded so the entire family could enjoy the day out, not just the die-hard geeks. The show turned out great, and after a

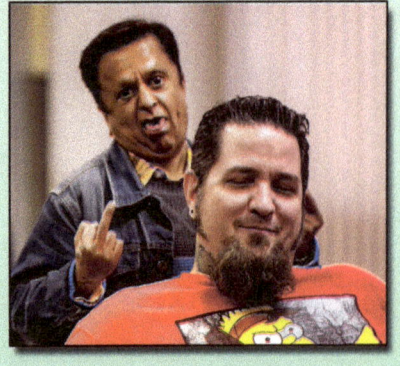

solid half day of rest, I was already planning 2017!

I am so proud of what Eucon has become, and as long as I am alive, there will always be a comic con in our small northwest area!

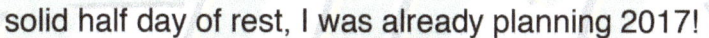

Deep Roy at Voodoo Doughnuts, Eugene

Greg "The Hammer" Valentine and I with the Geeksterink Tattoo guys.

25

EPIC INK
(Take 6)

TATTOO TRIAL BY FIRE

Day one of filming. First tattoo, three cameras in my face. No music in the background to get lost in. It's completely quiet, and everyone is watching and judging. The shop is closed for business, so we're losing money, and the past-due bills are mounting. No reason to be nervous . . . so I start doing what I was born to do. I do what I know how to do better than anything on earth . . . on a design that's completely not my style. It's the type of tattoo I haven't done in a decade, but it was the only thing I could choose that remotely resembled a pop-culture-themed tattoo. The producers cast a bunch of shit art subjects, mostly based on the client's story and personality, forgetting that we are here for the art first. So, this realism artist is gonna have to do a half sleeve of solid, bold outlines that he hasn't done since two presidents ago. It's okay, I remember my roots. I got this. I mean, at least it's *Teenage Mutant Ninja Turtles,* so I will

just focus on my love for the subject matter at hand.

I start tattooing . . . and they make me stop. "What do you mean my tattoo machine is too loud?" They clarify: "We can't hear you talking with your mic right under your throat because your archaic machine is too damn loud." "Oh, you mean this machine that I have done every tattoo with for the last fourteen years— this one?" "Yeah, that one. You can't use that one, it needs to be quieter." I explain that this is a coil machine and they are all this loud. The only thing quieter is a rotary machine, which is a totally different beast. It's like driving a monster truck and then getting into a Ferrari expecting to hit the same dirt track. I physically cannot use it. Never have. Told myself I never will. It's what all of them young, cocky, whippersnapper kids are using, and I'm old school, yo! "Well, we can't get you talking on your own TV show then, sorry," expresses a producer. "Chris, try my rotary," offers Josh, who is sitting next to me, "I know your style and you can handle it. It's what I made the transition with." No problem. New type of machine I've never used, doing a style with outlines I haven't done in ten years with no music to drown out my nerves, all while being filmed and going broke

with only one million people going to see it. No pressure at all. This is what I worked so long and hard for though, so I was gonna get it! Nothing was going to stop me now, not when I was this close. Adrenaline, pride, and even stubbornness all kick in to help me through. That, along with Josh's help yet again . . . and maybe a strong desire to have a successful geeky reality comedy TV show.

That was my initiation into reality television. After that, shit just seemed to get easier.

(Above) My cast mate Heather Maranda during a routine day of filming. This is an example of what it was like daily, for three straight months.

WRONG PLACE AT THE RIGHT TIME

Like Ken Griffey Jr. past his prime, I was always the one getting injured. Maybe it's because I tried the most physical comedy, or it might be just because I was the clumsiest.

Whichever the case (I prefer to think it's the first), I always sacrificed my body for the scene and never really considered my personal safety a factor.

Don't let me brag (or make fun of myself) too much, because we were pretty stationary and didn't really do much in the way of dangerous activity. But, we did do lots of interstitial scenes. Interstitials were the funny little action skits we did between scenes, and they usually aired when the show returned from commercial breaks. They required your basic athletic prowess, including a gnarly dodgeball match. Please keep in mind that for sedentary tattoo artists, basic athletic prowess feels like hardcore Olympic training because we don't get to move much while sitting on our asses all day long. So basically, tattooers are more like assletes* than athletes!

My first injury happened in a scene that never aired. Long before I got my TV show, I'd had a retrofit ambulance made into a tattoo studio. It was so unique that I suggested to the producers that they incorporate it into a segment. They agreed and decided that the cast would design each other as aliens to replace the old, outdated graphics on the vehicle. We spent hours and hours on these scenes, and it's a waste that they never aired because they were extremely funny. Luckily for us, the producers made a couple of the production assistants manually scrape off—with razorblades—all the old vinyl stickers that had been on the ride for almost a decade. So in the end, we had the much easier job making that scene. Get to the point here, Chris. Okay, so the final scene entailed some silly banter, unveiling the funny new graphics, and then jumping in the "Manbulance" for a maiden voyage to the local comic-book shop.

The producers had a bottle of champagne ready for us that magically appeared to christen the new and improved vehicle with some classic naval tradition. It was cheap champagne, as to not be too classy, but a strong-ass bottle nonetheless. Apparently, it was too strong for this weakling.

Enter scene one: Mr. 51 bashes the bottle on the

diamond-plated steel bumper in a most impressive barbarian-esque swing, yet the world's strongest bottle refuses to break and literally bounces off the bumper and laughs at Mr. 51 on its ricochet. Laughing ensues from the cast and entire production team, even the ones sitting in the back of the shop hundreds of feet away, and I hear it all, and it feels like I just missed a free throw to win the game.

Scene two. Let's try this again, C51. Second swing: this time I am as focused as Jose Canseco at the plate, aiming for a home run . . . or in the bathroom before the game, aiming the roids syringe for his vein. Either way, I'm not gonna let that stupid bottle get the best of me. It gets the best of me . . . again. What the fuck, is it filled with concrete? I hate this damn bottle. More boisterous laughing reconfirms my pussiness.

Scene three. Fuck this bottle. I take the hardest swing ever, a swing that would impress Mike Tyson himself. I break that sumbitch in half. Only problem is, I break it on the front half by the handle, and I feel a sudden sharp pain, followed by coldness on my hand. I know what happened, but I'm not about to lose the scene we finally got, so I quickly put my hand in my pocket and continue on. A minute later, we enter the truck to exit the scene driving away, and boy do I speed out of there. When I remove my hand from my pocket, it looks like I just fisted a woman during shark week. Josh is

Cleaned aftermath, 3 inch wrist slice

riding shotgun and lets out the proverbial, "Holy shit, dude." I play off my agony cool but exaggerate it at home to my wife for added sympathy. In the end at least we got the scene, even though it was never used.

My next injury was a simple hamstring pull, but as those of you who have pulled a hammy know, it's no joke when it initially happens. Enter scene. A picnic-heist interstitial. We recruited a mom and her baby to sit with one of our crewmembers and enjoy a loving family picnic on a green, grassy knoll. My role was to casually stroll behind them and stop in mid-stride when I noticed a plate of chocolate-chip cookies adorning their sweet setup, like a pot of gold under a glorious rainbow. Since chocolate-chip cookies are one of the most important things in my whole world, this idea wasn't far-fetched at all. I continued to bend over and reach for a cookie while the adults were focused on their infant. Like a stealthy ninja, I grabbed one and dashed away. Well, I wasn't exactly ninja-like, because as I sprinted away I made it about ten strides and fell to the ground in agony. I pulled a hammy, but never dropped my cookie, and proceeded to eat bites through tears of disappointment in my fat ass. I limped off in shame and pondered why I didn't do my pre-ninja stretching exercises.

Of course, that scene never saw the light of day, but they did use a funny-ass one with the same setup where Heather rolled down the knoll past the picnicking family, like a three-year-old, all giggly and hyper.

My third injury was the worst, but not at the time. This time the scene was actually used in an episode, so it was worth it in the end. During another interstitial, I was standing king-of-the-mountain style at the top of a big, curvy slide at a playground. The producer told me to go up there and just do something. If you know me, then you know I'm not about just doing a normal something, nor am I about just normal sliding. I take my playground sliding serious, cause there is always an audience at the slide. I told the punk kid in my way at the bottom to gangway, turned my hat around backward for better aerodynamics, and dove headfirst. It felt as graceful as a Lynn Swann TD catch, but looked more like a Peyton Manning scramble. I jerked and banged my body all the way down, because strangely, the slide curves weren't made for my curves, a six-foot-tall, 250-pound bear-man. I hopped up like a baseball player who just got beaned by a fastball like it didn't hurt, refusing to brush myself off. I went straight to my wife and complained that I think I heard a pop or tear in my shoulder and it was real sore already. She laughed and said that she'd just told Caroline right before my stunt that she bets I complain that I get hurt. The nerve of her being right!

I was sore for a few days and lost some range of motion, but I didn't think it was anything serious. I'm an avid weight lifter, and I noticed that my strength went down significantly over those next few months. The nagging soreness persisted. Months after filming, I got an MRI and it showed that I indeed tore my rotator cuff in half. Turns out, I wasn't such a wuss and had valid complaints to my know-it-all wife, ha! I win! But not really, because over two years later, I'm still in pain and have no time for surgery. Sure, I could make time, but then I would be sidelined from tattooing for a couple months, and I just can't have that. I'd go crazy.

In the end, it was all worth it, and I would do it over again and again for the opportunity to entertain with my friends. We had so many adventures together while filming, and the only pain that remains is it being over.

Not all of our adventures ended in soreness or injuries, in fact, most of our outings were downright Epic.

EPIC ADVENTURES

THE ENCHANTED FOREST

I couldn't resist nagging the producers to film at Oregon's historic Enchanted Forest. It's a small, quaint, nursery-rhyme theme park built into the side of a forested mountain. It's a filming paradise complete with a haunted house, an old western town, a log-flume ride, and eerie trails winding through creepy witches' houses and Hobbit-type trees. The producers eventually agreed to take us there, and we got a very memorable field trip day out of it.

We must have filmed a dozen different scenes there. We used one scene on an episode where we were all bored around the island counter at the shop, so Jeff used his wizard magic and whisked us away through the time-space continuum to land in the middle of the theme park. We skipped down the trail and out of the scene. It was so brilliant and cheesy at the same time, which made it so endearing.

In one effort, we shot a scene where the whole cast was piled into the cutest little kiddie train, going for the ride of a lifetime (which happened to be a thirty-foot circle). It was ridiculous, but hey, that's what we were all about.

In other scenes throughout the day, and in about every location of the park, was Heather chasing around Caroline with a fly net. Caroline wore a unicorn costume and Heather was the animal-control catcher lady. They jumped in and out of rides and buildings, simultaneously scaring onlooking parents and making their children laugh.

None of us have ever seen any of this unused footage. The mysterious network executives behind the curtain keep it all locked in a vault at the secret Emerald City of A&E, and the yellow brick road no longer leads there.

THE GOONIE HOUSE

Early on, one of my producers asked me for fun field-trip location ideas for filming, and I immediately thought of things that I like to do with my kids. It seemed fitting since my cast mates were all a bunch of grown kids. Other than the local ballpark and Enchanted Forest theme park, I suggested a water park near Portland.

Evergreen Water Park has a giant 747 airplane sitting atop its roof with water-tube slides coming out of the plane's exits, which wind down into a huge pool. I called the water park myself and set up the trip, but the producers decided against it. I'm not sure if it was a network financial thing or a liability thing.

Then my inner geek took over, and I remembered that the house where the 1980s' classic movie *The Goonies* was filmed was in Oregon. Though I had never been there, I knew we could make the most of it however the house turned out because we were all huge fans of that movie. I mean, who isn't? In fact, if you're a child of the seventies or eighties and you don't like *The Goonies*, I don't trust you. There could be something mentally wrong with you. You should get that shit checked, homie.

Astoria, Oregon, was a good four-hour drive away, so I didn't hold my breath that we would ever actually pack up the whole cast and film crew on our small budget and make the

trip happen. I didn't hear about it again until one day when we were told to come in the next morning prepared for a field trip.

We packed into a couple huge vans and started heading north. I got a pretty good idea of where we were headed just by paying attention to the roads, but the crew did a great job  keeping the details secret. They wanted to film the cast's real emotional reactions and energy when we pulled up to the famous location. The producers even called ahead and got special permission for us to film on the porch, which was completely off-limits to the public.

We filmed a scene where Caroline all made us do the "truffle shuffle" in order to join her on the porch. I immediately did mine without hesitation because I was so excited to hop up on that porch and immerse myself in the nostalgia that was running rampant through my veins. Turns out, I did the famous fat-kid belly dance too quickly because the cameras caught only the remaining cast doing it as I jumped out of the scene.

Being on that famous porch where Data crashed though the front door coming down his zip line was mind melting. You can actually still see the hole that the zip line was attached to above the neighbor's top-floor window where Data's room was. From that porch, on a steep hill, you can look out over a quaint residential community and spot another famous movie landmark. The elementary school where *Kindergarten Cop* was filmed lies right in the middle of all the surrounding homes and hills, like out of some storybook of pop-culture epicness.

Later that afternoon, we visited the small jail where *The Goonies'* opening escape scene was filmed. The now historic Astoria Film Museum still bears the original jail cell that Jake Fratelli was held in, even the contraction that he fake-hanged himself with to induce his escape plan. Parked outside is the Jeep Cherokee escape vehicle that Mama Fratelli picked her escaped son up in, complete with bullet holes above its rear bumper. We filmed various little scenes there to add to the day's adventures, but unfortunately, none of them ever escaped the cutting-room floor. I have still never seen any of the classic footage we made, which was hilarious as always.

Above) The original hanging contraption made by Jake Fratelli, still in the cell in which the scene was filmed.

(Left) The cast left a signed note at the museum. As you can see by the Area 51 Show portion, we did not yet know the name of our show at the time.

I have since been back to the historical house with my wife, and the new homeowners have disallowed all fan visitation. Fucking lame. If people don't know what they are getting into when they buy that house, then they don't deserve to own such an important piece of geek history. I told my wife that one day I will buy it and retire there, just selling Goonies merchandise in a booth out front. Seriously, I would be completely content making and selling original Goonie fan art and apparel, and taking fan photos for a small fee in front of the house. I would grill up hotdogs and serve hot cocoa and own that shit! A geek can dream I guess, because Goonie dreams never die.

DODGEBALL CHALLENGE

I can barely put into words how fun this adventure was, and even more so how funny it was. Collectively, this memory has to be one of the cast's favorites. We came together as a team of athletically challenged misfits, and achieved victory over another pretend team of athletically challenged misfits.

This scene was the only one we filmed that was almost entirely fabricated, just to be over-the-top silly and outrageous. The producers had the idea for us and another local shop to play friendly pranks on each other throughout the season. One prank had an artist from the other shop come in to get a third-nipple tattoo, and we were the gullible butts of his joke. We retaliated by tagging his truck with Area 51 Tattoo and alien graffiti art (in washable paint, of course). The back and forth pranks finally escalated to a challenge with Epic repercussions, as the losing shop had to buy beers for everyone.

Now this is where shit got real. I reached out to a local tattoo shop called Eugene Ink to participate in the fun, thinking that some camera exposure might also help them out. You know, spread the local love. The owner, who was an acquaintance, must have thought I was full of shit or something, and he refused. I explained that I was trying to help him out cause I always heard he was cool, but he continued to distrust me. That's the tattoo industry for ya—even when you try and help out a fellow artist or shop, they immediately think something scandalous is going on. Oh well, his loss. So, I called my friend, Josh Docherty, from Level Up Arcade and asked him to put together a

fake team for me, chosen from his favorite, most personable tattooed customers. I purposely called them Springfield Ink to mimic that Eugene Ink shop that wouldn't help us out.

Dodgeball was the sport of choice to settle our rivalry with our longtime (weeklong) nemesis Springfield Ink once and for all. We got dressed in our fanciest, short 1970s-era gym shorts and loaded up in the ambulance to meet our pretend enemies at the battle court.

During the first play of the game, Heather slipped and ate shit, sending her out of game one. Several matches and lots of hysterical antics later, I found myself the last remaining soldier against two of the opposing team's best. I made quick work of them as I caught a fierce throw to force out one of their players, and rocketed that ball at the feet of their last survivor to seal our victory. In my recollection, it was a glorious victory, but on film it probably looked more like a lucky, out-of-breath fat kid heaving one last throw of desperation.

For our victory, Springfield Ink presented me with my own cherished Homer Simpson Buddha statue. WTF! They had somehow stolen it during our prank wars, probably by sending an inside man to perform the heist days prior, and I'd never noticed. I pretended to freak out and jumped into the arms of Bodwell and Chris Jones, telling them to hold me back. They knew where I was going with this gesture and made it look as real as possible, however corny. I spread my legs kicking and flailing like mad, which unknowingly caused my undersized jogging shorts to ride up, giving the cameramen a free ball-bag show. Now that was some acting!

Interviews about the match followed, and that's when the humor got out of control. We all had to stop watching each other because we were laughing so hard, and we had to do countless retakes. That day, Jeff and Heather were two of the funniest people I had ever seen and could've rivaled any stand-up comedian alive.

In the end, not one second of it aired. An entire day of filming, and the funniest moments that television would see that year, and it was scrapped. The network said that dodgeball was too cliché or something ridiculous. I promise you that they lost out on what would have been our best ratings with that one.

Mysteriously, a video surfaced on YouTube last year of the cast jumping out of the ambulance, all slow-motion style like a Michael Bay explosion scene. Decked out in our dodgeball gear, we walk off scene to the sweet sounds of Heather whispering about if it's possible to fart into someone else's butt.

None of us know where production got Heather's sound bites from; even Heather herself can't remember where and when she was talking all quiet and seductively about farting. Can you imagine all the stupid shit that came out of our mouths when we forgot we were mic'd up? To this day, none of us know who put together and released that video. I would give anything to see the rest of the footage.

STARS ARE BORN

My cast mates are a bunch of geeks, and they made a geeky show. *Epic Ink* deserved more than the normal cable-TV commercial or advertising-signage routes of promotion—it needed an Epic introduction made just for fellow geeks. We wanted to reach our kindred nerd spirits, and there's only one place where that can be done most proficiently and with the biggest splash: a comic con. And the most Epic comic con in the world is, of course, San Diego Comic Con. I had an idea.

When I first approached the producers about promoting our show's release at SDCC, the whole thing seemed wildly unobtainable. I was used to seeing new TV-show booths and advertisements all over comic cons I went to, which made sense since that's where the shows' target demographic was. But A&E didn't understand that because they had never produced a show so geeky, and they weren't really aware of the pop-culture heart of the beast that was SDCC. So, I made them aware! It was a subject I refused to give up on because I knew in my own heart that the grand master of all comic cons is where we needed to be. I knew that our personalities would help sell the show, but for that to happen we had to be live and in person to an audience of viewers made for our kind of show. I knew we needed to sell ourselves to the public as much as we did our characters on film.

Either the network had some kind of faith in us, or I nagged them to death and they wanted to shut me up, but they finally approved the trip. They decided to have a *Bates Motel* booth at the convention and bring us there as guests of honor to promote our show from their current hit-show's area. Do you know what an erotic feeling it is to put on a badge that reads "celebrity guest" at the world's most illustrious geek event? I had a boner for days that even Viagra couldn't touch. Then the network added their own plans and flare to the adventure, which would again change our lives forever.

First, A&E flew their Jedi-master executive out to wine and dine us. A $1,000 sushi dinner later, we started feeling pretty spoiled. Next, they put us up in a fancy hotel right in the heart of the comic con action.

During the days at the con, we handed out promotional temporary tattoos with the show's debut date and time on the back. Leading up to the trip, we had all designed a temp tattoo for the event, which seemed appropriate (pictured right). The network picked my design and Heather's to be printed (mine had some needed help from Caroline's photoshopping skills).

Our friends Butch Patrick and Daniel Logan (Star Wars' Boba Fett child actor) even stopped by the Bates Motel booth to say hi and help us out with a little celebrity clout (pictured left).

At night, the network had us attending a few red-carpet press parties, the first thing like that any of us had ever done. It was the last press party that would solidify us as true stars, or at least it felt that way.

Our limo had to circle the block a couple times to give the other celebrities time to finish their walk on the carpet. When it was our turn and the door opened, a whole new world opened to us. Camera flashes and bright lights were actually focused on us, these out-of-shape, most atypical, new Hollywood celebrities in the making. Hordes of TV and magazine reporters bombarded us with questions, and we were ready for every single one. Even without experience, we shined under this sort of attention.

We all agreed in advance to color coordinate our fancy ensembles for this event. Black and gold were the flamboyant colors of choice. We wanted to be different than the norm, just like our show, so the standard penguin suits just wouldn't do. Between my gold-flaked Adidas, Jeff's solid-gold Nike Air Force Ones, Chris's gold-sequined jacket, and our beautiful, tattooed women, we definitely stood out in the crowd. People might have thought something like, "Look at these assholes who have never been here before and don't know how to act," but, we didn't care; this was our moment to shine. After posing for pictures on the red carpet like actual stars, we moved into the magic wonderment that was a celebrity party.

My jaw dropped. This was a *Bates Motel* and *Playboy* joint event. A set replica of the actual motel from the show formed an entire side of the grounds. Patrón Tequila sponsored the party so there was top-shelf alcohol being shoved in our faces all night for free by girls in *Playboy* bunny suits.

We headed to the VIP area to find half of the cast of T*he Walking Dead* already there, along with celebrities from shows such as *Vikings, Bates Motel*, and others. We got to meet, drink, and hang out with all of them, as equals. It took everything I had to not fanboy out, and I tried to act respectful and like I belonged there. My wife was, of course, gaga over Norman Reedus, like every damn woman in the country. Actually, come to think of it, I was too. What can I say; he's a badass-looking dude, haha. You'll be happy to know, though, that I did not kiss him in a photo like my Katie did . . . I refrained from my urges. I talked a little with Freddie Highmore (*Bates Motel*) about what it was like to work for A&E and how they treated him. Ya know, some insider business to make me look like I was speaking the common tongue instead of getting tongue-tied. I think it was probably obvious to him that I was still a little giddy though (pictured right).

Our network-press liaison introduced me to Vera Farmiga from *Bates Motel*. She was as beautiful as she was charming. She gladly took a picture with me, and even asked about my new show. Right after my new crush walked away, I was introduced to *Lost* and *Bates Motel* star Nestor Carbonell. He wanted to

show me his neck (why?). He was sporting my temporary tattoo that I designed for the comic con promo. I saw him taking pictures with it on his neck all night at this important event. It made my day even better—if that was possible.

Nobody wants to admit that they love being treated so lavishly with such attention... but most would be lying if they didn't. I'm the first to admit that it sparked something in me. It was an injection of chaos, serenity, and fantasy all at the same time. It was a feeling that I would try to duplicate for the rest of my life, like a drug that I couldn't get enough of. I told myself I could handle this drug and that it would never change my morals trying to score it. That promise wouldn't stop me from constantly craving it though.

26

BASEBALL PHOTOGRAPHER

Those who can't play the game become fans. Then there are Superfans who get season tickets and buy the expensive jerseys. Then there are the few Supermegafans who want more, because being just a spectator won't do anymore. I didn't just want more, I needed more! And who was to stop me . . . only me.

I was a season ticket holder for the Fort Myers Miracle of the class A Florida State League. There is something about the quiet chaos of a minor-league baseball game during sunset after a hard day's work that is indescribable. It is simultaneously nostalgic, exciting, calming, and serendipitous. Add a hot dog, peanuts, and Coke to that combo, and you have the recipe for a perfect evening, of which I have enjoyed thousands of times in my life. I digress; I still wanted more.

As a geek, I (of course) collected baseball autographs and memorabilia. When there were no photos of newly drafted or traded players to get signed, I started taking my own. I would print out two, giving one to the player as a keepsake if he would sign the other for me. With great response and appreciation from the ballers, this practice soon took over normal, complacent collecting, and I began to think outside the (batter's) box.

After developing one batch of kick-ass action photos (on film), I arrogantly decided that I was to become the team's next photographer. I had two things that the current photographer didn't. One, I was as young as the players, so in their eyes, I was on their side, almost one of them. The other dude was a lame old-timer who was stuck in the past. Two, I was FREE! I didn't charge anyone a dime. I always looked towards the bigger picture. I was confident that once I made a splash on the scene, I would get the money I deserved. When you aren't greedy and don't focus on money, you can redirect your focus on the task at hand. I talked to one of the staffers who I had befriended a little and told him my idea. He brought me to the GM and introduced me. A couple days later, I started my own sports photography business.

I didn't know the first thing about photography. I was just a baseball fanboy with a fanboy camera. That didn't stop me. I didn't need to know. I knew I could do it, so I did it. I just read some reviews online and found a good, user-friendly camera. I turned it to the green auto setting and I was set. I knew nothing of filters or lighting, but I was blessed with the natural Florida sun and the vast knowledge of baseball.

I now have a close relationship with my local Eugene Ems from filming Epic Ink there. I no longer do photos because I prefer family time at the ballpark.

Not only did I know the sport so well that I could tell when batters were going to swing and base runners were going to steal, but I knew the players so well from hanging out. We spent time together outside of the park, whether it was parties, dinners, or fishing. That allowed me to understand their tendencies and routines, strengths and weaknesses, and capture it all on film. I knew what Michael Cuddyer was going to do on a 0-2 count, and I knew when Matt LeCroy was going to swing away. I understood the perfect time to get the optimal picture. This was crucial because nothing was digital back then, and film was expensive for a blue-collar plumber taking pictures on the side. My shots had to be exact and creative—that was my niche.

The other photographers never got close to the players. It was just a job to them. It was a passion to me, and the guys were my homies. They saw my passion and trusted me because of it. It was a mutual respect for the love of the game. Before I knew it, they were showing me naked pictures of ballclub groupies and inviting me to their parties.

No longer did I buy season tickets, or even sit in the stands for that matter. I was on the field, behind the mound, and chilling in the ball boy's chair. Soon the manager was inviting me to sit next to him in the dugout during games.

I kept it fresh, and more importantly, I kept it fun for the players. Standard team photos were anything but the standard. They were no longer boring rows of emotionless minions, but juxtapositions of every uniform combo outside of the stadium, around the fountain, and even in the decorative fountain! Baseball cards and program inserts weren't just blurs of repeti-

tive live-action sequences, but a truer definition of what these players were: grown kids. The photos showed pranks, funny poses, tough-guy stances, and just about anything else. In fact, a lot of times I let the players give me ideas and try things themselves. I kept to the tradition of the past with some classic images, but tried to balance the modern age by infusing some anti-conformography*.

The players loved the different approach so much that they would do anything I asked, no matter how silly. I took them on the practice fields alone with heaps of different jerseys and equipment to pose for me and do fake

action shots and over-the-top dramatic stills. Not only did they love it, but so did a few baseball-card companies. I started getting calls from the "show." For a minor-league photographer, true accomplishment was getting your pictures published in the newspaper or Baseball America, but the "show" was getting your work made into a baseball card. I ended up getting a half-dozen cards made, and I still didn't know what the fuck I was doing (haha). I was just having fun and exerting my passion. Upper Deck, one of the biggest card companies in the world at the time, even called the Fort Myers Miracle about my services and sent me on a special assignment to capture a couple hot prospects in the league.

The lesson here is to push. Push yourself, push traditional boundaries, push your will. Push people around you to do better and visualize greater . . . or push them out of your way to success. If you never stop pushing, you never slow down, and nobody can impede your progress.

Even though my professional sports photography days are long over, I have rekindled my joy of the art form through my children's love of sports. I started making them their own football cards to give their friends. I Photoshopped vintage cards from my own childhood as templates and put all of my boys' statistics on back. My kids' friends liked them so much that the parents from their siblings' teams started wanting them. Before I knew it, the whole league wanted me to make sports cards for their young, aspiring athletes.

When you are passionate enough about something, that love shines through in your work, no matter what it is. And there is nothing that evokes more passion than your children.

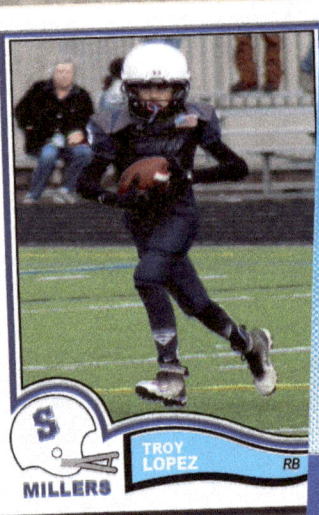

Here are some examples of my photos made in to baseball cards; from Minor League team sets (*on following page*) to Major League prospects for major card companies (*below*).

You always have to research everything! The Florida State League used dozens of my photos for their All-Star set (*example on right*) without my permission or compensation. I was honored they used them, but it wasn't done right, so I made sure it ended right.

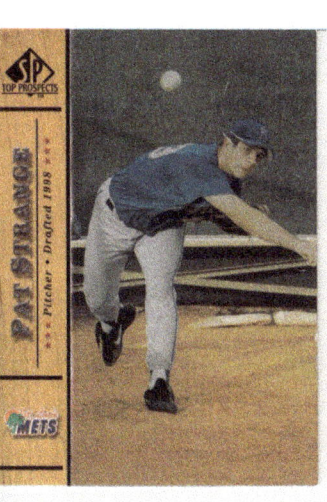
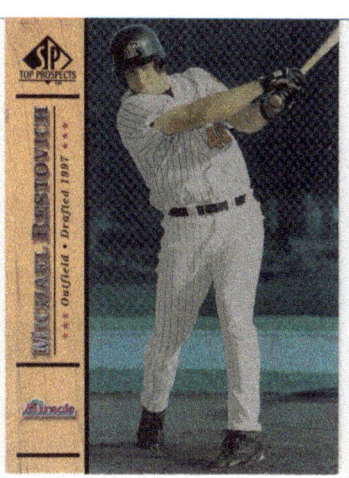

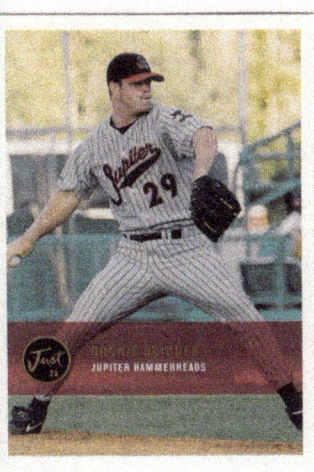

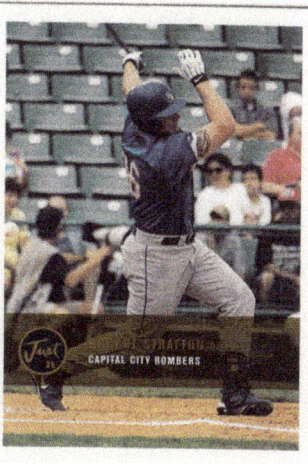

Spring Training in Fort Myers, Florida, was a candy store for me when it came to taking sweet baseball photos. I always enjoyed catching players in obscure, rather than ordinary poses. Here, I got Hideo Nomo (left) delivering his famous windup, and Deion Sanders superstitiously drawing in the dirt before his at bat. I loved the capture of the golden cross dangling from his neck.

27

GOING PRO: MY FORTIES

It is a very peculiar and astounding revelation to discover that you are in your mental prime. This chapter is a message about a personal revelation of self-awareness. Maybe it can help you, because there is nothing better to help boost your confidence as a maturing man than having the courage to try anything without fear or hesitation.

One day, when I was forty, I was telling my mother about all the new projects that I was working on. Not the high-profile stuff, just the books, paintings, trading cards, and such. She always humored me with interest and offered balanced pros and cons. This particular time, she commented that I reminded her of my dad at my age. That statement, as complimentary as it was to me, really made me ponder my immediate situation. I always respected my dad's business-minded intelligence, and it just seemed like there was a point in his life when he could do anything in his career he wanted, and

didn't need instruction or harbor hesitation. It was as if he always had the knowledge hidden inside him just waiting for the right time to reveal its prowess.

I had inherited that same trait, like The Force that is passed down from father to son, and I was going to use it to accomplish great things. My brain was at its climax for entrepreneurial release, and I was going to stimulate my cerebellum until it exploded. I tried my hand at every idea my mind presented me, and they seemed to come easily and frequently. I just knew how to do new things through common sense, life experience, and intuition. I honestly felt like I could accomplish any mental exercise, and turn it pro without even a training camp to speak of. And, that's exactly what I did. Although not all my ideas came to fruition, usually due to time restraints or lack of monetary reach, they all landed right where they needed to in order to motivate or manipulate the next fruitful endeavor. I failed at a few things, but I didn't let it stop me. Like trying to follow any set of Ikea instructions ever, you too will fail and fuck shit up, but those are the necessary steps in the manual of life that teach you resilience and clarity.

My dad was like a white Mr. T. My painting, "Mr. T Got Robbed...Fool"

Suddenly, I was painting anything that came to mind and visualizing art pieces faster than I could produce them. I freed my mind of hate and aggression and turned those mind-bogging emotions into fuel for excellence. I imagined new companies or products in my dreams and was pursuing them by that next afternoon, throwing caution and worries to the wolves in the complacent canine buffet in which they belonged. I was completely mindful of my mind, and nothing was stopping me. I also knew that power had a temporary shelf life, so I wasn't going to waste it before I got brain arthritis to match my old sports aches and pains.

There is no such thing as being bored when your mind reaches this level of clarity. There is no downtime. In fact, there is never enough time to accomplish all of the things that your brain can conjure up. It is more likely that your hands won't be able to keep up with what your mind wants them to build or create.

There are clues to recognizing your mental prime, and it doesn't take Sherlock to figure them out. Are you extremely focused on just one project, or do you want to start new projects before

He had no fear, so "The Fucking Annoyance of Scrappy," seemed fitting here.

the current one is even completed? That is your mind telling you it hungers for more stimulation. Feed it! Are you waking up from dreams about what you want to do rather than what you've already done? That is your subconscious trying to motivate you. Is depriving yourself of sleep to find time to work on projects more important than wasting time snoozing? Would you rather stimulate your brain with pen, paper, paint, an instrument, or computer over a video game console? Has your TV become more of a reward than a necessity? If you can relate to these questions, then it's time to be like Tony Micelli and show life Who's the Boss! You don't have to act like a grown-up to grow, you just have to overcome childlike fear.

Like usual, I probably sound braggadocios, but I assure you that my moral agenda is sound. I just want to help open your eyes and squash your intellectual inhibitions. Your mental prime time will come for you, and you need to be prepared to recognize it, capitalize on it, and sideline the fears so you can go pro!

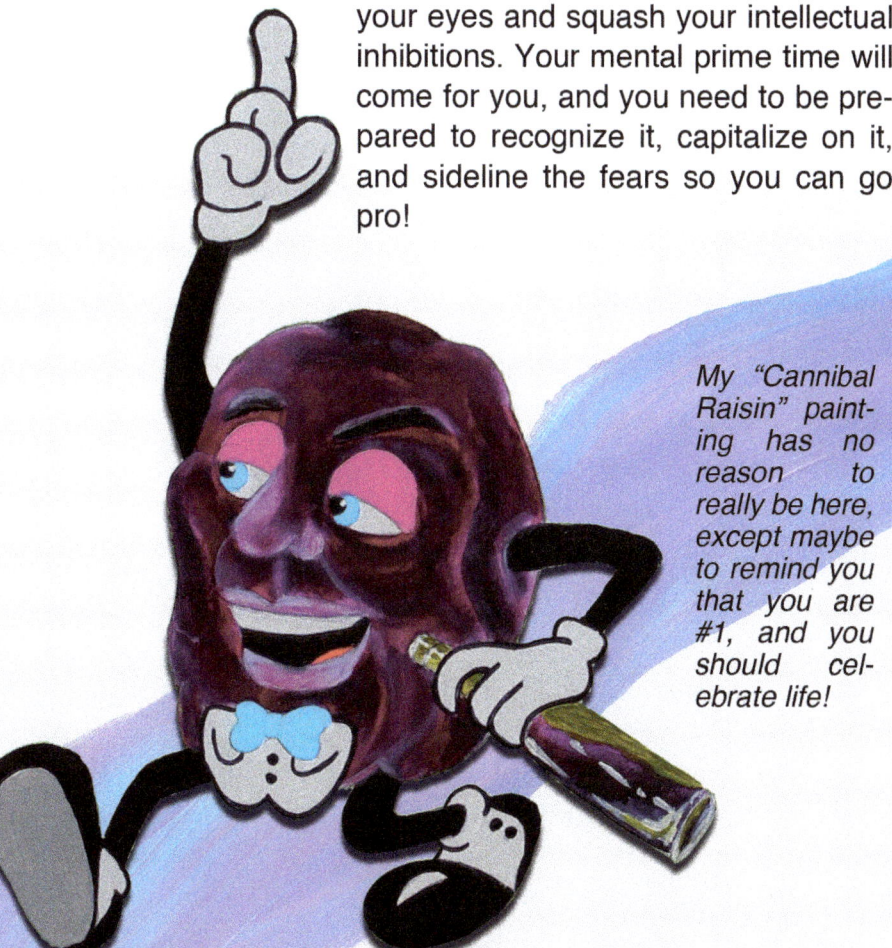

My "Cannibal Raisin" painting has no reason to really be here, except maybe to remind you that you are #1, and you should celebrate life!

28

FATHERHOOD UNDERSTOOD

If you honestly can't say that being a father, not just a provider, is the most important job in the world . . . well then, you are missing the whole point of living in the world. Allow me to define the difference between the two concepts for you. A provider is a man who provides a roof for his offspring to live under, clothes to wear, and food to eat. Very important, yes! But, a father, a real father, not to mention a real man, instinctively does all those afore mentioned duties while filling that home and everything within it with love and attention.

Procreation is why we exist and continue to exist, not the drive for monetary wealth. True wealth is obtained by

measuring your success on your child's success, to know you nurtured them right. Nothing can replace the feeling of being a proud father. You can burn dollar bills, but you can't extinguish that pride ever.

If you don't hear that you are a great father, then maybe you need to try harder. You know those people who always brag about what they are doing with their children every day on social media? Well, that's me. I own that shit!

If Facebook "friends" want to ridicule or make fun of you or me for spoiling our kids with our time and hard-earned money, then they aren't really true "friends," so fuckin block them. If they are tired of seeing those posts, tell them to either match them with activities done with their kids or delete you. They are probably negative because they know they never did "that" or thought of "that" with their kids—and that's the worst part of all, that they don't!

I will be the first to admit that I used to be a selfish prick at times—well, maybe a lot of times. If the birth of your new extended soul doesn't change that in you, you were not meant to be a parent. In an instant on November 16, 2009, my entire philosophy on life changed. Everything I thought was important and "mattered" didn't mean

My son at the H.R. Giger castle at six months old. It wouldn't have been the same without him.

shit anymore. I wanted to live only for him, and everything I did from that point forward would ensure that, not to mention change me. It took my son being born to actually become a real man. Does any of this sound familiar? I hope so. That is fatherhood understood. That is never wanting to be apart.

Embrace your new life. You are responsible for another

being now. Your priorities have suddenly changed quicker than Christina Aguilera's weight fluctuations. Guess what you can't do anymore: stay out late drinking, work twelve-hour overtime days, or have sex or masturbate regularly. Sure, you will make time for these things later again (especially the masturbation), but hopefully there are some that you won't want to do so much anymore.

If you are still working long-ass days, get your ass home. Not just to help out with baby duties, but because YOU SHOULD WANT TO. The most important thing you can give your child is your time. Time with an infant or toddler equals one thing: an unbreakable bond. Don't cheat yourself out of that bond that will cement your relationship for the rest of your life. If your boss won't allow you to spend more quality time with your child, then tell him to suck your dick. There will always be other jobs and more understanding bosses, but there will never be another munchkin like you have awaiting you at home. All your child wants from you is your attention, that's it. Spoil them rotten with it and be the wealthiest man alive.

Once, when my son was two, he asked me to play and I told him sure, like always, but I got caught up working on my computer. When I finally went out to play with him, he was sound asleep around the toys he got out for us to play with. I fucking cried. It happened only once, but that was enough. I promised myself at that moment that ANYTIME my son asked me to play I would drop whatever I was doing, no matter how important it was, even if for only a fraction of time. I would get down on the floor at his level and play whatever he wanted, no matter how silly. Nothing hurts like your child's heartbreak, and I will die trying to prevent ever seeing that again. The whole point of me working is to ensure that my kids have the best life—so how would the work itself be more important than the goal I am working for? Have you ever asked yourself that question?

If you had a child too young, and you still have the urge to party, then YOU especially need to reevaluate your situation. First of all, you should have worn a rubber and not been so selfish. Don't make your child suffer for your mistakes. Time to be a real man and tackle this situation head-on like Marshawn Lynch headed to the goal line. If you are still going to go out and party all the time, then you don't deserve that child. There are far too many people who can't have children that would kill to have what you do, and would be more suitable parents, real parents. Adopters can be "real parents" way more than some birthing parents ever could be. And think about this: every time you do go out and party and drink and drive, you are risking those kids growing up without a father. What an embarrassing legacy that would leave behind. My daddy was a doctor, my daddy was a teacher . . . well, my daddy was an immature asshole who died young cause he didn't care enough about me to stay in and play with me, so he perished in a DUI accident . . . oh, and he also killed the father of a kid my age who actually was a great dad! If your child's smile and laughter can't replace the joy of getting fucked up, then you are fucked up, there is something seriously wrong with you, and you should get that shit checked out. That's why they make counselors!

Maybe all of the youthful partying and irresponsibility isn't an issue with you. Maybe you have one of the other toughest jobs in the world . . . stepdad! If being a great dad is a piece of cake, then being a stepdad takes building the whole fucking bakery's worth of patience pie.

I am a stepfather, and I am so proud of it. I am lucky. My kids get along great; we are the *Brady Bunch* without the cheese dickery . . . and with a much hotter wife! I don't call them my stepchildren because I don't think of them as not my own. They have been with me for over half of their young lives now, and we have a history of love that can never be described as "step." I'm not saying there aren't strenuous moments, but luckily, they're not because of us; they're because of their insensitive father. If you are a stepparent, then you are fully aware that dealing with the birth parents can be the most challenging, frustrating, bang-your-head-against-the-wall part of it all. Because my daughter, Jaiden, will read this book immediately after it's published, I will refrain from saying what I really want to say about her "real" father out of respect for her. Just know this, baby girl: I will always be here for you whether he is or isn't.

My beautiful daughter Jaiden and I.

As an unrelated segue to a new topic . . . I can't fuckin stand deadbeat dads. A man who doesn't support his child is not a real man. Period! Seriously, I want you all to burn in hell. There is a special spot for you there.

Now, I understand that some guys get raked over the proverbial coals by some cunts who just want party money or are lazy as hell. A small percentage of women are pure evil and feel entitled to a man's money just because they opened their vaginas for you. But even then, you have to understand that even if you absolutely know that your hard-earned dough is paying her house rent, drinking habit, or boyfriend's video game fund, your child still lives in that house. Don't you want *his* house to be nice? Or, would you prefer your child growing up in a dirty environment or in a crime-infused neighborhood? Without the aide of your financial support you increase that possibility exponentially. I don't care what she did to you or what she doesn't deserve, your child deserves better than suffering from your spite and pride. Your child deserves you to work your ass off to help make their time away from you the best that it can be.

And yes, shit does happen. People get laid off or fired. Maybe you can't always make a timely support payment. Love your child enough to put aside differences to work out a payment plan. You would be surprised at how many women just want communication from you, and what they are willing to do—or forgive—for it. Don't let your child suffer because you can't be a real man and learn how to verbally communicate with another human being because of hatred or sorrow.

. . . By the way, don't even get me started about all the men who are pure evil and abandon their responsibilities to let so many women fend for two lives.

It is so hard for me to comprehend how so many fathers don't appreciate who they have waiting to love them at home. How do so many fathers abandon their own blood?

As you can see, I feel strongly about fatherhood. The topic warrants a little punch in the face and a lot of profanity to get the point across to some dads. And maybe that's just what we need more of to open some eyes.

QUALITY TIME

Sure, you've heard of it. But do you practice it with your children? What do you do to bond with them? And no, video games and TV don't count. What do you get out of the house to do together? Do you have traditions, go on weekend adventures, or build things? If you can't answer yes to at least one of those, it's time to make a change before your children change and it's too late for you. There's nothing worse than growing old with that repeating phrase of "I wish I would have" ringing in your head, making you mad.

I will give you an example of what I do with my family that bonds us and makes us a cohesive, loving, family unit. Maybe you can learn from it or apply something similar to your life, if needed.

We are a Seattle Seahawks family. Now, you can do this with any team in any sport (although I recommend the amazing Seahawks for best results). You can do it with plays and musicals or concerts. Just find an event or outing that the whole family will enjoy and make a tradition out of it.

Fortunately for me, my family gravitated towards the Seahawks because watching their games was what I already loved to do. I've had season tickets for a dozen years, and once I started taking my kids to games, they all fell in love with the grandeur of it all. The mighty cathedral of a stadium, the loud energy and music and bright

My tough lil' Seahawk gangsta boys.

lights—how could they not be mesmerized? Even my wife, who wasn't a football fan, began to love our games together. It's a place where we can all forget the stress of daily life, work, and school and just be free. We can all be kids again, all of us! We all have our favorite players and ask for their jerseys for birthdays. We even go out for wings or nachos just to watch away games.

Unfortunately, the tickets are expensive as shit. I have to save all year and make payments on them, and it straps us. But you know what . . . it's worth every penny and every sacrifice when I see the joy on their faces at the season opener. You cannot put a price on an activity that your entire family loves to do together. Do you

(Top) Mashup of the two best things in any world; Star Wars & Seahawks. (Above) My kids in awe of the stadium at Superbowl XLIX in Phoenix.

know how hard that is to find in this day and age?

I encourage every dad out there to find his own "Seahawks" for his family. Make the monetary sacrifice, and more importantly, make the time. Whether it's minor-league baseball games, or hunting or fishing trips, you know they will remember every effort for the rest of their lives and so will you.

INCOMPLETE RANDOMNESS

Do shit with your kids! Their young, impressionable minds are there for the molding, so don't just let them sit around and grow mold. Get them off their asses and out in the real world. Let them experience culture, art, and music. How else are they going to find passion or motivation if they don't witness firsthand all that this life has to offer?

This doesn't just mean taking your kids to the movies. This means actually spending your money on them, which is just as much of an investment in their lives as a college fund would be.

My seven-year-old loves *Three Days Grace*, probably because daddy always blasts them in the car. Nonetheless, he took to them immediately, and my other kids soon followed because his passion was contagious. My wife and I took them all to their first concert at the Roseland Theater in Portland, the perfect setting for a real, dingy, dirty rock show—exactly as rock shows are meant to be!

They were traumatized, at first, when a girl collapsed fifteen feet in front of them, (probably from drugs), and the lights came on. Ryker (who was five at the time) asked what happened. We were able to teach them a valuable lesson on "that's the stupid shit that happens when you use drugs," and they will never forget that teaching. But then the lights went off, and the guitars began crunching heavy riffs. Lasers filled the room, and I literally watched my children's minds blow. We wanted to show them the rock 'n' roll culture shock and see if they would love it or fear it.

Not only did they love it, they all wanted to play musical instruments afterwards, and constantly begged to go to more concerts. We couldn't have paid them to try an instrument before, but now, who knows; we may have the next Beethoven, Cobain, or 2Pac on our hands. We would have never known that hidden talent if we didn't take them to that first show, and they may not have ever found the passion for music that an iPod just can't deliver.

My five year-old took this photo from atop my shoulders. What a view!

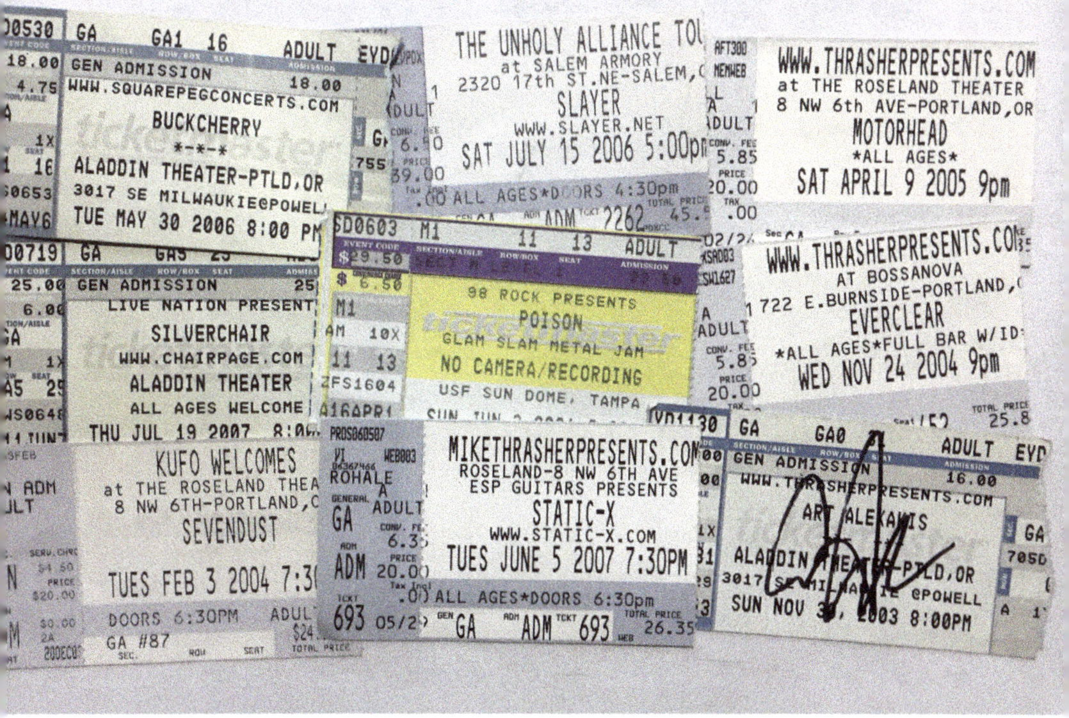

29

GOODBYE DADDY

I lost my dad this year. He was the strongest man I have ever known. I both feared and revered his strength right up until the end. To see that power be reduced to a jar of ashes created a hole in my soul that can never be repaired.

My dad taught me everything about respect, honor, loyalty, work ethic, and morals without ever saying a word about them. He didn't just lead by example—his actions engrained those traits in to my every fiber. He demanded respect . . . and he got it!

"Pops," as he was referred to by everyone, was a tough motherfucker. He was a man's man, strong in every way. His hands were like vise grips, his legs like tree trunks. He could hurt you with a stare alone, yet cure you with a smile. In his prime, he was a macho grease monkey. A lady-charming, fast-car-speeding badass.

He was a genius

made for muscle cars, music, and just about everything pop culture from the 1960s through 1970s. The man could fix anything he touched.

When I was a young boy, he was the judge, jury, and executioner wrapped in to one unyielding gavel. I'll always remember his belt on my bare ass as much as the sense of safety I felt around him. Nothing and nobody was going to fuck with his boys, and we knew it. It seemed every lesson had to be learned the hard way, but every lesson was taught, remembered, and eventually appreciated. There was no way he would allow us to grow up and not be strong, responsible men.

Dad and I in 1974, Ft. Myers, FL

When I was a young man, I thought that dad placed too much importance on work. Our lives revolved around his work. I hated it! He never had time to play catch or go fishing with his boys. What father turns down a chance to play catch with his sons? I couldn't even fathom doing that with mine. He worked twelve-hour days and weekends sometimes. He rarely attended our school sports or functions. I despised this and vowed to never duplicate it as a father.

Now that I'm closer to the middle-age side than the drinking-age side of things, my views have somewhat changed on my dad's priorities. Although I will never agree with or forgive how much time he missed out on in my childhood, I now understand why he did. While some of my friends couldn't afford new cleats for sports, I always had them. I got new skateboards, while other kids had to buy my old used ones. I was the one picking up and dropping off my friends from school because I was the only one with a car. All my buddies always wanted to have sleepovers because our cabinets were full of good food, and now I understand why.

We were not spoiled by any means, and dad made us do chores and work for everything, but we also never had to worry about anything because of dad's unyielding work ethic. How do you respect and despise someone for both things at the same time? I guess it's all about finding that balance.

When Pops sacrificed time with us, he unknowingly taught us some of the most important lessons in life. I look back at it all now that he is gone, and some of these questions begin to answer themselves. I am no longer mad at him for missing so much time with us, but I feel sorry for him. I also look up to him for giving up so much to ensure that his boys had the best life and future possible. Fuck, writing that sentence just made me cry . . .

I know that a lot of sons and fathers have difficult relationships, especially when they are a lot alike. I always envied the kids who could just hang out with their dads like they were best buddies, with the greatest relationship. Even in the most difficult times though, please take a step back and really evaluate the problems you have.

Take it from someone who has lost his father: there will be a day when you pick up the phone to call him with a question, and he will no longer be there to answer it. Then it will hit you. People will tell you that you remind them of him, and it will simultaneously feel like a knife to your heart and pat on the back.

Look for the good in him. Did he work hard for his family, encourage you, and teach you? It may not seem so now, but you will view things differently when you have to do that for your own family. Remember, dads fuck up. There is no manual, and you learn as you go. You have these little lives you have to worry about and work even harder for now, and sometimes you do stupid shit to ease the pressure. You can understand this only when you become a father yourself.

The thing he would be most proud of now is that he raised two wholesome boys who both became excellent fathers themselves.

The last time I saw my father was when he came to visit for my son's sixth birthday. He traveled from Florida to make it, and to try and make amends with my mom who had recently divorced him because of his old-age, retarded, late-life-crisis misdoings. Looking back, I don't even know how he made it with his health the way it was. We didn't know it at the time. but he wasn't supposed to fly or even really be alive by that point. But, he was a hard worker in everything he did, and he wasn't going to let his deteriorating body and some doctors stand in the way of his final trip to do the right thing.

He made it to see me put on my first comic con (Eucon), which he was very proud of. He made amends with my mom, and he made the birthday pizza party.

When we left the pizza place, we all hugged good-bye, and I noticed how he walked away differently. I pulled my children back and whispered to go give him a second hug before he left.

(Right) *The last picture taken of my dad, on his last night alive, at his grandson's sixth birthday.*

They ran over to him, and the smile that formed on his face brought everlasting life to his soul. That was his last defining moment as a man, I could just feel it. Somehow, I knew, without knowing his health situation, that that would be the last time they saw him. I still can't go back to that pizza place; I well up every time I even drive by it.

My brother drove him to his friend's house in Portland that night, so thankfully, they had a couple hours in the car to have a heart-to-heart. Dad expressed all of his sorrows and regrets. My brother still can't talk about it either. My dad passed away at his life-long best friend's house that night. I like to tell myself that if there was any way he would've wanted to go, and with anyone in the world, that's how it went. He did what he came to do with his family and he stayed strong. He told death to fuck off for one last week because he had shit to take care of!

I never got that heart-to-heart that I needed with my dad before he left. I was still mad at his stupidity for ruining forty years' worth of family history with my mom.

I would give anything to have one more hour with him and tell him that I forgive him and that I am proud of everything he had done in life. I would tell him that he should be proud because his children grew up to be kind and loving adults. He did good. I would tell him that I love him and never stopped, even through all the hard times we had. I would tell him that I was proud to have him as a father.

(Above) *I had to include this toy of mine because my dad was totally Fred Flintstone. Their mannerisms were the same, from the temper to the compassion. That's probably why I love the cartoon so much.*

EPIC INK
(Take 7)

Everything that went on film, or was even talked about on film, needed clearance and legal releases. This was our number one nemesis. Legal clearances and releases were our Lex fucking Luthor, Darth fucking Vader, Cobra fucking Commander, and Montgomery fucking Burns. Thorns in our side from day one to day last! I am sure the network's legal department hated us, and we hated them.

I nagged the producers daily (DAILY) to get me releases! My geek passions were the whole reason for making my TV show, and I couldn't even wear a fucking *Star Wars* T-shirt! I was so aggravated sometimes at their lack of importance placed on the matter that I would take it into my own hands. I stayed up late at night e-mailing companies to get permission to wear their brands or display their toys or art in the background of filming. I wasn't about to wait on somebody else. Don't get me wrong, the producers did a great job—just not great enough for me because I don't settle. I would take control because nobody could stop me. What were they gonna do, fire me?

I refused to wear boring, plain T-shirts on air. I went to local businesses to get their shirts and help support not only them but also the local community in general. I went to the Eugene Emeralds minor-league baseball team, whom I grew up with, and got permission to sport their team-logoed hats and apparel. Not only did they graciously and thankfully give it, they also gave me a ton of free shit to wear. You can see me wearing Ems hats in most of the episodes, even though I had to put colored gaffer's tape over the little MLB logo, or Sharpie it out. That's also when I got the idea to film at a baseball game and presented the idea to the showrunner, Sara.

The first release we got was for the *Teenage Mutant Ninja Turtles*. The powers that be at TMNT were the best! Turtle power! They gave us permission from the start for apparel, décor, and tattoos. That's why in an early episode most background décor is TMNT. In fact, I traded my *Nightmare on Elm Street* pinball machine for a TMNT one with my friend, Josh Docherty, who owned the local barcade, strictly because I had a release to show it!

The second release was for my beloved *Simpsons*. Unfortunately, we got only two of the three facets we needed. We could wear the clothes and show the art and toys, but no tattoos. As you can imagine, that put a huge damper in my inking arsenal, but nonetheless, I was still happy FOX and *The Simpsons* were on board.

One by one more releases started falling into place as the season progressed and companies saw the legitimacy of the show. *Aliens, Terminator,* and *Star Trek,* and then finally *Star Wars* about two-thirds of the way through the season. We weren't really allowed to show *Star Wars* tattoos, but nobody was going to stop us from that, so we found ways to reference the iconic universe indirectly. You can take the kid away from *Star Wars*, but you can never take the *Star Wars* out of the kid.

We actually even filmed a whole segment about moving all

of our *Star Wars* toys and collectibles into the shop. I had the idea of justifying it like we just hit the motherload of all Craigslist sales or something similar. Casey Baker played the delivery guy and helped carry in my *Star Wars* pinball machine (he also played the parts of other random delivery-service men). It was another fantastically funny and nerdy portion that never aired, forever lost in the A&E vaults.

Marvel basically told us to fuck off and wouldn't even consider giving us a release, and plenty others never even answered. It's funny because now that I have become a well-known geek ambassador, some of those very companies that denied us releases want to hand me free shit and see me endorse it. And guess what I tell them???

One morning, I went in early with my Snoopy shirt on . . . and with my snooping eyes I went through the showrunner's office. I was familiarizing myself with all the goings-on of the behind-the-scenes secrecy because they never told us shit. The cast was the last to know everything. But this was my

building and my crew, so I had the right to know . . . or at least that's how I justified it. Anyway, I saw the legal-release folder and wanted to see if there were any updates. I happened to see one bit of juicy information that I just have to tell you. Can you believe that *The X-Files* wanted $2,000 PER poster PER episode to allow us to show the three I had hanging in my shop? Can you believe that? We were trying to promote them, in a positive light (one that could only help their reputation and maybe bring some current life to it), and they wanted that much (bahahaha). Needless to say, they were happily replaced with TMNT and *Simpsons* art.

I wrote the Seattle Seahawks a letter to ask if I could sport a shirt on the show. I mean, I am a twelve-year-season ticket holder after all. They were nice but said the NFL would never allow it. So, I improvised. I had a plethora of unlicensed, knock-off fan-art shirts that I had purchased on the roadsides over the years. I wore one that just said L.O.B. on it. Now, any football fan knows that L.O.B. stands for the Seahawks' famous defensive secondary, Legion of Boom. One morning, my producer asked what it stood for, and I said the initials  of my favorite player that I had specially made as to not infringe on anything. A bold-faced lie (and I am sorry, Angie), but I was desperate and had to support my team. I got away with that one.

My set designer, Emilio, was a lifesaver. He understood both my frustration and passion, especially with his background designing the set of AMC's *Comic Book Men*. I gave him a list of my favorite artists to reach out to for set decoration. He pulled through amazingly. As I mentioned before, all my favorite artists donated, and I was so happy to help support them. Guys like Brian Rood, Joe Corroney, Steve Anderson, Emek, Alan Forbes, Jermaine Rogers, and others all sent stuff that I never could have afforded to obtain over a lifetime.

EPIC TATTOOS
(And those that didn't make it on TV)

Like I talked about, everything we did had to go through the network's legal department and all the proper channels to make sure nobody would get sued for using something on air, talking about something on air, or showing something on air that they weren't allowed to. It got downright silly and retarded at some points. When we were filming at C2E2 con in Chicago, they wouldn't even let me wear a *Bates Motel* shirt. That's their own fucking show, same network! What the hell do you have to check on about that, knowing I would be promoting your show to a whole new demographic for free?! I even had to tell them to send some *Bates Motel* posters to the shop so I could hang them in bare spots. Why wouldn't that be one of the first things they ask me to do? I swear, sometimes I felt like I had to think of all that shit.

Anyway, tattoos were no different in that department; in fact, they were the hardest things to get approval for. The whole show was about tattoos, and we went down to the wire on getting permission to do almost every one. At the time, no reality tattoo show had had to deal with it, since they were all primarily dealing with artist's original, non-infringing artwork. We just had to be difficult, and we were proud of it. Even when we did our own original fan art, we still had to fight corporate rules and regulations to use it on TV. If we didn't have a release, they wouldn't touch it. Everyone was so afraid of everyone suing, it was sickening. I say use the art, and then promote the controversy to help ratings and get more social media trending, but what do I know?

On the following pages you will see and read about some Epic tattoos that you have seen on the television and those works of art that you have no idea ever existed.

SAITO SISTERS' MONSTERS

Jeff actually tattooed Elysa (the older sister) on our sizzle reel for the Syfy channel. "I was lucky enough to be chosen for the first round of filming, when they were just trying to land a show. I got my *Futurama/Star Trek* crossover piece," says Elysa.

I liked her personality and taste so much that I invited her back to be on a real episode of *Epic Ink*. "Then I got even luckier when Chris 51 reached out to me again to be a part of an episode for his new show, *Epic Ink*!"

Elysa brought her younger sister, Emily, and we decided to tattoo both of them as a battle of Epic proportions. Not only would Jeff and I be ink battling, but the tattoos themselves would be battling. I had the idea of giving the sisters two separate pieces that would match up as one cohesive battle scene when lined up side by side. They wanted a robot and a monster done in a *Pacific Rim*-meets-old-Japanese-monster-movie style, which was the perfect subject matter for such an undertaking.

"For my sister and me, getting to be tattooed by two of geekdom's most famous tattoo artists was the coolest way to

show our nerdiness with pride," Elysa says. "Not only did we receive beautiful permanent art, we also got to become a part of the inked geek community. It's awesome to meet other people who were also tattooed on *Epic Ink* too. We still get to see the cast and crew of *Epic Ink* at nearly every comic-book convention we go to!"

In the end, I think everybody was a winner because both tattoos ended up, well, Epic, and both sisters were happy as could be.

MINNIE KOBEISSI

Minnie was actually an old client of Josh Bodwell's. When she reached out to him to be on the show, he suggested that I do her tattoo since what she wanted was more my style of work at the time. Minnie wanted a scene with a blood moon, bird, and tree from the Gilbert and Sullivan opera The Mikado. It was a stretch to represent the geek factor Epic Ink was after, but since choices that early on in filming were so limited, I decided to do it. And I am so glad I did. "I described my idea and left it in Chris 51's hands. What he created was beyond anything I could have imagined," explains Minnie.

It was one of the first tattoos I made on set. Although I had been tattooing geeky stuff my whole career, I didn't promote it that much before the show because I was known more for tattooing subject matter of a realistic nature. That's what my name in the industry really grew from, and I had just started coming out of the geek closet a couple years prior with my ink company branding. I was trying to shed that old reputation, but once I met Minnie in person, and saw her passion for her ideas, I couldn't resist. I knew that I could make her happy.

Minnie walked through Area 51's doors in a full kimono, ready to get tattooed. She had no shame in her game, and that made me even more stoked to work on her. This girl was one of us, a total nerd, with extraordinary dedication for her fandom.

During the tattoo procedure, she educated me about The Mikado. She even had me singing its famous song before we were finished. I had so much fun doing the tattoo, and there were moments that I forgot the cameras were even all up in my shit. "I spent the day laughing and joking.

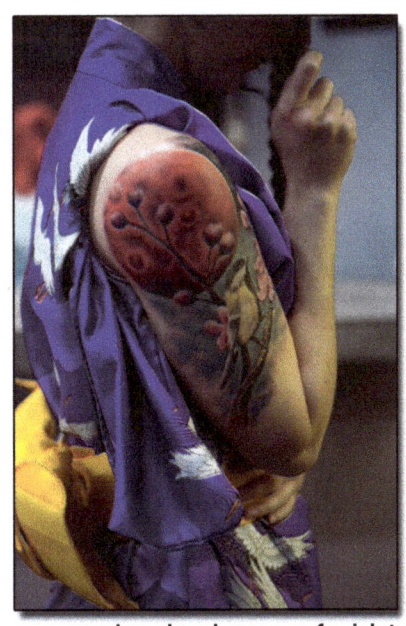

The whole shop has the best vibe ever! And in the end I was brought nearly to tears when my piece was revealed to me! It's my favorite tattoo, and I can't tell you how many compliments I get! I cannot wait to come out to Area 51 and visit Chris 51 again," admits Minnie. At the tattoo's conclusion, she gave me a gift for a tip . . .

Now, I don't know if this gift was her idea or the producer's, but it was clever as hell. I honestly had no idea what it was. As you can see in the episode, I was afraid to open it, thinking my cast mates put something like a snake in there, knowing how afraid I am of snakes. Once I quit being a little bitch, I went and put the gift on in the bathroom. It was a full-on kimono with a samurai-style wig.

I knew they were gonna film me in it; it didn't take a genius to figure that out. But what the crew didn't expect was that I don't get embarrassed easily. They thought they might get some shy little red-faced boy; instead, they got me proudly flashing my chubby belly to the camera. You have to own those opportunities because you don't get many. "Chris was super cool about me showing up dressed as a geisha," says Minnie. "He even got dolled up as one himself."

What the network didn't show on the episode was me singing the song Minnie taught me while doing a little song-and-dance number with her. I was bummed that part didn't air, cause it was funnier than anything. I mean, I can't sing or dance worth a shit (now that would have been embarrassing).

TANNER'S T. REX

Having a T. rex-tattoo request fall into my hands was a godsend after a couple of the nongeeky tattoos that I had already faced. I was so excited I could've roared.

Tanner wanted a particular scene from the *Jurassic Park* movie, but unfortunately, I couldn't give it to him, not because of my skill set, but because we didn't have a legal release to use characters from the movie, even if they had gone extinct millions of years ago. In addition to that steaming pile of dino poop, we couldn't even reference the correlation between the tattoo and the movie during our banter. We were allowed to talk about why Tanner liked the movie and how it inspired him in his youth, but we couldn't mention that the tattoo was taken from the actual movie. It's still ridiculous to me that you can't promote something you love on film without legal permission, especially something as lasting and memorable as a tattoo.

We made it work though. And in the end, I'm glad we couldn't use the *Jurassic Park* reference because it forced me to get creative. I actually found some amaze-balls T. rex reference in my son's dinosaur children's books that I used as inspiration. Tanner was totally stoked with it, as was his mom, who came along for support. I think she was there more to investigate my legitimacy and the legitimacy of the show. She even said that she wanted the tattoo to be "badass!" But in the end, I had her in happy tears over the tattoo. Being a mama's boy myself, I have a way with making moms feel secure and comfortable.

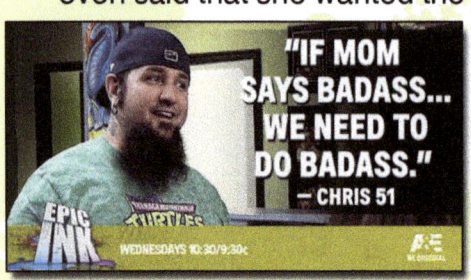

(Above) A&E used these humorous quote cards on social media to promote key parts in episodes. This one is from when I was talking to Tanner's mom.

"The experience was unlike any other. It was my first big tattoo, and due to the recording process of the show, I had to do it all in one sitting. We spent nearly eight hours there. I had initially wanted a mural of Jurassic Park scenes, but Chris knew that simply wouldn't fit. What I got was more than I could ever ask for. Chris has since made a customer for life out of me, and time and time again he's shown his skill and talent to be out of this world," says Tanner.

I love when Tanner's turn comes up at Area 51 Tattoo because I always know I'm in for another memorable day. We always reminisce about the *Epic Ink* experience, and it brings joy to us both. His T. rex is now becoming an entire leg sleeve of dinosaurs. I still use the same children's books for reference, too.

(Right) I tried something a little different in Tanner's Tyrannosaurus. It had so many similar colors that it needed a severe contrasting element or two. So, I added some bright green foliage on one side for a pop of color contrast. Then, I added some solid black with negative-space fossils on opposing side. This added dark contrast and some artistic flare, utilizing the bare skin itself as an important part of the tattoo.

LORD OF THE RINGS DAY

One particular day of filming was all about *Lord of the Rings*. It was, well, Epic! Heather did an entire chest piece of Balrog with flames and Gandalf in his "you shall not pass" pose. She even tattooed over the dude's nipples, during which we all chanted, "run the nips, run the nips, run the nips." It is still one of the coolest tattoos I have ever seen. I did an entire half sleeve of Treebeard carrying a hobbit, which I was pretty proud of too. They were two giant, Epic pieces, probably two of the biggest of the whole season. They were all set for a LOTR episode. We got the release, so I had already spent hundreds of my own dollars (like I always did) on background décor. Every time we got a new release I would go eBay crazy on that subject to fill the wall voids, and boy, did it drive my wife nuts. Back to the episode. The shop looked great, our banter was funny and witty, and the tattoos were unreal. At the last second, we got word that LOTR never "officially" gave a release to do tattoos. I think the network was taking a chance that they would, and it backfired. Needless to say, Heather and I were heartbroken. We worked so hard on those tattoos, as did the clients who sat through the pain and nearly ten hours of getting them. What a disappointment. Unfortunately, this happened more than a couple times. But we got used to it and just kept our heads up.

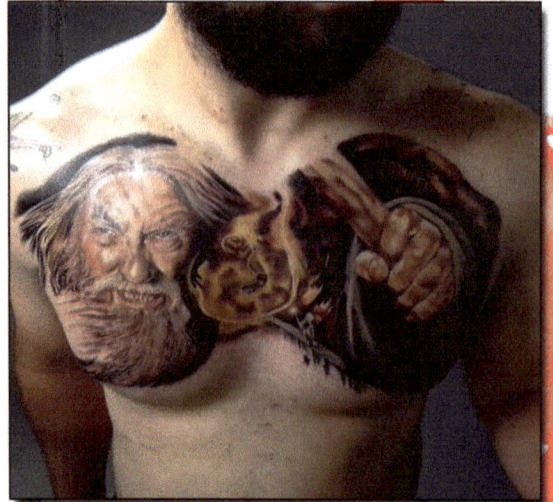

TMNT SAVIOR

Luckily, I got to do a giant half sleeve of comic-book-style, old-school *Teenage Mutant Ninja Turtles* (as seen earlier). That tattoo single-handedly changed my entire career from the minute it aired. All of a sudden, clients from all over the world wanted me to tattoo nothing but comics and cartoons on them. I still get a boner thinking about it! That was one of those life-changing moment tattoos. Thank you, Kevin Eastman, for allowing me to do your amazing artwork and changing my life in the process.

I got the chance to meet Kevin Eastman *(above right)* at San Diego Comic-Con while I was promoting the release of *Epic Ink*. I showed him the Turtle tattoo and he loved it. His approval made all the stress of filming the episode worthwhile.

(Above) *"HomerAngelo" oil on canvas. I painted this on-set, during down time from filming. I would always try and keep myself busy so when I needed to be high energy for a scene, I was ready.*

THE JELLY BELLY DONUT

What started out as a simple homage to one of my favorite foods and *Simpson's* images turned out to be the most famous and talked about tattoo done on *Epic Ink*. In fact, it has surpassed its notoriety from the TV show and become an Internet classic.

The whole doughy idea started at the famous Voodoo Doughnut in Eugene, Oregon. Heather, Jeff, and myself (pictured) had a work meeting, which was really more of an excuse to eat Voodoo's delicious offerings, and decided on the spot to do the tattoo on me. We went straight back to Area 51 Tattoo and started setting up for the sweet procedure.

The tattoo was slated as a "tramp stamp" for my lower back, but an old surgery scar excluded that from being the ideal spot. So, I decided on my stomach. It made better sense anyway since I already had the Springfield hillside sign from *The Simpsons* there. I thought, maybe I will just make my whole stomach a *Simpsons*-themed collage. It was a good idea . . . until the pain started.

Either Heather didn't take it very easy on me, or I am the biggest pussy alive (probably the latter), but goddamn that hurt. I endured almost five hours of pure torture, and I had to, because the world would be watching. Luckily for me, the   producers actually cut out a lot of the bitching and whining coming out of my mouth. That footage was not pretty.

I don't remember who came up with the idea, but after the tattoo, we topped off the afternoon with a donut-eating contest. Every single person was competing, even the skinny Caroline, and maybe even a few audio guys on the sidelines. I was totally cocky. There was no way in hell that any of those sugar-eating novices were going to beat me at eating one of my regular staples.

The PA went back to Voodoo to get a bunch of their Tex-Ass sized glazed doughnuts for the contest (pictured). Now, one cannot truly understand the grandeur of a Tex-Ass until they lift it from its pretty pink box. Not only is it the size of a ceramic dinner plate, it weighs more.

The contest was simple. Whomever I lost to got to "set" my tattoo. In the tattoo world, setting a fresh tattoo means slapping it—hard. It hurts like a motherfucker. It's a cruel old-school tradition that is completely retarded. But, I was so cocky that I didn't care. I knew I would win, so I didn't care if it was a one-sided bet.

As the contest got underway, I was all smiles. I had this in the bag. I had to. I was the donut ambassador now, wearing my new ink medal of honor on my belly and representing legendary donut masters everywhere.

As the contest neared the end I started to panic. Heather was actually kicking my ass. I conjured up my Jedi donut-eating powers from deep within my prediabetes intestines to catch up to her, but it was a little too late. One damn bite too late, to be specific! No joke, no camera tricks—that bitch beat me by one fucking bite haha! I was devastated. I let down my donut comrades everywhere. To worsen the blow, I now had to face the contest loser rules and own up to the bet.

I prepared the cameramen. I warned them all to be in the right place, positioned and ready. Same goes for the audio guys. I told them they had one take at this because it was gonna kill. If they didn't film it properly . . . tough shit, their loss. I pulled up my shirt to reveal my fresh ink, still pulsating from the tattoo just a couple hours prior. Heather pulled back and gave me a total fakey, which made me flex my nonexistent abs, which hurt by itself. Finally, she reared back—far back—and let her little T. rex hand rip like a slingshot out of hell. "The slap heard round the world," is what I like to call it. It resonates in my nightmares to this day. It hurt so bad that I dropped to the floor. The credits started rolling, and as the scene concluded I could say only one thing: "I gotta poop."

She literally slapped the shit out of me.

The whole ordeal remains a fan favorite, and everyone always asks me if they can see "the donut" wherever I go. I am happy to show them.

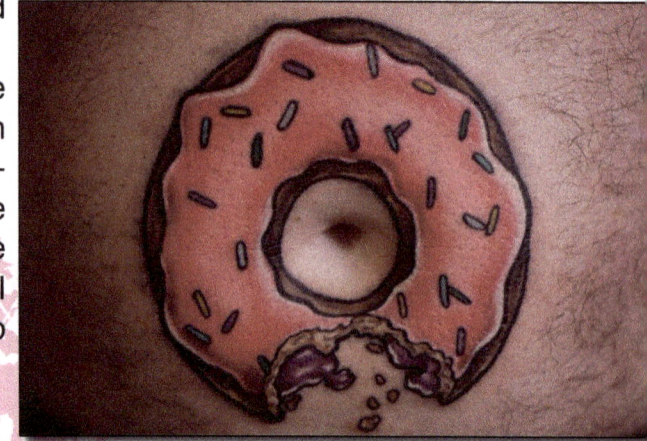

(Above) Of all the fun people who have asked to see my donut, one special person will always stand out the most. Yeardley Smith, Lisa Simpson herself, cracked up over it and definitely approved!

A BEATLE ON A MUNSTER

Butch Patrick (Eddie Munster) and I have been friends for years, ever since he endorsed some of my tattoo ink for my old company. I asked if he would come appear on my show and let me tattoo him on it. Not only did he do this for me but he paid his own way to do it! He is that kind of gracious, loving guy. I decided to do a "Simpsonized" version of his childhood TV character riding in The Beatles yellow submarine (his other love). I did all original art and completely changed up the submarine as to not get in legal trouble. It barely looked the same compared to the album cover, but Butch liked it. We combined it with our Friday the 13th fan-favorite episode featuring Elvira, Mistress of the Dark. A little cartoon Munster fit the show's overlaid theme perfectly.

You can probably guess that in the end, we did not get a release to use the tattoo, even though it was completely my original artwork. The legal department laughed at the idea of us using

anything referring to The Beatles because I guess they are very sue happy. So, even after I got preapproval to do it, and my friend flew out here on his own penny, it was all for nothing. Well, at least he could still be on the episode and add some cool geek clout for the shop party ...

NOPE! I was told that the network felt it was too much of an improbability that we could have two celebrities at our party. WAIT! First of all, this show was about the opposite of that; it was about pop-culture fantasy and over-the-top silliness. That was the whole point. Second, both celebrities were already there, and only because I knew one and Josh Bodwell knew the other from working for years at comic cons and forming relationships with them. We worked side by side with them, in the public eye, so it was a more real scenario than most reality shows could produce. It was such compelling television too, hearing Elvira and

(Above) I'm showing Butch a drawing of his tattoo.
(Right) Bodwell & Elvira in curious conversation as Butch, Kyler Shinn, and I look and stare dumbfound-

Butch tell stories to each other about the old horror TV days. That was pure gold, and fans would have shit themselves hearing those insider stories. It still baffles me to this day how ass-backwards some decision-making people think.

So who looked like the asshole now? Me! I called in the huge favor and produced an iconic celebrity, and our work never even aired. Thank god Butch is an understanding guy. If you watch closely in the show promos though, you can see Butch. He is wearing an alien mask and a Hawaiian shirt at the front counter. You cannot ever see his face, but trust me, that is fucking Eddie Munster!

DELETED SCENES

Some of our favorite scenes never saw the light of day. Whether it was because the network nixed them, they weren't relative to the storyline, or there simply wasn't enough time, they will be locked away in the A&E vault forever. As a collective, we were very disappointed when we saw the final version on TV (we never watched it before it aired), and funny scenes that we were expecting to see had vanished. We had worked so hard as a team on them and had so much fun, that it was like they took away a small piece of our history.

THE MURAL

One of my favorite deleted scenes came in the form of THE MURAL story. We decided to paint a mural on the back, bare wall of Area 51 Tattoo. Since none of us had any experience in this giant art form, our haphazard efforts quickly escalated to an all-out paint-fight war. Paint-filled balloons, flinging drenched brushes, and filled buckets were the ammunition of

saturation. In the end, we hired a local muralist who worked his magic on the wall. His art wasn't shown either because it was full of amazing pop-culture references that we didn't have releases for . . . of course.

We were picking paint out of our orifices for days after that shoot, but it was worth every ounce. It was the most fun I have ever had working on television, and I will never forget it.

Even though we have moved on from that landmark building now, the decoupage mural remains. It also still bears our *Simpson*-ized portraits I made with our autographs under them. And, if you are ever near 700 Q Street in Springfield, Oregon, it's worth the visit (it is a Pokestop too).

(Above) I'm picking paint out of Josh's eye so we could do our after-scene interview.

(Left) Our Show Runner, Sara was brave to pose with us after the paint fight.

THE AMBULANCE AND ALIENS

Another scene that we all missed seeing come to fruition was the ambulance redesign. We shot a continuing story for days about aliens. It seemed appropriate since we were at Area 51 Tattoo. It began with us all making a competition out of an alien design for a client who was coming in to get an alien tattoo with one of us. We all love aliens, so it was a no-

brainer for us. The tattoo scenes and competition actually made it to an exclusive clip that we put on YouTube. Jeff won, and ended up doing an excellent shark-alien tattoo and it was very funny. What you don't get to see, though, are the shenanigans that happened after the tattoo, with the ambulance I told you about earlier. The graphics ended up being the cheesiest cartoon versions of ourselves as astronauts and aliens. Heather drew mine using fart propulsion as a blast off, and they got crazier from there. We filmed the funniest banter, almost pissing in our pants laughing at all the graphics.

Whenever we started talking on film, it got ridiculous. It always ended in some dirty innuendos or poop and fart stories. We constantly had to stop filming skits like these because not only would the cast be hysterically laughing, but the entire crew couldn't help but fall victim to them too. Every day was a new adventure on set.

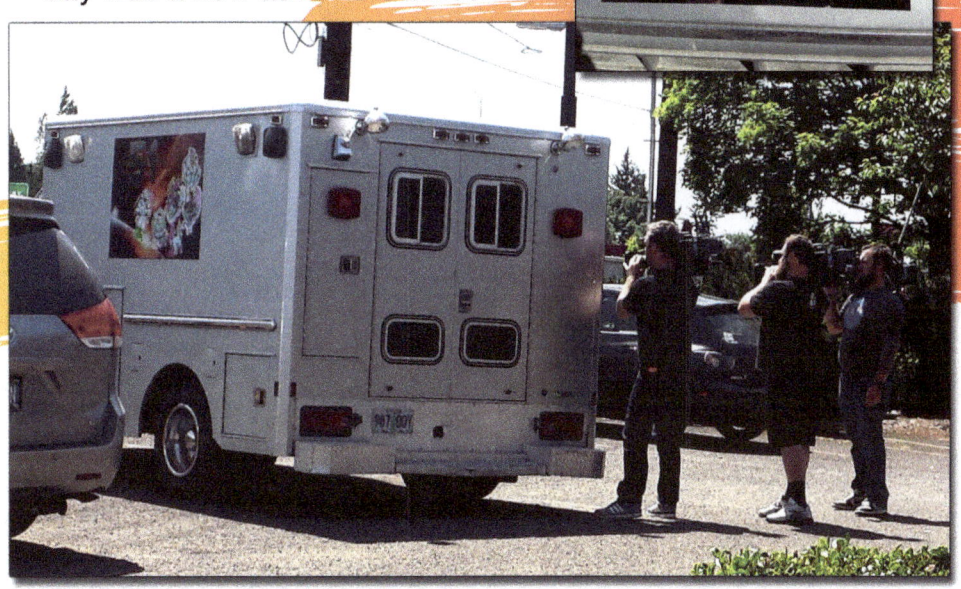

I have since sold the ambulance/tattoombulance, but the memories remain rich in my heart. I never actually tattooed out of it because of state licensing rules. I also never really paid for it, as I traded tattoo work for all the interior work, paint job, and mechanical work. I do miss how sexy she looked in my parking lot though.

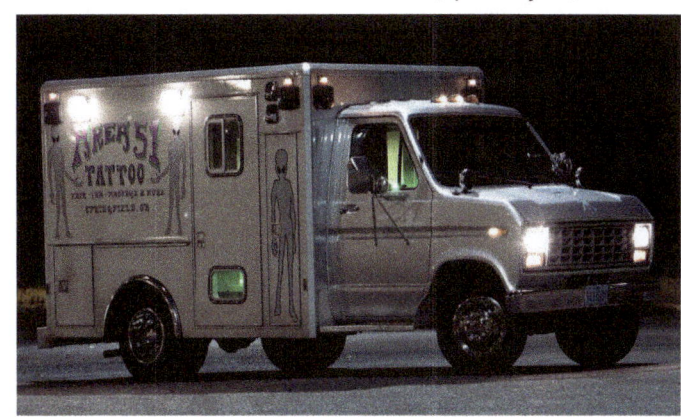

THE CATCH

My all-time favorite scene to film was my birthday baseball game. Although parts of it were used in episode nine, "Take Me Out to the Ballgame" some of the best moments were cut like a fat rookie in training camp.

The episode started with a birthday surprise from my producers. Knowing my love for baseball, they arranged for me to throw out the first pitch of the game. I had a flawless, Greg Maddux-esque professional wind up, but the delivery was more like a Little Leaguer's. The ball fell about eight feet short of the plate, an embarrassing feat for a dream moment. I couldn't revel in my inadequacies long, though, because they quickly rushed us up to the skybox to start filming the next scene.

Did I seriously catch a foul ball during filming, while still holding onto my first-pitch ball that I had thrown just minutes prior? I absolutely did. Nobody believed this actually happened, so we had to send the whole stream of these photos (taken by the local Register-Guard newspaper photographer)

(Top) A kid looking on in disgust at my first pitch moment.
(Left) We may or may not have had a few drinks while filming at the ballpark.

to the network as proof! It was the second pitch of the game, and we were literally telling Jones (on camera) to be cautious of flying foul balls being hit up towards our area. Then it happened, and I leaped from my chair and caught it! One in a million chance it could happen. It still blows my mind. You couldn't fake our reactions with any trick photography.

The network also cut all the other scenes from this game, like the unforgettable one in which the mascot smashed a birthday cake in my face, and it escalated to the cast having a cake-food fight atop the dugout in front of a cheering crowd. I almost fell off the dugout roof onto the field but got caught by the net. None of this was ever scripted, so we were very disappointed when it wasn't used. Nevertheless, it was still one of the most memorable birthdays of my life.

(Above) Notice the cameramen even ducking, more proof that nobody was expecting that foul ball.

THE SEXY CAR WASH

By far the most erotic deleted scene was our sinfully sexy, all-male car wash. As you can see from the photos, we were very scantily clad and not embarrassed by it one bit. I think this skit was almost certainly cut by A&E due to sheer provocative overload.

Originally, the skit was us dudes sitting around bored in Speedos with our car wash signs, wondering why we aren't getting any business. Then we hear some commotion and see some girls in bikinis (models we hired) doing the sexy car wash thing next door and taking all of our business.

I then had the idea to reverse the scene and show it from the other perspective with the girls bored and us guys doing the car wash in bikinis.

There was actually one part where I was wringing out a sponge

full of glistening, soapy water onto Josh's chest and lathering it in. Of course, from there everything began to look more like an old Whitesnake video of us doing splits on the car hoods and seductively spraying the hoses in slow motion on arched lower backs and other provocative body locations. It got so bad (or good, depending on how you look at it) that a few cars driving by called in to complain. That just told me it was a win!

TATTOOED KID

We were always looking for fun and unique ideas to film our interstitial skits.

My lead cameraman, Patrick, always came up with gems. Knowing that I wanted to get my kids involved on camera whenever possible, he approached me with this idea (pictured below), which I totally approved of.

First, the camera would focus on my son's facial expressions of anguish as you hear my tattoo machine running, as if he's actually getting a tattoo. Patrick would then turn his camera to my facial expressions of focus, and zoom out to show the top of my machine moving in tattoo-type motions. Finally, the camera would zoom further out, revealing that I actually have a Sharpie marker in my machine rather than needles. Then our joint expressions would turn to laughter and silliness.

We thought it was genius. A&E network DID NOT! They said absolutely, positively, hell no. They thought that too much controversy might come from it. Wasn't that the point? I guess they didn't want either the boost in ratings or the social media frenzy from airing something that had never been done.

(Left) My producer Angie probably explaining how to not look like a douche bag on camera, considering the puzzled look on my face.

(Right) Angie working her magic with a client again, while cameramen J.B., Josh & Patrick take a well-deserved break.

(Left) Heather drew penises on whatever she could get her hands on. She even drew the entire crew as penis caricatures, aka, dickatures.

31

IT'S NOT GAY TO BE GAY

Let me begin this touchy subject with a simple proclamation: I don't give a shit if you are gay, bi, trans, or whatever. The only types of people I hate are assholes. You don't have to have a dick to be a dick. Whether you are fat, retarded, anxious, or socially inept, it is your strength that determines who you are and what people will ultimately see in you.

Here are three simple questions I ask. One: how are some people so high and mighty to judge others when they themselves don't have a fart in their own piles of shit together? Two: who the fuck are those judgmental people to decide what and who is right and wrong? Three: what business is it of yours or mine what others do with their lives? If you disagree with any of those questions or even have an answer for one, then you are one of those high and mighty assholes I am referring to. You may think you have or know the answers, but in the grand scheme of life, you truly are a nobody, and not many people really care what you have to say anyway. The same goes for me!

Society as a whole has become so overly sensitive and politically correct that it has disabled mental toughness and fortitude in the younger generation. The tattoo generation today fears everything. Are they saying the wrong thing or the right thing? Are they pissing off the wrong person or insulting the right person? Will others accept them or ridicule them? It's time we teach our youth to invest in themselves and quit putting so much stock in what others think of them.

I have never wanted to be the grumpy old man who just bitches about the youth of today. In fact, my job surrounds me with people who are much younger than I am, so I feel quite in touch with them and their environment. But, I cannot help but notice underlying problems that are constantly reaffirmed by today's tattoo generation.

Honestly, it's not really their fault! It's the authoritative figures in their lives. It's the lack of parents present and the lack of parenting presence that fails them.

When I was in middle school I watched the space shuttle blow up live, right in front of my face on TV at a school assembly, and we had to finish the school day with the usual dose of homework. I watched some crazy man attempt to assassinate my president live on TV, and I still had to finish my vegetables before I could be excused from the family dinner table. Youth today need counseling and grieving time off because the president they didn't want got elected to office. They are burning flags over the same issue, which is like spitting in the face of every man and woman in uniform who is fighting to protect the rights of that same flag. They are quick to judge and even quicker to retaliate, because they haven't been taught any differently. Our asses would have been whopped by a belt of tree swatch if we acted in such a way. Sometimes respect is a lesson only learned by a little fear of pain or repercussions.

Growing up is hard enough, but without a new type of "real life" education, our future generations are doomed. High school certainly doesn't prepare you for the real world. Instead, it teaches how to fit into protective social cliques and beat the attendance and testing systems in place. And college may show you how to perform higher levels of mathematics and English composition, but there are no classes on how to behave at a job or what to expect once you secure one. All the formal education in the world doesn't mean shit if you don't have the social skills or courage to get a job and keep it.

After you realize all of this, being gay seems like it should be the least of anybody's problems today, doesn't it? The fact that people even think being gay or different is a problem is the problem itself.

I have several friends who are gay. Some I knew were gay from the start, and some I found out about later. It has never made a lick of difference to me. I have found my gay friends to be the most loyal and caring people I know. And they know that I will always support and defend them. I will be there for them no matter how gay they are or what gender they turn into . . . just as long as they don't turn into assholes.

I will say this though: I use the word gay in a sarcastic connotation often. I am a child of the '80s and that's just what we said—it had a different meaning then! It has no correlation with the fact that someone prefers the same sex or not; it's only slang for something being lame or retarded. And yes, I say retarded too but don't think I am making fun of mentally handicapped people; I am just a gay retard from the '80s with a very limited vocabulary who can't outgrow his generational incorrectness. I love you however you are: gay, retarded, geeky, nerdy, or a stupid jock . . . just as long as you aren't an asshole!

I've gotten a lot of flack over being so brutally honest with people in my life. Some appreciate it, and then there are those whom it either scares or repels, because they can't handle the truth. I don't sugarcoat things. If you can't be real with somebody, then is that somebody you really want to be around?

If you are fat, then you are fat, not big-boned or harboring a "weight problem." Who gives a shit; wear that weight with pride! Look at the people who really judge you, and ask yourself, are their lives so much better than yours just because they are skinny?

If you are a pussy, then you are a pussy, not overly sensitive or sheltered. Either face your fears one at a time, lift some weights to gain some cosmetic confidence, or be a pussy and not give a shit about what others think.

I don't discriminate, and I am never racist. But I am honest.

If you don't like your predicament or social standing, then change it. If you think your life sucks, then you probably suck. You are sucking the life out of yourself with your own negativity. Whether or not your life sucks is your choice. You can accept it, or you can do something about it.

The only way to dig yourself out of a rut is either with your own hands or by building your own shovel. You must risk getting dirty to do it. You must risk the pain of falling back in your hole. If you do fall, don't just rise out of your self-loathing and failure—elevate yourself. Why aim for just the solid ground when you can climb a mountain? If you are happy and don't care what others think about you, then you have found a home on the summit, and are already ahead of society's curve. Good for you!

If you surround yourself with people who are offended by your honesty or sexual openness, then maybe you are surrounded by the wrong people. Sometimes you'll find that there isn't good to be found in everyone. Don't take time away from the people who really matter in your life. In the end, the people in your life define your life, so choose them wisely.

So be gay, fat, retarded, ugly, geeky, nerdy, or whatever else you are, and be that way proudly. Take comfort in knowing that there are those of us out there who only care about what you consist of on the inside.

32

NOT ENOUGH TIME IN THE DAY

People always tell me they are too busy to do certain things, and I laugh. Parents will find reasons to not attend their kids sports practices, musical lessons, or school functions. Single adults would rather be at a bar then raising the bar at their profession. Peers will say they are too busy to create new projects. These people are making excuses that hold them back from finding greatness and success (because of their busy lifestyle), and they are the very same ones who spend hour upon hour playing video games or talking about different TV shows they watch every night! If you want to win, if you want to never worry about competition, and if you want to seduce greatness, you have to make the sacrifices that the greats make—and then make more!

The hour you spend on video games every night of the week could give you seven hours designing a new website to promote your new idea or work and to reach a new clientele. The hour of TV you watch every night could give you an easy seven hours to network and market your idea while the rest of the competition is in a Kardashian's idiot trance. Shave two hours off your nine to ten hours of sleep, and see how much more you can accomplish.

I am not saying that you don't deserve or need a little "you time." Every brain needs to unwind. But make it an earned treat one night a week, or late at night when the family and rest of the world is asleep and you have peaceful, uninterrupted time.

Of course, you can also melt away into oblivion as just another spec of normalcy, and play all the video games and watch all the TV you like. But you are probably reading this book because either that isn't you or you no longer want to be that drone. I am here to help.

The time is there. You just need to reevaluate your clock's priorities and set the hands in motion.

Here's an example of my typical work day; see how yours compares:

8:00 a.m. - Wake up. Take kids to school.
8:30 a.m. - Hit the gym or jog.
9:30 a.m. - Starbucks!
9:45 a.m. - Get to shop early to: draw tattoos, answer emails, work with health depts for permits for Geeksterink tour, research reputable comic cons to expand tour, make travel arrangements, order tour supplies from sponsors, update websites for Area 51 Tattoo/Geeksterink/Chris 51 brand, manage seven social media pages, work on current art project (pins, patches, trading cards, prints). Mentor younger artists.
12:00 p.m. - Tattooing.
6:00 p.m. - Finish tattoos. Take wife out to dinner and/or
        take kids to football/baseball practice.
7:00-9:00 p.m. - Play with kids. Toys, sports, games.
9:00 p.m. - Work on computer. Work on portfolio. Graphic design and promotion for all three of my companies. Advertising and networking. Do commissioned artwork. Continued education for career advancement.
10:00 p.m. - Spend quality time with my wife.
11:30 p.m. - Personal time; writing books of all genres, painting, digital art, reading do-it-yourself books, eBay-ing like a motherfucker for collectibles.
12:59 a.m. - Trip to fridge for a diet soda and dark chocolate.
1:00-2:00 a.m. - Bed time...if I can actually sleep.

Sundays are strictly spent with my family. We go to sporting events, movies, toy hunting, or on some kind of out of town adventure. I try to mix it up every weekend and keep the kids out of the house, and away from the couch and lure of video games. Sundays are off-limits to work, unless I am out of town at a convention, and I average about 18-20 of those per year.

As you can see, there is not enough time in my day to waste any of it, unless I want to sacrifice the little quality time that I have with my wife or kids, or want to fall behind in my career.

Write down your schedule this way so you can see where you need to make time adjustments to get the most out of your day and get ahead in your life and business.

Go, Chris 51. Go!

33

GEEK INK

When an Intenze Ink representative approached me about featuring their ink on the (possible) second season of my TV show, I was intrigued. I'd already had Eternal Ink on the first season, and although they provided me with my requests, they didn't follow through on sponsoring the whole cast or really see the value in the bigger, promotional picture. I was ready for change. I was ready to go with a company that was more in tune with the "Hollywood" mainstream marketing side of the spectrum. I have nothing bad to say about Eternal Ink, and I remain friends with the owner to this day.

Enter Intenze, the biggest tattoo ink company worldwide. When they talked I was all ears. Unlike other companies, they had the potential to keep up with me. Their owner, Mario Barth, is intense, just like his brand. He is flamboyant and edgy, and not afraid to take new risks in the industry. I can relate! I love that about the company, and once we started talking, I caught the Intenze fever.

When Intenze approached me about the TV-show sponsorship, I used that as a springboard to dive headfirst into something with more grandeur, something more personal and beneficial to both parties. I had no idea if the show would have a second season, and I didn't want to rest on my laurels. I suggested that we capitalize on the popularity of my show and its association with all the current comic-book and geek-based movies and buzz, and make a "Geek Ink" set of colors. Intenze already had a few top sponsored artists with their own sets, but nothing was branded towards a specific cultural phenomenon or really anything outside those artists' fan bases. The company agreed and sent me a few dozen empty bottles to play chemist with.

Playing chemist turned into becoming mad scientist. Mixing new colors came easy to me though. It was something I honestly never thought I'd do again because of the bad taste left in my mouth from that fucked-up ex-partner, but this time was dif-

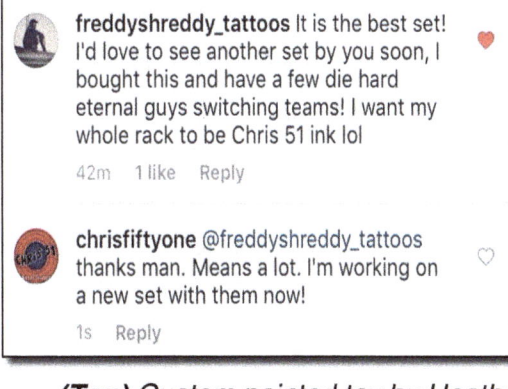

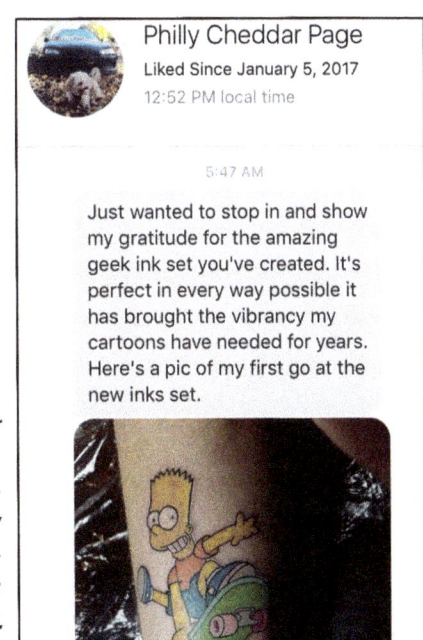

(Top) Custom painted toy by Heather Maranda.
(Above and right) Social media comments and messages like this is why I put my heart and soul in to my projects. Helping younger artists inspires me to do more and work even harder.

ferent. I could just create like an artist without worrying about the production, bottling, packaging, distribution, and other shit that comes with it.

I worked on those colors day and night and in between tattoos. I started out with eight, expanded to ten, and finally rested with twelve. I honestly could have done twelve more. I sent each color back and forth with the color masterminds at Intenze. Over and over I returned them. This one was too thick, that one too runny. This one too dull, that one the wrong hue. For almost a year I perfected the recipes.

I worked on the names and branding for months too. I wanted enough geek reference to cover many facets of the

My Fellow Geeks,

I am the Alpha-Geek, boss-nerd, Chris 51. Through my Comic-con tattoo tour, Epic Ink TV show and multiple other geek-art endeavors I have discovered one major Force that binds us pop-culture artists together...Our love for cartoons and animated art!

The most important element in animation is the vibrant colors. The brightest hues somehow give two-dimensional characters a third depth of life and movement. The only problem was finding a collection of all of those brilliant colors in one place, and from one company...Until now!

I have intensely formulated the ultimate color set with INTENZE to give you the only ink you will ever need to bring your geeky cartoon, toy, video game, TV and anime characters to life on the skin.

In this set I will reveal my tricks and tips to get your tattoos out of the dark side and into the bright! Enjoy.

Geeks Unite,

Chris 51

(Above) Front page of box set insert booklet.
(Right) I had an idea to include a limited-edition, autographed trading card in each set. I mean, this stuff was geared towards geeks, so it seemed logical to include a little geeky collectible to fit the motif. I even paid for them, because in the end, it's a small price to pay to expand my own brand.

culture; choosing names or slogans derived from super heroes, cartoons, science fiction, fantasy or horror. But, I had to be careful to not legally infringe on any copyrighted material, not the easiest task.

Then I really became the control freak I am. I wanted complete control over every graphic, box design, booklet insert, and more. If I was going to attach my name to the product, it had to be 100 percent made by me and supported by me. I was honestly probably annoying as hell to the staff, but I didn't care. They would thank me when the final kick-ass product was unveiled.

I was a picky little bitch too. Intenze wanted the tough-guy-with-arms-folded pose for the box front, as to stay cohesive with their other sets' graphics. I understand the desire to keep the branding similar, but I wasn't having the stereotypical tough-guy, frowny-face, I-hate-you, ass-kickin pose! That goes against everything geeks stand for. We hate that attitude. We are actually happy because we like fun, happy shit. *Epic Ink* made fun of (almost mocked) that exact type of thing in our industry that all of the other TV shows portrayed. So, as a joke, I made an image of me in the arms-folded pose into a Simpsonized character with a huge smile. I worked for hours on it, meticulously drawing every tattoo I have on its arms. If

(Photos) *I still constantly make all of my own promotional flyers and ads to support the company that has supported me so much. They notice this, and share my work on social media in return, allowing me to reach new fans and future clients.*

this set was going to be aimed at my beloved geek demographic, then it sure as hell would have a cartoon on the box! To my amazement, Intenze loved it! What was kind of a smart-ass gesture turned into the design department's favorite project to work on. It was a testament to compromising a little, but sticking to your guns of integrity.

The design team told me that I was the only artist of theirs who had ever designed a whole project from start to finish. It felt great, and it feels even greater seeing my hard work being sold all over the world now. This shows you that there are so many opportunities to succeed in business, but sometimes you have to create them yourself. As soon as that sun shines on you, plant the seed. Plant a big-ass seed that the garden isn't expecting but will be forced to grow. If you put in the hard work, it will pay off for a long time and open other doors you weren't expecting.

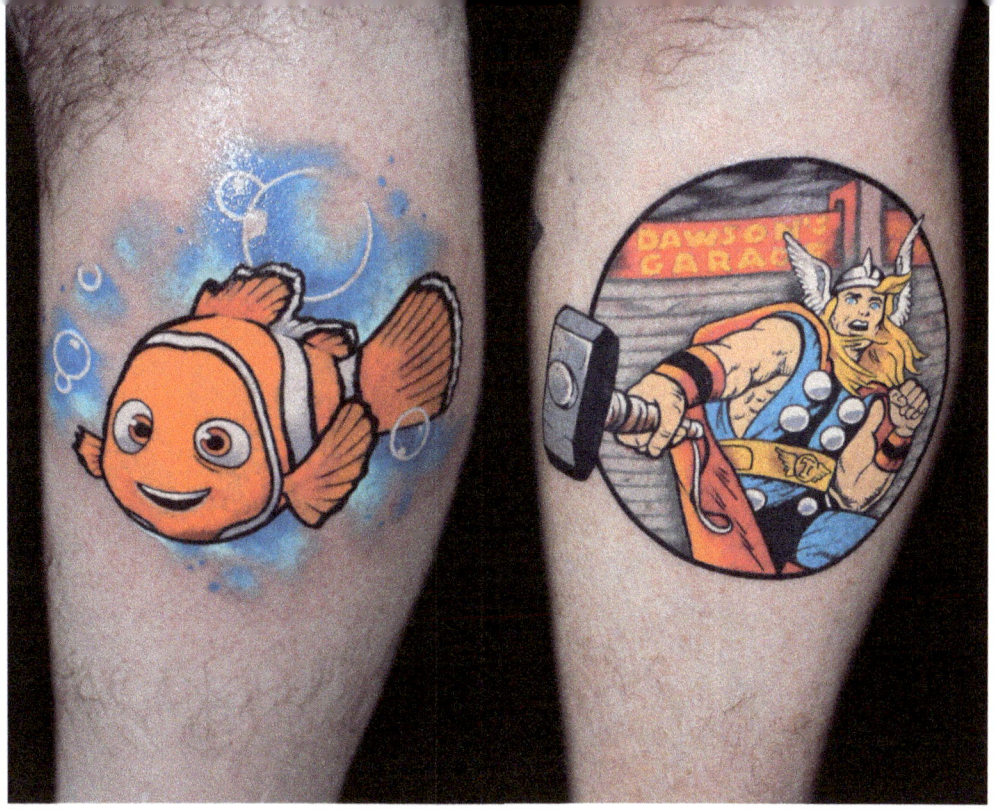

"Chris 51 became the face of Geek/Vintage Cartoon tattoos with his show, *Epic Ink*," says Bill Gross. "As part of my duties with Intenze Tattoo Ink, I shot a promotional video at one of Chris 51's many GeeksterInk events around the country. Chris and his wife Katie went out of their way to make me feel like family. After two long days of tattooing, Chris was more than willing to go the extra mile to promote his upcoming Geek Ink Set. We sat down and worked for several hours on various sound clips to use in the promotional videos for his set. Chris was tireless in making each and every color exactly what he wanted it to be. Whenever Intenze has an idea for a promotion, Chris is the first one to go the extra mile. He has been the easiest and most enthusiastic artist to work with since I joined the company."

I am so grateful to Intenze Ink for including me in their family and allowing me to spread my wings with nothing but their support. For that alone, I will stay loyal to them until the end.

34

EPIC INK
FINAL TAKE

In our eyes, *Epic Ink* was a smashing success. The fans thought so too. Everyone loved it. Its positive message and incredible tattoos blended perfectly with its geeky message and over-the-top, real-life characters. It was fun and it was REAL!

Its debut had nearly one million viewers—a huge number for any network. *Epic Ink* was paired up with shows that had no rhyme or reason, but it endured. All season long we pushed between a half million to 750,000 viewers. Tons of support was shown through letters and social media. But the overwhelming love from our fans wouldn't sway the network's decision to renew. In the end, it came down to a new network executive simply not wanting to have a tattoo reality show on the channel anymore. This was a battle we would not win. It was a change in direction for a network whose overall viewer numbers were plummeting, and all the love and support in the world couldn't change it. *Epic Ink* fan groups started petitions and sent hundreds of e-mails. But the network wanted change.

No matter how sad I was to not get renewed, I was still the happiest man ever. I had a dream, a very far-fetched dream, that became reality. I made that dream come true with my best friends, and it changed their lives too. "Filming the show was the hardest, most exhausting, most exciting and fun time I have ever had," says Heather Maranda. We all worked hard, struggled, and flourished as a cohesive team and kept our integrity and friendships. We didn't sell out, and we made magic happen on camera the likes that had yet to be seen in the tattoo world. We single-handedly helped combine the worlds of tattooing and pop-culture and brought them together to a new demographic. We inspired children to become artists while remaining positive role models. We did it all without any drama or insincerity. Together, we did what millions of people dream of but only a handful get to do: we made a wonderful, funny, and entertaining TV show that nobody can ever take away from us.

And, that is why we didn't get a second season (HAHA): there was no drama, fighting, lying, or cheating. Nothing immoral. It's a sad state of affairs when you need sad affairs to get a second season on TV, but it's true. People like to hate characters and talk about them with their friends. People like to get mad at stupidity and realize they can do better than those they are watching on television. People return to the boob tube for the buildup of who's gonna fight whom or sleep with whom this week. We had none of that. We were too real and too likable. We were actually told this by industry insiders. We were too good at what we did and not too bad at anything else. But looking back, I wouldn't change a thing.

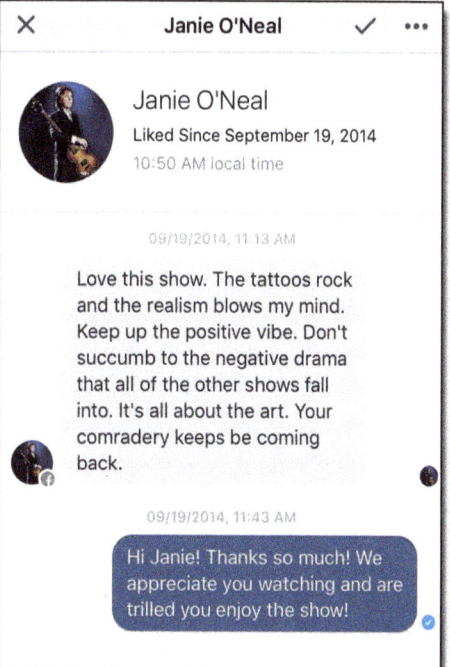

I am so proud of what my cast mates and friends and I did. From the caterers to audio guys, cameramen to producers, everyone had a role and performed it perfectly, beyond expectations. Even though we had a cast of six, the ones with the real talent were the twenty other souls making us look good behind the scenes. I am still in awe at how cohesive and powerful a unit of strangers from all walks of life can become after working their asses off towards one common goal.

"I loved the whole cast, they were like a crazy bunch of cousins in my family," claims executive producer Jerry Carita, "except Josh Bodwell, he's a real dick (haha)." Jerry continues, "Also, I made up all the nice things I've said in this book so that Chris 51 will keep letting me be Facebook friends with his gorgeous wife!"

After the show ended, Jeff and Caroline and Heather and her family all stayed in Springfield to work at Area 51 Tattoo. We never pretended that the cast worked there to begin with; in fact, I say in the show's opening credits that I assembled an all-star geek dream team at my shop. Josh was content with his life in Pennsylvania, and Chris Jones wasn't going to relocate to America unless he were to get hitched to an American supermodel.

Heather still remains at Area 51 Tattoo and has settled into a good life in Oregon, surrounded by people who love her and probably wouldn't ever let her leave at this point (haha). Her clients travel to Area 51 from all over the country.

Jeff and Caroline lasted one year in Oregon. I don't think Caroline ever adjusted to life away from home, and we never saw her even when she was here. Jeff wasn't built for working for somebody else, I can see that now. I'm not sure if he was ever truly happy at Area 51 Tattoo; I think it was just a pit stop

on his life's track to explore other things. I could never fault him for that, and I wish him all the best of luck and happiness.

Chris Jones never really needed *Epic Ink* to boost his career, as his artwork spoke its own famous language. He has an intelligent and innovative mind, and his talents with a tattoo machine are never-ending. He is a true ink-Jedi master. I still visit him every year in Wales, and he visits me here in Oregon. I confide in Jonesy a lot because we have similar stubborn streaks and pride about certain things.

Josh Bodwell is just the same old, peaceful-go-lucky Bodwell he always was and always will be. He takes great pride in *Epic Ink* and is always ready to jump on a new project with me—he's the first one I would call to do so, too. Nobody understands my business passion and drive like Josh, and nobody deals with it better. He is the Riker to my Picard and the Luke to my Vader.

Yes, we had only one season on major-network television, and maybe I treat it like more than it was in the grand scheme of life. But, it is something that we created and put on this earth that will stand the test of time through recorded history. The fact that I still get letters from parents thanking me for giving their child a new direction or goal in life, being a positive role model, or bringing a family together to laugh one night a week still brings tears to my eyes. Reading those letters assures me that I did something right in my life, something that my own children can be proud of me for. Reality shows may be a dime a dozen nowadays, but I can tell you that my experience will always be a special accomplishment for my family and me. How many people in the world can say they were lucky enough to get that opportunity, and to make a positive and meaningful impact on people's lives through entertainment?

I am constantly writing letters to A&E to get the show on Netflix or DVD. I search other networks to air it, and I'm fueled daily by my fans to continue to push it. They motivate and inspire me. I am also working on several different incarnations of *Epic Ink* and have pitched three different new shows to other networks that involve parts of the original cast and, of course, all of the extreme geekiness.

The *Epic Ink* fans can be only described as . . . EPIC! They support everything new I do. I owe our fans everything, and I will never stop giving back to them, whether through art, entertainment, or just my time.

(Above) Some of the Epic crew still get together regularly to work at comic cons across the country. (Right) The amazing Voodoo Doughnut still surprises us at local cons with artistic mouth-watering masterpieces. I don't know if it's my now-famous donut tattoo or because I visit there weekly, but we have developed a sweet local bond.

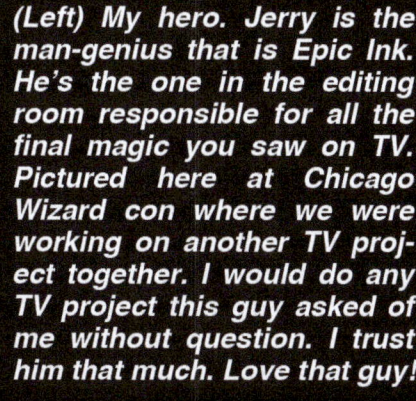

(Left) My hero. Jerry is the man-genius that is Epic Ink. He's the one in the editing room responsible for all the final magic you saw on TV. Pictured here at Chicago Wizard con where we were working on another TV project together. I would do any TV project this guy asked of me without question. I trust him that much. Love that guy!

Joe Dove
A whole hour of epic ink! !! So epic!
13 minutes ago · Unlike · 👍 1 · Reply

Chandra Arnold Shores
I freakin' LOVE this show!!! #mykindapeople
20 minutes ago · Unlike · 👍 1 · Reply

Khoa Phan
We the fans want another season!! 👍👍👍👍👍
22 minutes ago · Unlike · 👍 1 · Reply

Shawn OneTon Steinle
I love the idea of this giveaway. I can't believe the show is over for this season already. I want you to all to sign the box when I win.
41 minutes ago · Unlike · 👍 1 · Reply

Keri Willis
From the very first episode I fell in love with the show and the amazing art you guys do. If there's any justice in the world there WILL be season 2 and 3 and so on. If I win I want signatures. But even if I don't win, I will still watch and follow religiously. I was actually in Gamestop the other day telling all kinds of people about this show. They had not heard of it and sounded stoked to watch it. I hope I gained you guys some more viewers. I have every episode recorded on my TV. And one of these days I'm coming out to get a tattoo done. I want all the female characters from Mortal Kombat tattooed around my thigh.
#epicinkfinale
43 minutes ago · Unlike · 👍 1 · Reply

Brandon Smith
If A&E don't renew you guys I'm rioting.
57 minutes ago · Like · Reply

Becky Snook
Done. How about some autographs? ?
59 minutes ago · Unlike · 👍 1 · Reply

Adam Michel
Best tattoo show out there on tv, where the only competition comes in the form of geeking out! (Hands down Josh Bodwell is winning so far!)
1 hour ago · Unlike · 👍 1 · Reply

Jon Smith
Done and done ! Now let's let A&E know we want a second season !! #goodtv
1 hour ago · Unlike · 👍 1 · Reply

Crystal D. Lowe
I LOVE EPIC INK! It's always good for a much need laugh in a world full of chaos. Every artist at AREA 51 is AMAZINGLY talented. Could you possibly offer up a free tattoo instead? Collectible figures are great but we want the real ultimate fan prize.....one that will last forever! Heather Maranda I am dying for you to get your hands on me, a tattoo virgin! Cheers to you all and hopefully an #EpicInkSeason2 Please tune in for the #EpicInkFinale everyone. ;-) #1FanEpicInk
Friday at 6:37 PM · Unlike · 👍 1 · Reply

Aaron Sanders
#epicinkfinale everyone watch!!! Love this show.
#epicinkseason2
Friday at 6:26 PM · Unlike · 👍 1 · Reply

Jason Malczewski
Hoping to see another season #EpicInkSeason2
Yesterday at 2:40 PM · Unlike · 👍 1 · Reply

Matthew Welzenbach
Cannot wait for season 2. I also badly want to get a tattoo do by Josh Bodwell!
Yesterday at 1:18 PM · Unlike · 👍 1 · Reply

Duane Allen Smith
Chris, "cookie". No drama is nice. It's time the tables turned on what people watch. You guys will get another season.
Yesterday at 10:38 AM · Unlike · 👍 1 · Reply

Tommy Frederick
Let's do this!!
Yesterday at 4:47 AM · Unlike · 👍 1 · Reply

Mike Reifschneider
Se you guys on TV makes me happy that there's still awesom people in our town of Springfield, plus if i win you wouldn't ha to ship it far since our area codes are the same :p
Yesterday at 12:26 AM · Unlike · 👍 1 · Reply

Andrea Rose Cripps
Wooo hooo!!!!!! Awesome!! :D <3
Friday at 9:19 PM · Unlike · 👍 1 · Reply

Catherine Kitty Lutton
Damn the season is getting ready to end already? I can't wait for season 2 then, you guys are awesome!!!!!!
Friday at 8:14 PM · Unlike · 👍 1 · Reply

Patrick Curtis Slayter
after watching you get your donut tattoomy 2 year old son no keeps asking for a donut tattoo on his belly button
Friday at 7:26 PM · Unlike · 👍 1 · Reply

Keena Bear Morris
I'm so in! Signatures from the cast AND its on a Clone Troope Oh my collection NEEDS that in it's life. Reposting, changing here and instagram. Can't wait for season 2! Gonna miss my Wednesday routine. But thank gobstoppers that theirs reruns until then. #epicinkfinale
Friday at 7:08 PM · Unlike · 👍 1 · Reply

Shane Wiggans
Totally want another season, and seriously am planning a trip from Texas some time on the future #epicinkfinale #epicinkseason2
Friday at 7:02 PM · Unlike · 👍 1 · Reply

Chris Lucas
Love the show! Can't wait for the #epicinkfinale
Friday at 4:37 PM · Unlike · 👍 1 · Reply

James Ryan
love this show hope you guys get renewed!
Friday at 4:37 PM · Unlike · 👍 1 · Reply

Mark Sylvestre
A second season would rock!!!
Friday at 4:17 PM · Unlike · 👍 1 · Reply

Sara Knox
Its easy to tell im an addict because every time I open my phone keyboard it predicts I start every sentence with #epicin
Friday at 4:15 PM · Unlike · 👍 1 · Reply

Amanda Betzold
I'm totally watching!! My whole family loves your show!!!!
Friday at 4:10 PM · Unlike · 👍 1 · Reply

35

NAMING NAMES

I have been fortunate enough to meet many celebrities because of my small taste of fame from *Epic Ink*. I get to sit and schmooze with iconic stars whom I normally wouldn't be able to get within twenty feet of. Yet, no matter how many times I am in that greenroom with some of them at comic cons, I can't help but to fanboy out (internally). I mean, after all, I am a geek first and foremost, and I love and admire those actors, the Epic roles they play, and the cultural impact they have had on my life.

When you are sitting at a greenroom table, and you've just finished scarfing down chicken so you can get back to work on a tattoo you're in the middle of, and Nathan Fillion asks to sit and join you, what the fuck do you do!? I mean, c'mon, Captain Malcolm *"Castle"* Reynolds is speaking to you in the flesh . . . I think you can stay an extra couple minutes and act like you need a second helping of food. But when he starts talking to you about tattoos and then hands you his phone to scroll through a section of pictures of fans who have gotten his likeness tattooed on themselves, then you really freak out inside. You have to stay calm and cool on the surface as you flip through his phone . . . but then you realize what's happening and think, holy shit I am holding the Browncoat Captain's phone, and your balls start to sweat a little.

Then there is the time in Sacramento when William Shatner is in a rare talkative mood and asks you about your tattoos. "Did Captain Kirk just talk to me for reals?" I ask my wife. Fast forward five minutes later, and we are laughing and talking about the tattoo I did on my penis, and he is completely intrigued by the conversation. He probably thought I was the biggest freak, but oh well. Now I can honestly say that I have talked with the most legendary starship captain of all time about the tattoo on my cock! My wife is still embarrassed that the conversation took that phallic turn (haha).

Oddly enough, I had another memorable day in that same greenroom the year prior. Billie Piper (of *Doctor Who* and *Penny Dreadful* fame) asked me to tattoo her finger. She wanted it done privately as to not attract attention. It definitely attracted a different kind of attention though. Suddenly all the celebrities in the greenroom were taking turns to come investigate the buzzing and commotion. The best part was seeing Sean Patrick Flanery (*The Boondock Saints*) gasping with looks of pain while watching the whole thing.

One time, I brought my producer with me to Chicago to film for a crowdfunding campaign we were planning so we could get a new version of *Epic Ink* back on the air. Since I had done a couple press events with Michael Rooker (*Walking Dead, Guardians of the Galaxy*) in the past, he knew of me and agreed to do some camera time together. We filmed a mock interview of me asking him for some money for my project, but in reality, I was just getting the bullet points of the campaign across to him so people would actually listen to me. Unplanned and unbeknownst to me and my producer, Michael decided to throw me in the service elevator and call security on me. It was so damn funny, and I was stuck in the elevator listening to all of them cracking up outside the door. He then pulled me out and patted me on the back saying, "Good job." What an honor it was to hear that and to work with such a professional, albeit so briefly. Michael did all of this on the fly, making it up as we went along. There is no telling Rooker what you want or think should happen, he is going to do it his way! But, his way turns out better than you could ever imagine anyway.

So there are a few stories of celebrity encounters. Trust me when I say that name dropping is the furthest thing from what I am trying to convey here. Remember, I am all out of fucks given to anybody who thinks I have any brag-a-licious intent. What I am really trying to do is show you what hard work can lead to. More importantly, I am fanboying out because I am one of you! These stories don't come from a movie set or high-budget filming location. These encounters and relationships aren't fabricated in tabloids or through "he said/she said"-isms. What I tell you is the real deal coming from one of your own. I am just a geek who probably has no worldly business being with these high-profile actors anyway—but I act like I do, so I do! I'm just spittin' truths from the cold concrete floor of comic con life and travel. I have no reason to lie to you or about them. I want you to see these celebrities through my eyes and experiences, and not judge them by a wrongful rap they might have gotten from a single bad day or a rude fan.

Sean Gunn (Guardians of the Galaxy), is always down for fun with fans; seen here doing the speak no, hear no, see no evil pose with Josh Bodwell and myself.

Jason David Frank

I consider the Original Green Power Ranger one of my true friends. Yes, I have tattooed Jason David Frank, but that just led to a bond that went way deeper than any ink.

The moment I walked into my first greenroom at a comic con, Jason greeted me. Some celebrities keep to themselves and keep their heads down. Not Jason. He saw my tattoos and immediately struck up a conversation. He welcomed me in and showed me the celebrity comic con ropes. My new-found reality stardom was greener than any Power Ranger, but that didn't matter to him.

(Top) Jason asked if I would tattoo him on his reality show and of course I said yes! We ended up doing the logo for his skydiving gear line Tunnel Rats. *(Above)* Filming the tattoo live at Wizard World Comic Con, Sacramento.

He truly is a good soul, always giving and always thinking of others before himself. He constantly uses his celebrity status for morally good deeds.

One night, I was walking into a convenience store after a comic con we both worked. I ran in to get some milk for my kids, and I bumped into Jason leaving with arms full of food. He had everything from candy bars and bags of chips to sodas and bread, probably fifty to one hundred dollars' worth of food. I was like, "Dayam, you are stocking up tonight, dude . . . you hungry or what, haha?" Without skipping a beat, he looked at me and said, "Dude, it's not for me, it's for the two homeless guys out front." He said it so matter-of-factly, like duh! That's the kind of guy he is. After a long, tiresome weekend of working at the con, and an annoying plane delay, it was still second nature for him to help out those in need. To top it all off, it was on his birthday! I felt like an asshole because the thought of it never crossed my mind; I was just thinking about my own kids. What a great example Jason set for my children though. I made sure to point out what he did for those two guys, and told my kids to remember that anyone can help out others. I tell this story when I speak at panels with Jason, because the audience needs to know that there is much more to his time here than just Morphin' time.

(Above) JDF showing my son Troy how to make a proper fist.

(Right) Jason was kind enough to appear for free to help launch my own first comic con. He was such a huge draw and could have charged us tens-of-thousands, but he is not greedy and did it to just help out a friend. I will be forever grateful.

Christian Kane

Christian Kane (*The Librarians, Leverage*) is another guy whom I consider a true friend. He was humble and sweet from the first time I met him at a comic con press event. I always tell everyone that he is waaay too good looking to be that nice, but it's true, he is that nice.

If you haven't heard Christian sing, I suggest you do . . . just don't take your wife because his voice is a panty greaser! Even I get a little chubbed up (haha). Seriously though, he is one of the most well-rounded men I have ever met on the talent wheel. The first time we met he treated me as an equal, never asking or wondering why this ugly, tattooed reality TV guy was doing the same press party as he was.

The next time I ran into him I wasn't sure if he would remember me from a dozen cons prior, but to my amazement he bro-hugged me like no time had passed.

We went out that night to sing karaoke. I got on the mic and jokingly laid down the strict law that Christian wasn't allowed to sing because he was the only legitimate professional in the

(Above) Christian and myself at a fan Q & A at The Hard Rock Cafe, St. Louis. *(Left)* Christian harassing me while I tattoo. He's always stopping by my booth at comic cons to screw with me (haha.)

group. He said, "Fine, I'll rap!" Before I could get out a chuckle, he jacked the mic from me and blew our minds with some Snoop Dogg, completely memorized and flawless. Some people have more talent in their left nut than the rest of us have in our whole bodies, and Christian is one of those with a huge left nut full of skills.

This dude is always down for a party, but when it is time to work he is all business. He treats his fans like gold and makes time to talk and listen to every one of them. When he sings live, he takes requests, answers questions, and tells stories to the fans. And believe me, there are a lot of them, especially the ladies. There's a whole society of female Christian Kane fans out there called Kaniacs, and they are the most loyal and supportive group of close-knit fans that I think I've ever seen. I have tattooed his lyrics and autograph on many of them now, so one day I am hoping I will have my own "51iacs" (haha).

Christian texts me often about tattoo ideas or about the night he got a crazy drunken tattoo in Thailand. He's invited me to *The Librarians* set several times, but unfortunately my schedule hasn't allowed me to go yet. I would love to see him in action, blowing up some shit.

(Right) Christian stopped by my Geeksterink Tattoo booth in Chicago when he heard I was tattooing his autograph on a die-hard Kaniac. He then made her day by hanging out to watch.

Lou Ferrigno

Lou is larger than life in more ways than one. Although he may look intimidating, to say the least, the giant of a man also has a giant heart. I have worked over twenty comic cons with Lou, and we've done press together at most of them. Doing early 6:00 a.m. press live in studio or sitting in a greenroom before going out into the center of the Mall of America for a massive Q&A will get you close to (or hating) anyone real fast. Luckily for me, Lou and I got close. I wouldn't want him hating me because I wouldn't want to see him angry (sorry, bad Hulk innuendo)!

I think some people misunderstand Lou. First of all, he has bad hearing, and if you don't catch him in his good ear, you may think he is totally ignoring you, when in reality he has no idea you are even talking to him. I have also heard people call him an asshole because he didn't stand up from his dinner (that he'd been waiting all day to eat because he was posing for pictures for his job) to pose for another picture or sign an autograph for someone walking into the convention center. I don't think that the common comic con goer takes into account that this is his job, and means of income. When Lou signs an autograph on the show floor, he is losing out on forty dollars that someone might other-

(Photos) Lou and I always have a good time when doing press events together. *(Top)* Doing a crowd Q&A at Philly Hard Rock Cafe. *(Right)* Screwing around on the red carpet.

wise spend on getting his autograph at his booth (not to mention that the promoter will give him shit because that means the show loses out on their cut). So, you can see that if this was a frequent occurrence, not only would the promoter not have Lou back, but he couldn't afford to do more shows, and then we all lose out on meeting an icon in person. I will defend Lou every time, and I do.

When you are alone with Lou he talks about important things. He asks about your family first, and career second. He genuinely cares. Then he starts telling his stories. For reals, the dude has the best stories in the world. He talks about being Michael Jackson's personal trainer. He speaks of Arnold and the old weight-lifting competitions. And, he always expresses his love and admiration for Bill Bixby, whom he credits for teaching him everything in the acting world.

I have seen Lou choose to talk to children at school about staying healthy and drug-free over getting worshipped at press galas by drones of Hulk fans. He always does the right thing; that's just the way he's built . . .

(Above) Lou always stops by the GeeksterInk tattoo booth at cons when he hears there's Hulk ink being done. **(Right)** Doing a live Q&A with Lou, Barry Bostwick, and Disney artist Clinton Hobart in Mall of America.

Charlie Benante
ANTHRAX

A true legend. The drummer for one of the biggest and greatest metal bands of all time, and he wanted to meet *me* . . . WTF?!?!

Anthrax's Charlie Benante was a fan of *Epic Ink*. When he heard that we were at the Chicago Comic Con he asked the staff to introduce the two of us, as he shared my love not only for tattoos but also *The Simpsons*!

I knew who he was right when I saw him. Before he could say a word I was fanboy-ing out! This guy has rocked my world for thirty years!

I couldn't believe how sweet and truly genuine he was. As soon as we started talking *Simpsons*, we were immediate friends. *The Simpsons* has a way of doing that. Mix that with awesome metal, and it's a recipe for a blooming bromance!

Charlie asked if I could redo the Krusty the Clown on his leg, and even though I was totally booked, you can bet your ass I said "hell yes" without hesitation. As I was tattooing him we started making future plans for an entire *Simpsons* leg sleeve. We still text to this day when we think of new ideas to add to it, and I surprise him once in a while with *Simpson*-ized portraits of him or his friends just for fun.

It's always such a great feeling when you meet someone you truly admire and he turns out to be even cooler or more gracious than you were hoping for. It really does leave a mark on you, especially on younger fans, and it's important to leave a positive memory instead of a scar.

Charlie and I have since had a couple fun adventures together at cons. In 2016 in Chicago, we got together and fanboyed hard when we got a picture with Princess Leia herself, Carrie Fisher (below). We practically ran to the Celeb Photo Op booth when we heard she was there, and skipped away in a joyous frolic with our new picture. That photo meant a lot to me; not only is it with the best heavy-metal drummer ever but also an iconic Star Wars actress.

Picture courtesy of Celeb Photo Ops

Anthrax came to Portland, Oregon, in the fall of 2016, and although I have seen them live several times, that show was a lot different since I am a friend of the drummer now. It felt way more personal, and I even developed a kind of

(Above) Behind the scenes. Charlie and I filming a segment for my new TV pilot about the GeeksterInk Legends tour. Photo by my boo, producer Nick Floyd.

pride for Charlie and his playing. Every song that I grew up headbanging to had a totally different meaning to me. We went on his tour bus after the show, but unfortunately there was no time for more tattooing.

The future holds a lot of geekery for Charlie and I. I just tattooed him for the third time for a new TV pilot I am co-producing for Walker Stalker con. I have also talked with producers from AMC's *Comic Book Men* about appearing on an episode with Charlie as avid quasi-celebrity *Simpsons* collectors, searching for that ultimate *Simpsons* rarity. Although Charlie already has the entire life-sized *Simpsons* family in his basement, and I own virtually every *Simpsons* toy made, there is still that holy-grail piece you may one day see Charlie and me fighting over on TV!

Bruce Campbell

The master of horror is as awesome as they come. He's nice, humble, and funny as hell. He's also the best dresser I have ever seen. The man is crazy dapper! Every time I see him at a comic con he is in an expensive, flamboyant suit, that few other grown men could pull off. Whether it's full lavender, solid white, or blood red, Bruce dresses the part of a superstar, yet never acts like one.

I have worked at least a couple dozen of the same shows as Bruce, and I have never seen him moody, frowning, or not on point. He is always on his game, whether it's talking to one fan or one hundred!

He is a huge fan of tattoo art and culture. He routinely visits the GeeksterInk Legends booth to investigate the work being done, whether it is *Evil Dead* related or not. Not only will he check out the work, he will dip in and out of the booths to take it all in, spending lots of time talking to both artist and client.

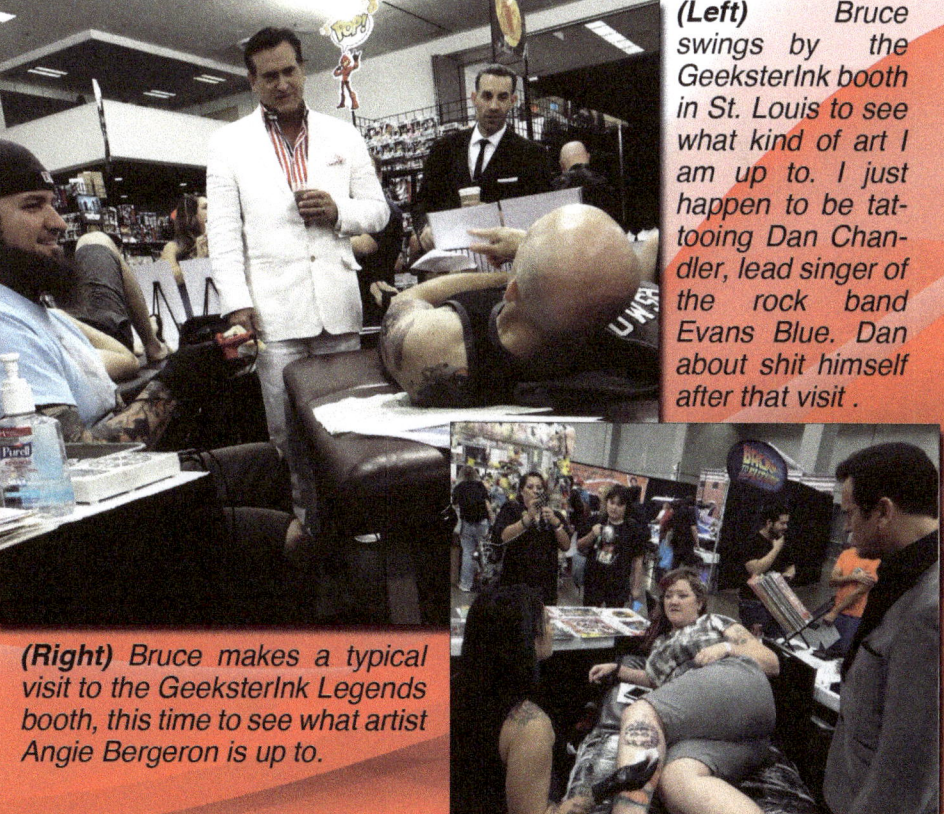

(Left) Bruce swings by the GeeksterInk booth in St. Louis to see what kind of art I am up to. I just happen to be tattooing Dan Chandler, lead singer of the rock band Evans Blue. Dan about shit himself after that visit.

(Right) Bruce makes a typical visit to the GeeksterInk Legends booth, this time to see what artist Angie Bergeron is up to.

Butch Patrick

I don't even know where to start with Butch. Mr. Eddie Munster himself. He is an icon to me and most of us horror pop-culture fans. But more personally, he's a father figure to my Hollywood life. He has helped me more in my career than anyone else and is always a phone call away if I ever need professional advice from the man who has done it all and seen it all. When I had questions about agents and management, he was there, sharing his secrets. When I had questions about entertainment lawyers, he was there. Or when I just needed to vent or bitch about production and shooting schedules, Butch always made me feel better.

I met Butch at HorrorHound Weekend in Columbus, Ohio, in the late 2000s. I went to his table to get an autograph and talk *Munsters*, and before I knew it, we were talking business. He was so humble and easy to talk to that conversation just naturally escalated to our future plans. Butch said he was always down to hear new business opportunities, so I presented the idea of naming a tattoo ink after him from my Formula 51 Ink line. He loved the idea! Surprisingly, he already knew several tattoo artists and was very knowledgeable of the industry. Months passed, meetings passed, and eventually I made two ink colors with his namesake: Eddie Munster's Skin (a light greenish grey) and Eddie Munster's Suit (purple). It was a risky yet radical idea that had never been done in the tattoo industry . . . and it worked. I later sold the ink company, but Butch and I remained friends, and then our real relationship through television

(Right) Butch introduced me to another icon at SDCC in 2014, Metallica's Kirk Hammett. I had a total metal boner in this picture. It's small but it's there trust me.

forays and Hollywood experiences began.

The last time he visited me, he didn't want to party or be "shown off;" he just wanted to hang out. He even went to my son's football game as a show of support; that's the kind of guy he is. He never gets off the phone without saying, "Give your wife my love," and he's always happy when I talk to him.

I can guarantee you won't find anyone with cooler stories than Butch either. He possesses over fifty years of classic Hollywood memories in his Munster brain and never shies away from talking about them, whether they are about going on unauthorized joy rides in the Munster Koach with Grandpa or sneaking onto movie sets and having free reign on the Universal Studios lots. He is proud to be a part of the magical history and culture of both Hollywood and *The Munsters*. I have heard lots of his stories, but every time I see him he surprises me with a new one; they are never-ending.

Butch has been through a lot in life. With childhood fame and the allure of money, drugs, and women, he has risen above the challenges, unlike a lot of child stars you read about in the tabloids. I am proud of him and even prouder to call him my friend.

Butch had to see the official Simpsons mural on his last visit to Springfield.

Michael Rooker

What can you say about a guy who has done it all? When you have played everyone from Yondu the Ravager to Jared in Mallrats, you have earned my respect.

I have had the pleasure . . . no, excitement . . . no, craziness (yeah, that's it) of filming a segment with Michael. He is definitely a character, to say the least. He's nothing like the racist swine he played as Merle Dixon in The Walking Dead, but I could see him easily surviving a zombie apocalypse.

You never know what you are gonna get with Michael. I don't say that in a derogatory way. What I mean is, is Michael gonna be calm and cool? Loud and crazy? Or is he going to be sweet and hilarious? The best is when he is "D," all of the above! I have been around him enough doing promotional press for comic cons to know that no matter what mood he is in, he's fun to be around. He's a contagious dude; you just want to be around him and see what happens next.

He is a true entertainer, and he does it because he loves it, not because it's a job.

(Above) I about shit myself when my wife showed me this pic she took of Michael watching my live segment in a Portland studio. **(Left)** Michael, Myself and Josh Bodwell having a laugh during a live red-carpet press event for Wizard World Comic Con in Chicago. Michael always has a way of making everyone around him laugh whether it's from shock value or pure comedy.

Katie Cassidy

Katie is a sultry and talented actress who starred in *Supernatural* and *Arrow*, and movies like *Taken*.

I have tattooed Katie a couple times now at comic cons. We have always kept the tattoos on the down low as to not attract too much attention on social media.

She was very standoffish when I first worked on her, and rightfully so. She didn't know my intentions or personality. Was I just a super fan doing her tattoo for the publicity or maybe just wanting her money? But, as soon as the Seattle Seahawks came up in conversation, we were immediate friends. She's a huge football fan and regularly attends the games, even from the sidelines (which has this guy super-fuckin-jeally).

The first time I tattooed her I did some black canaries on her finger as a tribute to her TV character, the Black Canary. I've also done some text on her that I will keep private out of respect. I was lucky to tattoo her, and I hope to again someday.

It's truly impressive how much she's done with her career in such little time. I have never charged her a penny, because I am a fan of her work too. I've only asked that she share the tattoo work I've done on her with her fans, and she has always gone above and beyond that to help support me.

Robin Lord Taylor

Robin is one of the sweetest and most gracious men I have ever met. My wife has such a huge crush on him that she had to get The Penguin's autograph tattooed on her. He was so excited about it. He was shaking with nerves because it was the first time he had ever signed his name on someone specifically to get tattooed. He watched me do the tattoo with the biggest smile on his face, and when we were finished, he actually thanked us for doing it. We ran into him later that night at a VIP party, and he talked to my wife like they were lifelong besties trading stories.

(Above) Robin couldn't believe his name was going to be tattooed. **(Right)** Of course it attracted quite a crowd at the GeeksterInk Legends Tour booth at Wizard World St. Louis.

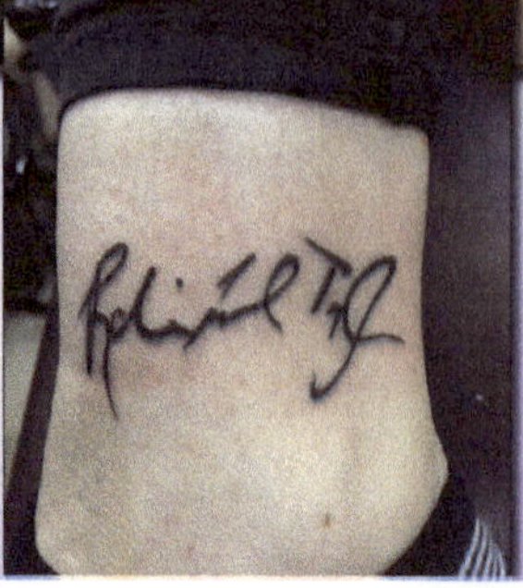

(Left) Original "Simpsonized" art I made for Robin as a thank you. **(Right)** My wife's finished ankle.

Erin Richards

This chick is amazing. Not only is she beautiful and talented but she is funny as hell.

I bumped into her at a Wizard World comic con when I went to the Celeb Photo Ops booth to visit my friends who own the whole photo operation. I hadn't seen owners Kitsie and Chris in a couple months, and when you do lots of shows together you become family and truly miss those good people in your life. Anyway, they weren't in the booth when I poked my head in but Erin was, sitting by herself. She said hi and just started talking to me about the Foo Fighters shirt I was wearing, like she had known me for years. She had no idea who I was, but I certainly knew her since I am a HUGE fan of *Gotham*.

She asked me my favorite Foo Fighters song, and before I knew it we were singing the hook to "All My Life" together- and in tune, I must say (haha). She was a hoot!

Before long, we got on the subject of tattoos. She said that she's always wanted a tattoo of a camel on her toe so she could walk into a stuffy room and literally ask people if they wanted to see her camel toe, then whip off her shoe and get a laugh out of them. That's the crazy kind of girl she seems to be, not much different from her role on *Gotham* . . . minus the insane killing aspects, of course! We planned to do that tattoo later on in the weekend, but we both got super busy and made a rain check for a future show. Unfortunately, I haven't seen her since, but you can bet that when I do, I will go straight up to her in the greenroom full of quiet celebrities and ask if I could see her camel toe.

Paige - WWE

WWE Wrestling Diva, Paige is simply a cool, fun, down-to-earth chick! I have hung out with her, partied with her, karaoked, and more, and she is always a riot. Paige is the shit!

I constantly see her go above and beyond for her fans, even going out of her way to make their day. I have seen her come out from behind her autograph booth to meet and hug every young fan she can.

You can often find her in the GeeksterInk booth during comic cons, either getting tattooed or harassing us all.

She got thrown into the limelight at a young age, and I think she still needs to find her exact place in life. Whether that's in the wrestling ring or not, I just want her to be happy.

(Above) That one time Paige stole my tattoo machine and freaked out my client pretending she was gonna ink him. I think she could have though, she's pretty damn talented! *(Below)* Kyler Shinn tattoos Paige's finger at Wizard World con Portland, OR

(Above) My Wrestling fan-boy friends Casey Baker and Kevin Becvar, and I enjoying the moment. I think at least 2/3 of the men in this photo got in trouble for it with their wives!

Ruth Connell

Unlike her character, Rowena, in *Supernatural*, Ruth is no evil witch. She is actually the polar opposite. This little Scottish woman is the sweetest, most polite female celebrity I have ever met.

We hired her to appear as a special guest at my Eugene Comic Con, and it was one of the best calls we have ever made. My wife and I had dinner with her beforehand, and I had no idea she would be so pleasant . . . and eat so much steak (haha). Not only did Ruth dazzle her fans but she melted their hearts with genuine gratitude. She was down to do just about anything to make their day and ours (as promoters) brighter.

During the convention, she took much interest in my tattooing. She started asking questions, and before I knew, she was asking me if I could tattoo her. We discussed several options, and she decided to see what her fans thought via Twitter (pictured above). With an overwhelming 99 percent positive response, the masses supported her and encouraged the ink. Unfortunately, her mom also saw the post back in Scotland and quickly put a halt to the idea. I was disappointed, but completely understood. I have never been, nor will I ever be, a tattoo pusher under peer pressure. It is a lasting life decision, and you have to be ready. I don't want anyone to ever regret the art I put on them.

I honestly just wanted to tattoo her because I got to know her and respected her grace as a person and celebrity.

(Right) *Two lovely ladies; Ruth and my wife Katie.*

Jake "The Snake" Roberts

I was always a fan of Jake as a kid. He was larger than life. The day I met him, he didn't disappoint.

I had tracked him down to endorse my tattoo ink. I had another lucrative marketing idea to have a bottle in my ink line named after an iconic wrestler (pictured on next page). It had never been done in the industry before, and the whole celebrity-endorsement deal was already working well with my line of Eddie Munster (Butch Patrick) inks.

Jake was all about it. We met at a Chicago Comic Con and solidified the deal weeks later. Although the ink line quickly fizzled out after I sold the company to my ex-partner (like that writing wasn't on the wall), it was a unique product that introduced a new demographic to both sides of the playing field.

Jake was a character, to say the least. He had lived a fascinating but rough life. The drugs and fame had definitely taken their toll on him. I was honestly terrified of him—not of his physical stature, but of his mental stability.

During that weekend, I heard the best stories of my life from him, shit that you couldn't make up if you tried. He had true tales about taping wads of cash to his thighs to hide it from customs when traveling home from wrestling gigs abroad. He openly told me of his past drug use and infidelity, and that he actually hated snakes! He showed me the scars on his arm where his gimmick pet snake, Damien, had bit him dozens of times. By the time he was finished talking, and I'd picked my jaw up off of the floor, I had a new-found respect and amazement for this man. He had taken everything that life had thrown at him and survived, albeit with several permanent bruises. Some things were his own doing and some were due to hard luck, but he endured and got his life back on track. Like in the ring, he always prevailed.

Dan Chandler - Evans Blue

The lead singer of the rock band Evans Blue and I go back a long way. I first sought him out to endorse an ink color in the tattoo ink line that I owned at the time. Since I was a fan of the band's style of rock/metal, and they had a color in their name, I thought they would be a perfect fit for the branding and marketing scheme that I was going for. I reached out to a lot of my favorite bands, and Dan was the only one to respond, and thank God he did because our relationship has gone so much further than that small business foray.

Not only do I tattoo him regularly but we also talk families and careers all the time. He has given me so much good advice and helped me through a very tough time in my life.

"There are people who leave an impact on your life, and then occasionally, and I mean very rarely, you meet someone who leaves a *residual* impact on your life. They are people you look up to, people you truly value and can be inspired by, not only professionally, but personally. They are all-around good fucking human beings. I believe this is how Chris 51 feels about me (HAHAHA)," jokes the not-so-funny Dan Chandler. "We both turn to each other for advice, whether it's trying to under-

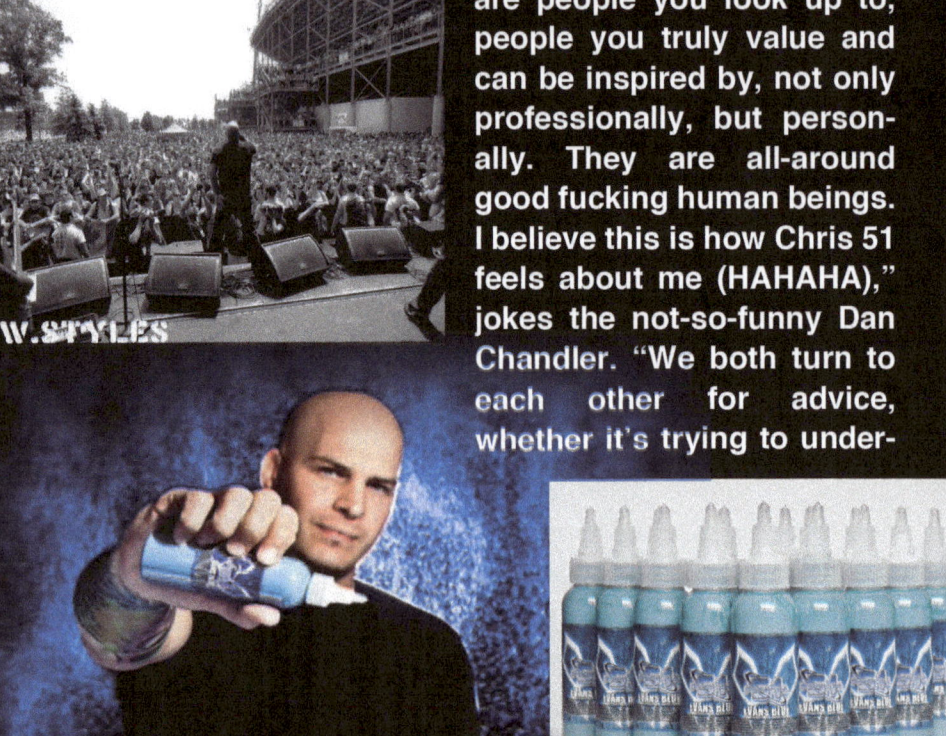

stand why people whom you've never met go out of their way to spread negativity, or simply talking about what our next chapter in this life holds. We never forget where we left off. I'm proud to know Chris 51 and that I get to call him my friend."

Dan faced haters and adversity when he replaced a lead singer in an already established band. I knew he would be the one to lean on when I went through some trials and tribulations of my own, both with my company and my new-found TV stardom. He is always there for me and always understands what I am going through.

Aside from tattooing a sleeve on my good friend, I have had the honor of presenting him at The Hard Rock Cafe St. Louis. I was doing some press at the famous restaurant, and I asked if I could bring my friend, who was not only a rock star but also a St. Louis native. The cafe didn't even know they had a rock star of their own living so close. Better yet, I told them that they should put some of Dan's memorabilia on their illustrious wall to represent the local music scene that made it big in the industry. They jumped

(Above) Just finished Dan's space sleeve at a Comic Con. *(Bottom)* Introducing my friend to The Hard Rock Cafe crowd.

on this, of course, and I know it meant a lot to Dan. After I finished my Q&A on stage, I brought him up and introduced him to the audience. The Hard Rock manager inducted him and his band into the cafe shrine. The greatest part of all was that Dan had played on that very stage with a small local band earlier in his career. What a way to return!

I don't know why it baffles me that a legitimate rock star can be so damn peaceful and humble. His persona on stage is so rugged and monstrous. But backstage you would never even know he's in a band. He doesn't flaunt it or use it to his advantage. He's just a cool dude and a great father.

It's funny because I used to be that guy who said, "Celebrities have it made; how nice would it be to be loved and admired all day . . ." What I never thought of was the fact that they are also the ones who are hated and despised all day, usually because of some fictional role that some morons can't separate from reality. There comes a point when they have to turn it all off to have some kind of normalcy to even breathe properly. The work is hard to take home with them at night, just like being a plumber all day and not wanting to go home and fix your toilets at night. So, when these celebrities are out and about, cut them a little slack and don't judge them when they want to have an uninterrupted dinner or some alone time with their kids.

I know that some of you wanted the gritty dirt on celebrities in this chapter, but I'm happy to say that I do not have much of that. I feel like if you show celebrities respect and patience, they will all do the same back. Please also realize that what they do is a job to them; they aren't just put on earth to entertain fans. They enjoy it, but it's just as hard of a job as you may have, and it's probably more stressful to always have to "be on" and energetic.

But yes, there are always assholes too. I have met my fair share of those people who just think that they are better than you simply because of their financial or celebrity stature. Those kinds of celebrities can lick my butthole!

36

MY TATTOOS

My tattoos are for me. I don't give a shit what anyone thinks about them, and neither should you. They are the ultimate form of dedication and self-expression. Hate my tattoos = hate me!

There are lots of reasons to get tattooed, and I am not saying that my tattoos are the right ones, just the right ones for me. I do get so annoyed, though, when some people have to explain every tattoo and the deep philosophical and spiritual meaning it holds in their heart, or what each and every star or pedal represents and why. Your entire family lineage from a bunch of old people you never met who could have been total assholes or creepy public masturbators is irrelevant. If you want to go there and represent all that, fine—but it's not for me.

My tattoos are no deep-rooted philosophical puzzle. They hold no religious or spiritual meanings. They are there for simply one reason, portraying one thing: happiness. They make me smile. That is all the meaning they need.

★ My donut on my belly reminds me of my Epic Ink family and the unbreakable bond we formed sharing something magical that forever changed us. It also reminds me of five hours of pain and my love for the *Simpsons*.

★ My silly-ass cartoons remind me of my wonderful childhood and moments with friends, from the Mystery Machine across my chest to the giant Hong Kong Phooey I did on myself, on my inner leg. I have Fred Flintstone coming out of a rose and Tom and Jerry popping out of tulips on my leg. The classic cartoon leg sleeve wouldn't be complete without Dick Dastardly in a coffin and Muttley laughing at him.

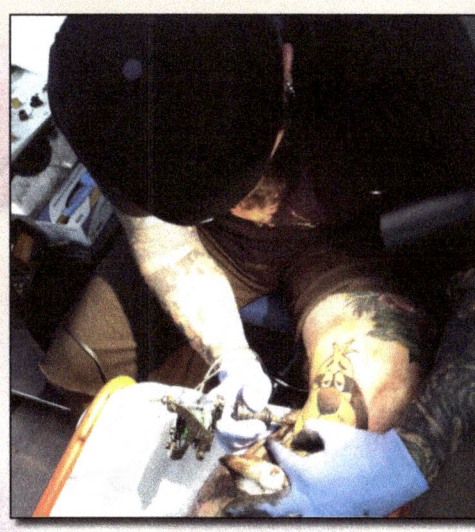

★ My monster chocolate-chip cookie on my ass reminds me to never take myself too seriously. It also reflects the fact that I just fucking love chocolate-chip cookies! I got it at a tattoo convention in Detroit by artist Jeremy Miller, in front of three thousand onlookers walking by.

★ My tattoo on my dick (that I did myself) is just funny and solved a bit of pain=location curiosity; it hurt like hell. I almost actually passed out from dishing my own pain on that

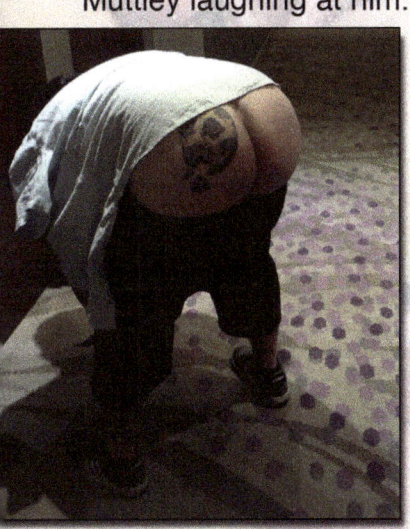

one. Yes, I said that right; I was stupid enough to tattoo my own cock . . . twice! It's only a stick-figure alien, but damn, it felt like an actual alien was probing me.

★ My tattoo on my balls (I did myself) reminds me to let loose and be stupid once in a great while, and to never sit too bored for too long at a tattoo shop. The outline was so painful. I kept thinking that I was tattooing through my ball bag skin and in to my finger it was wrapped around. Near the end of the procedure I made my apprentice (at the time) finish coloring it in for me because I couldn't inflict that much more pain on myself.

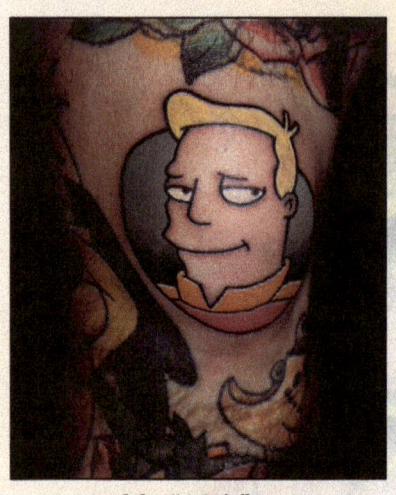

★ I also tattooed my own kneecap cause it was one of the last empty places that I could reach on my own leg. *Futurama's* sexy Captain Zapp Brannigan was the subject—pain was the outcome! Don't ever tattoo your kneecap if you don't have to. It blows.

★ My giant Spock on my thigh logically reflects my love for Star Trek, and of course, he is throwing up the gang sign for "Live long and prosper."

★ My "12th" text on my left fingers shows my passion and loyalty to the Seattle Seahawks, whom I have loved since I was five years old. I did that one on myself, which is never fun. I also have a classic Seahawks armband...yes, from the '90s' armband era of tattoos, lol.

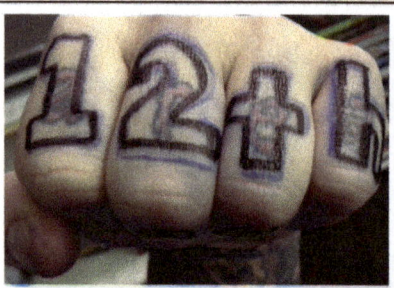

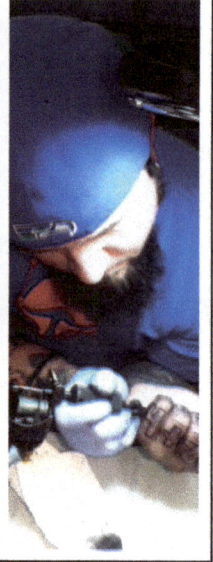

★ My Will Ferrell (as a bobble head) basketball card on my back is simply for my love for his character Jackie Moon in the movie *Semi-Pro*. He was genius in that movie, and Heather Maranda tortured me for ten straight hours on it, so now it reminds me of my love for both Jackie Moon and Heather Maranda. It, of course, says E.L.E on it, representing the famous movie quote, "Everybody Love Everybody."

★ I even have Mötley Crüe puzzle pieces and a rat for Ratt on my upper arm, punctuating my geekiness for old Butt-rock hair metal!

★ Stretching across both of my feet is my favorite inspirational quote of all time, "I'll make it to the moon if I have to crawl," courtesy of the Red Hot Chili Pepper's Anthony Kiedis.

★ One of my best friends in the world, Kyler Shinn, tattooed Gobo the Fraggle on the outside of my knee. Let me tell you about some pain when you start dipping behind the kneecap in the tender and soft "ditch" area. I hated every second of it.

★ Kyler Shinn also tattooed Scrooge McDuck's lucky Number One Dime on my right hand. This was important to me for a couple reasons. One, it covers up an old memory of a tattoo tour I no longer support (done by the owner I despise), so it closes the only remnant of that chapter of my life. Second, it is a good-luck piece and a reminder that you'll be rewarded if you always work hard. Third, it's from the fucking *DuckTales*, and that alone is reason enough.

★ My friend James Mullin has tattooed me twice. Not only did he do a killer coverup on my calf (pictured right) with a perfect TMNT Michelangelo (who we all know is the best turtle), but he put a perfect Great Gazoo floating on my neck, dumb dumb.

My geeky art reflects my personality and passion. It is who I am. It doesn't decorate me—it is me! The art was there all along; it just needed to be brought to life.

37

JUST THE TIP (FOR TATTOOERS)

Old-school artists who don't like to share tips and education to help younger artists can suck my dick. It drives me crazy when people are too cool or too busy to help those artists who look up to them. Either they don't remember that they were at that beginning point at one time and would have loved for someone to help them, or they are just grumpy, washed-up assholes who have to treat people like they were treated. I am not that guy. I hate that guy. I am here to help because I want everyone to succeed who deserves it. I want everyone who is looking for education in their industry to better themselves to get it. That being said, here are several tips, tricks, and stories that I hope may help you in some aspect of your career.

JUST THE TIP . . .

Here's a tool tip. The first question I always ask tattoo artists when I hold seminars is, "What is your most important tool in this industry?" Everyone with the social fortitude to speak up always replies "tattoo machine." Nope! Wrong every time. The correct answer is your camera. No matter how good of a tattoo artist you are, it doesn't mean shit if you take or promote shitty pictures. A picture isn't worth just 1,000 words anymore—it's worth 1,000 likes, 1,000 followers, and 1,000 dollars towards your next tattoo. A cell phone pic isn't the solution either. So many artists will spend hundreds to thousands on their tattoo machines, but settle for crappy cell phone pics with horrible lighting and glare as a representation of their skills. You need to spend as much, if not more, on a good camera. Why wouldn't you? It baffles me. If your tattoo image is the single advertising and marketing tool at your disposal, don't you want to put the best quality forward? You don't skimp on machines or ink, so why would you on your pictures? If you have to start out your picture post with the phrase, "It's a crappy cell pic," or, "Sorry for the bad pic," then why the hell are you posting it? All that's telling your admirers and peers is

that you are lazy and impatient, and maybe that the tattoo really isn't all that good under scrutinizing eyes. You might as well post, "Hey, I don't really care about this tattoo or myself enough to take the time and spend the money to get a good picture to show you all who are waiting to see good pictures of my tattoos."

JUST THE TIP . . .

Here's another hard tip to swallow. You suck, your work is never going to be perfect, and there will always be somebody better than you. The sooner that you realize this the better off you'll be and the faster you will grow as both an artist and a man.

A truly good artist is his own worst critic. You have to find flaws in all of your work to have something to improve and build upon. If you can't find mistakes, you are either not looking hard enough or you are already too arrogant.

There will always be somebody with more experience or more natural talent than you, so check your ego. As soon as you think you are king, your throne is already lost.

This tip certainly isn't meant to discourage you. Quite the opposite actually—it is meant to motivate you. Just because there is somebody better than you at what you do doesn't mean you have to lose. You can outwork, out-promote, out-market, and outsmart them! You just have to put in the effort and hours.

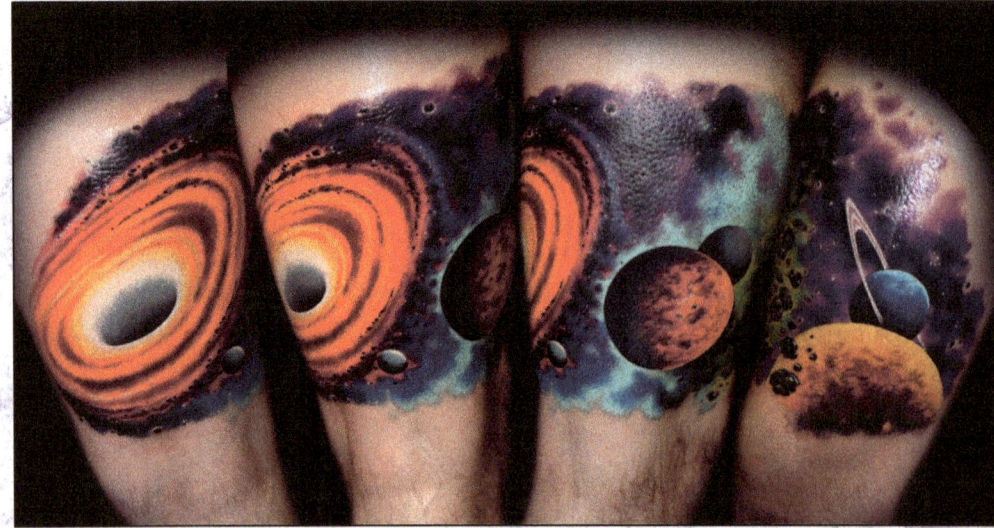

JUST THE TIP . . .

Here's a scary tip. Don't ever be afraid to ask for help. If you practice your craft the proper and respectable way, no veteran artist should criticize you. If one does, then that artist is just an asshole, so ask the next one in line. A lot of stubborn old schoolers don't like "sharing trade secrets," and I say fuck that, quit being cocksuckers. There is enough work to go around for everyone. In the end, I think those old schoolers lack the confidence to retain their clients or are threatened by the new wave of artists making a splash at their feet, so they protect the only thing they have left: knowledge. Most old-school tattooers drive me fuckin crazy with their outdated antics and superiority complexes all because they spent more time doing shitty street tattoos than some of us.

JUST THE TIP . . .

Here's a selfless tip. CUSTOMER SERVICE. Good customer service is the foundation to any business. Tattooing is a service industry, and your job is to provide a service and be of service to your clients.

If you are only good at being good at art, then you are not going to make it in this business. It is the intangible and unseen art of being good with people that will make you great as a tattoo artist.

Pay attention not only to your customers' art but to their comfort too. Are you providing them with a clean environment and an enjoyable atmosphere? Are they nervous or scared? Are they sweating or shivering? Customers will remember the smallest things that are wrong with their surroundings and overlook the hundred things that are right . . . and they will tell all of their friends!

Are you listening to speed metal while tattooing an old-timer? Are you listening to Tay-Tay while working on some hillbilly? Changing the music to match your human environment is a little touch that can go a long way to ease someone's comfort.

Make follow-up calls. Call your clients after a week to see how the healing process is going. Do they have any questions or concerns? Tell them to stop by next time they are in the area because you are excited to see how the tattoo turned out after healing. People like to know they are thought of and that you are truly concerned with your art and their well-being. A few seconds on the phone can mean the difference between a lifelong client or a one-time spontaneous fling with the needle.

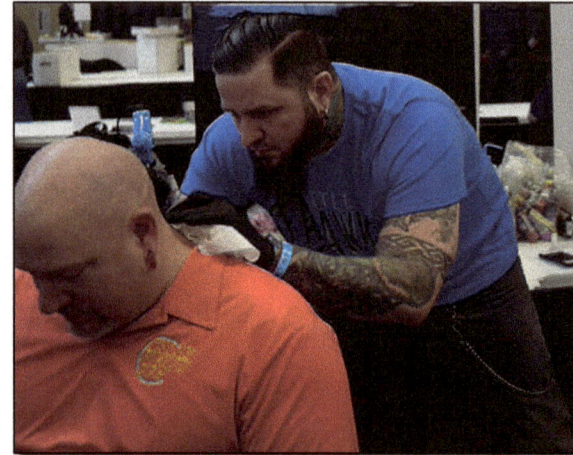

JUST THE TIP . . .

Here are some douche-proof convention tips. I learned more going to conventions and questioning and spying on artists than I ever did from my mentor. My stealthiness earned me more education than my apprenticeship, and it cost a lot less. I quickly learned that you must train like a gazelle before you can run like a lion. That being said, I have devised a douche-proof guide on to how to "not be" at a convention. Whether they are working or lurking, there are several types of artists that warrant this convention attention. Don't be one.

The Fashion Tool. This type of cute kitten belongs more in a Fall Out Boy video than in a tattoo booth. You have definitely seen this cat before; he makes sure of it. With the ironed bandana fitted underneath his perfect forty-five-degree cocked hat, his carefully planned ensemble is completed by just-washed skate shoes and sparkly things that make me wanna go fishing. To complete the tool time, he insists on wearing his sunglasses indoors because it is so damn bright inside the facility it burns his retinas, and the coolness will seep out of his eyeballs if they aren't well protected. We don't want to see this guy, and we don't want to answer his questions because he looks like he is only in it to get laid or get paid.

The Trophy Whore. This slut of the silver and digger of the gold insists on proudly displaying all his trophies won at every show he has ever attended. Although it may be a beautiful buffet of acclaim, we don't give a shit unless it was won at the show we are currently at. Guess what else . . . everyone is a goddamn award-winning artist, so quit printing it on your banner! I once won an award for a high school architecture project, so maybe I should brag about that on my banner too. Put pictures of your actual trophies in your portfolio if you must, or better yet, just put up the picture of the award-winning piece and let the public judge for themselves so that your fellow artists quit judging you.

The Apocalypse Packer. These herds are of the younger, less-traveled breed. After you show up with your one suitcase, you can sit back on it, grab some delicious popcorn, and be entertained. The display is like a U-Haul made love to an ant farm—lots of little worker ants marching in box after crate after chest full of sweet picnic treasures. These bugs use more time setting up gadgets and gizmos (not the lovable gremlin variety) than they do tattooing. Unless they flew Southwest, I would like to see if their baggage fees equaled their profit margin.

Please don't mistake my (attempted) comedy for bashing. As usual, Mr. 51 has a moral justification stronger than Mr. T's neck muscles. I simply want to drop some knowledge to help the younger players not make the same mistakes that so many of us have in this game. It takes a long time and a lot of hard work to earn the respect of your peers—might as well know a few things that will help speed up that process. Always remember, like a Barry Sanders touchdown (non) celebration, ACT LIKE YOU'VE BEEN THERE to get there!

JUST THE TIP . . .

Here's just the travel tip. Through the good and the bad times I have endured while traveling the globe to tattoo, I can tell you that even the worst times aren't really all that bad when you get to witness the majesty this world has to offer by doing what we love to do. I have tattooed in China, the Philippines, Brazil, New Zealand, France, Holland, Belgium, Switzerland, England, Ireland, and too many more to name. Every place helped me grow as an artist and a man. I encourage traveling to any artist in any field; nothing will help progress your skills faster. Sometimes, though, it all can get a little intimidating, so here are some tips that might help you avoid those bad moments during your endeavors. I want you to be able to focus on the artistic adventure that lies before you.

Pack properly. You are going to be walking—a lot! The worst thing you can do is spend fifty dollars on luggage that is too heavy to begin with, then carry that heavy bag around your destination trying to find your hotel or hostel. A hiker's backpack is ideal to fit all your tattooing and survival gear in one spot, and to carry your laptop and artwork on the plane with you. A suitcase on wheels will do, too, but it's not as practical when wandering around rural areas of town or cobblestone streets. I have always split up my machines by bringing one in my carry-on and one in my checked bag; that way if your luggage is lost, you are not. You would be amazed, though, at the generosity of local artists from different cultures who are willing to share their supplies with you should yours get lost. Don't panic if it happens.

Don't put too much in your carry-on because you will have to endure hellacious layovers and lengthy customs lines, and a heavy bag on your shoulder just fuels your frustrations. Include a laptop or an iPad (with an extra battery), your artwork and client info (which are irreplaceable if lost), a tattoo machine, and a universal plug-in adapter to charge all your phones, iPods, and laptops. Almost every country has different electrical outlets, but every airport sells the corresponding adapters.

Protect your ink. Get one-ounce bottles first. Any bigger, your bag will check in overweight and your wallet will lighten in weight. Inks are the heaviest things you will pack. You must take time and care in packing them correctly if you want to avoid explosions of Epic proportions. I retighten every cap, then pack them in color-coordinated groups of five (for ease of unpacking because you may not use them all). I wrap five bottles in plastic wrap, then put them in a ziplock sandwich bag, which fit perfectly. Finally, I put all the small sandwich bags of ink into a large ziplock freezer bag. This may sound like a lot of excess work, but once you have had to clean up an exploded bottle of ink that got on all of your other inks, you will reconsider my advice. Pressure buildup in a plane at 37,000 feet is intense in the cargo hold, so you should be prepared. Since I have instituted this procedure, I have not had one inkccident*.

Prepare for muscle aches. Damn I miss my stool and massage table from home when I travel. Apart from my family, those are the two things I long for most. You will have to invent some acrobatic ways to position your client that your body will not be accustomed to. Bring plenty of ibuprofen . . . and patience. Expect a sore back upon your return home; that is just the way it is. My advice: take up yoga. I have never been in a hotel or hostel not big enough to do some pre-expo stretching, and it will help immensely. If you are pairing your convention with a local shop guest spot, befriend the owners first because you may be able to borrow a stool, massage table, pillows, and other luxuries to aid in your comfort and your clients'. You can also try and make contact ahead of time through the convention promoter or one of your clients to secure needed equipment.

Foreign paper towels suck. No matter where I have been, Amsterdam, London, or Paris, it doesn't matter . . . their paper towels suck! In fact, paper towels are about the only thing that isn't better in other countries. The cuisine, the culture, the history, and the museums are all superior, but the paper towels . . . garbage. If you have extra room in your bag, pack a roll or two, and treat every piece like a slice of quilted gold.

Ship ahead of time if possible. Some foreign airports are very strict in customs. It is always easier to just ship some ink and basic supplies in a shoebox to a friend in another country. Do it a good month in advance, though, since international shipping takes forever and sometimes shit can get stuck in customs.

Customs suck. Waiting in lines, being judged by officials, bratty kids, sweaty butt cracks . . . all part of the airport customs' experience. ONE RULE: never, ever, under any circumstances, say that you are there to work. If you do, they got you. They will want taxes, work visas, and all of your time and money. You are always there for *holiday* (the proper foreign terminology for vacation). Don't post a bunch of stupid shit on social media about traveling for work, because customs will check if they are suspicious. I let them check in Canada, and luckily, I deleted it all before I got to the border. If you can't get around packing all of your supplies, always contact the promoter in advance for a letter. Most promoters understand international travel and the risks involved, and they will e-mail you a letter about attending their show as a guest who is there as promotion or for education in exchange for accommodations. This way, no money is expected from you, because you are supporting that country's economy, not taking from it, and there would be no reasons for pesky government issues.

Explore! Remember, you may never be back to this location again. Time, money, your wife . . . you cannot foresee the circumstances that may inhibit your return. Plan a couple extra days. My rule is one day to explore for every two days I work. If the show is two days and I guest spot for two days, I schedule a six-day trip. You will make new, local friends, and they will show you sights and delights that a guided tour could never offer . . . legally. I always wear a good pair of gym-type shoes because otherwise you will walk, and walk, and walk the blisters right into a pain-dominating existence on your feet. Or you could try and look cool in Converse and take taxis everywhere, blowing all of your bungee-jumping, lobster-eating, cave-diving, castle-searching adventure funds.

Make your trip an adventure. Try new things. I once ate a scorpion in New Zealand and then visited the Shire and stood before Frodo Baggins's front door. I further toured the countryside to find beautiful filming locations used in *The Lord of the Rings* movies, and stood upon the same battlefields that orcs and wizards once did.

I've had melted Belgium chocolate on a hot Belgium waffle in cold Belgium. I've tried the nastiest Chinese food in China and tasted the best Filipino food in the Philippines. I've sang Barry Manilow's *Copacabana* while sipping from a fresh coconut on Copacabana Beach in Rio de Janeiro. One day you will forget the tattoos you did, but you will always remember the adventure you lived! Don't be afraid to be a tourist and do touristy shit. That stuff is popular for a reason, usually because it is cool!

Be careful and always be on the lookout. Wear a chain wallet or keep cash in a couple different places on your person. Always scan your periphery for threats. Don't be naïve, because people will steal your shit and take advantage of you. I always just mind my own business and act like I know where I am. Never pull out a map in public; you might as well just paint a target on yourself. Don't let these things scare you, though, because no matter the small risks, the rewards of international travel are far greater.

I hope that some of my experiences can help you with yours. Life is hard, so let's try and make it a little easier on one another when we can. That's not hard to do.

Cliffs of Moher. I took this photo on my travels to Ireland. Tattooing can take you all around the world and enable you to see sights like this if you just work hard at it.

That shit right there is a castle, that's how giant these cliffs are!

38

MY SUPPORTING CAST

I am the man I am today because of two women, my mom and my wife.

My mother makes angels look like demons. She is Mother Teresa and the *Mona Lisa* wrapped into one priceless work of moral art.

If it sounds like I am a mama's boy, you're absolutely right. Why wouldn't I be? The woman had me when she was eighteen and gave up her whole life from there on out to raise my little brother and me.

From as early as I can remember, she was Wonder Woman. She could do it all, and still does! Mom packed us lunch every day and made us a three-course dinner every night. She found the time to make it to our practices and never missed a game. Mom helped me with homework nightly so I could get straight As, not just helping me to complete it but to understand it as well. She sat down for hours if needed, relating math equations to sports terminology so I could grasp them.

The woman handmade all of our pajamas when we were young and poor so we wouldn't look like indigent welfare children at night. She spent quality time with us every night, too, and I truly believe that all she did cast the mold for the type of father I would become one day.

She rarely raised her hand to me, only breaking a wooden spoon over my ass one time, which I totally deserved. Mom never belittled us or put us down. She was always encouraging and inspiring.

To this day, she's my homie. I never hide anything from her, and I'm never afraid to talk to her because I know she will have a positive ear and solid advice.

I still take her out to dinner and a movie once a week in appreciation for working for me as Area 51 Tattoo's accountant, bill payer, and general do-it-aller baller!

My mom is everything to me, and if more kids had a mom like mine, this world would be a more loving, more peaceful, and more advanced place!

Then there is my wife...

The third time really was the charm in my case. Two marriages down and I had all but given up on the female species. Then fate brought me a dream girl. She is a younger version of my mom. She has all the same qualities and the same moral compass, but wrapped in one small sexy package.

I'm talking drop-dead gorgeous. "Like, how the hell did I score her, kind of hot!"? She makes me weak in the knees and hard in the bones. I feel like I'm an eighteen year-old in heat around her, and I cannot get enough of her.

Katie is the whole package with a cherry on top! She has brains, looks, kindness, generosity, patience, thoughtfulness, and enough love to go around the world. She's so perfect it almost makes me sick (haha).

When I say that my wonderful wife saved me, I'm not talking about from drugs or alcohol. I'm talking about something way more devastating for the restless, strong-willed minds like me; I'm talking about saving me from myself. She saved me from my own undoing. She's my rock. A fuckin' solid and

(Top) *Photo by Kitsie, Celeb Photo Ops.*
(Left) *Photo by Bob Williams, me in awe.*

strong rock that kept me grounded and peaceful through the most dramatic and traumatic times in my life.

With ex-people in my life betraying me, cheating me, and trying to ruin me, Katie was my first line of logic and defense. She built the highest road and taught me how to take it and stay focused on it.

When fame and admiration hit me, she squashed any arrogance and entitlement I might have felt before they even had a chance to rear their ugly heads. She was around before it all and kept me sane through it all, no matter how rough times got or how busy I got.

She gave up everything to support me and let me fly, and was always there to repair my wings when needed, just so I could take off flying again. To say that behind every great man stands a great woman is a gross understatement in my world, because my great woman helped this guy become a real man! Katie has done way more than stand behind me; she has helped build me.

I would probably be the coldest, most bitter and arrogant asshole today without my wife. She calms me, relaxes me, and shows me alternative paths to anger or aggression. My wife is my best friend and I can't stand to be more than two feet away from her, ever.

Thank God for these two women in my life. They inspire me to be more and do greater every day!

Photo by Bob Williams.

39
MY ART, YOUR ART

Always wanting to make art, not how it looks, is what makes you an artist. A true artist is one who isn't afraid to experiment and think outside the canvas. It's in the very act of experimentation that the best art is created.

I have tried about every type of medium available. I gravitate towards oil painting because it is very difficult. Art that is easy isn't rewarding. Struggling through the difficulty and unknown is the most satisfying, and it's what keeps me coming back for more.

Most of my projects strictly depend on the time I have available to work on them, and the motivation at hand. If I have a free weekend, I will get out the paints, then I come back to my pieces frequently throughout the week to make finishing touches. If I have only an hour here or there between doing tattoos at work, I will do some mash-up sketches to scan onto the computer and digitize. When I have breaks in the day to color them, I then take those digital outlines to make trading cards or prints.

The point is that to progress as an artist, you must be constantly doing art. Whether it's a small project on the computer, large-scale masterpiece paintings, or anything in between, like sculpting, vinyl-toy painting, or sketching comic-book covers, it all helps you become a better-rounded artist. Once you commit yourself to this work, you will have little desire to play games or watch TV anymore. They become time-sucking digital leeches. The best artists I know are also the hardest workers I know- living, breathing, and shitting out art all day and all night long.

Art is always in the eye of the beholder, and I always see improvement needed in my own work. The point of being an artist is to always chase perfection, realizing that you will never obtain it. But once in a while you may get close or surprise yourself, so always keep trying.

The following pages show samples of different kinds of art that I typically do. Some are quick and simple one-hour projects and some are twenty-hour paintings. I have done thousands of tattoos, paintings, sketches, crafts, woodworks, photographs, sculptures, and other art projects of all types, shapes, and sizes. No matter what, I always aspire to do more and never settle for just what's sufficient. Nor should you.

The first artistic influence of my life was a Dr. Seuss book I was exposed to when I was three years old. The message still resonates in my mind today: *Go, Dog. Go!* Keep going, always.

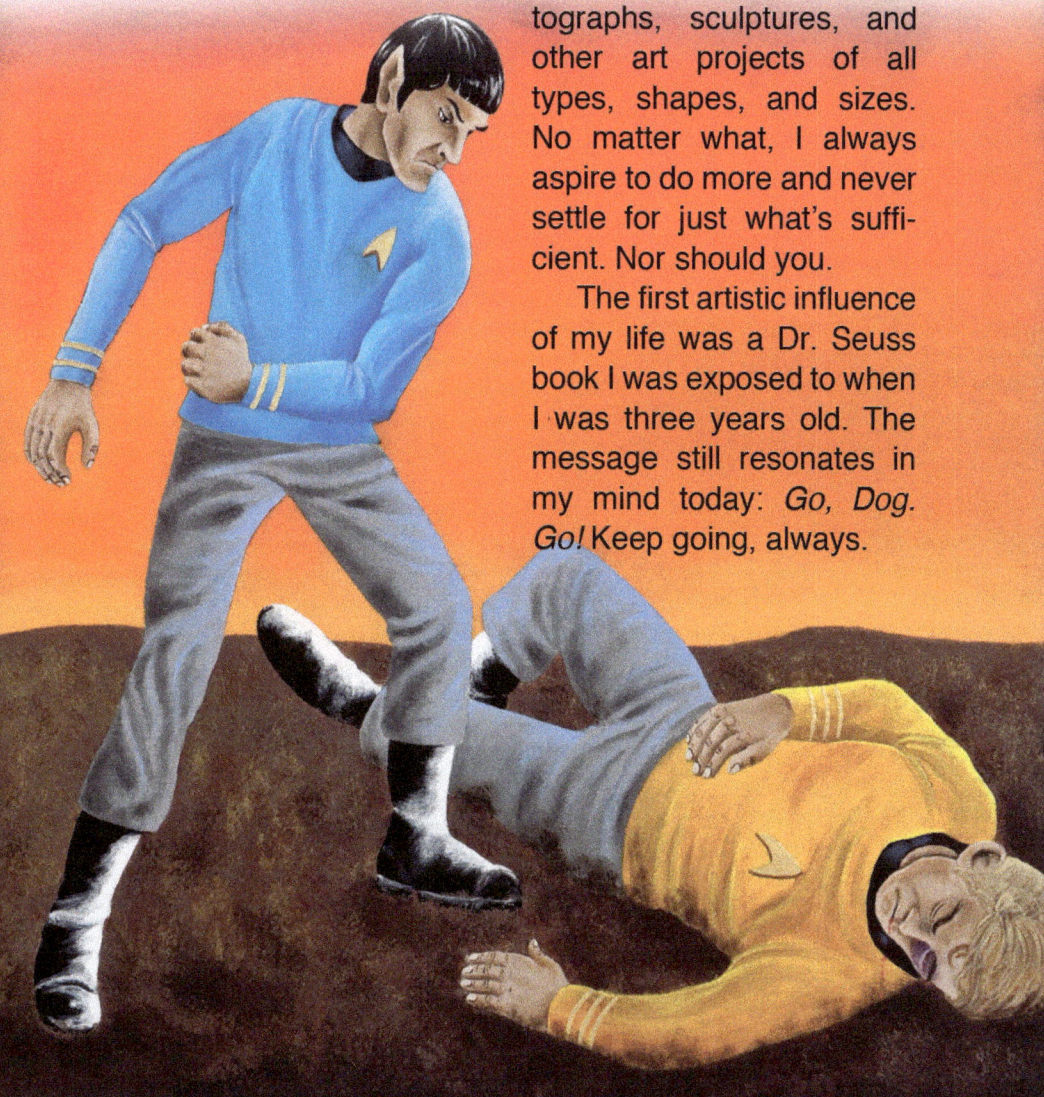

PAINTINGS

Great White Hope, oil on wood

Holy Shit!, acrylic on wood

What The Phooey?, oil on wood

The Great Moral Martian, oil on canvas

OIL PAINTINGS

Disgruntled Bartender

/150

Evil Business Tycoon

Overweight Mob Boss

PUDGY INSECURE BULLY

...URE BULLY

EVIL BUSINESS TYCOON
-CHRIS 51-

ARROGANT MANIACAL MASTERMIND
-CHRIS 51-

MEDDLERS

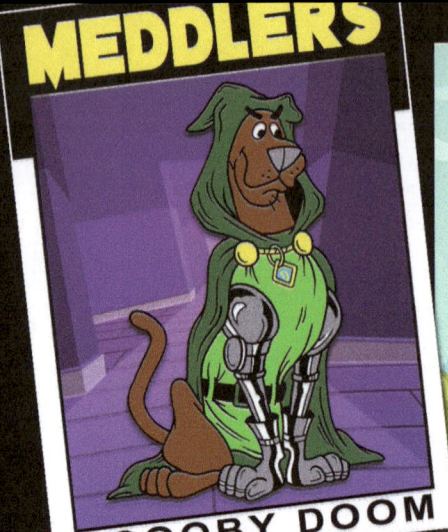

SCOOBY DOOM

LIONS — MUFAS-O

ADMIRAL
KIF ACKBAR
DEMOCRATIC ORDER OF REBELS

SCOTTY DOO

Peter the Pooh

TAKING NO BULL
CRASH & NUKE
Art by CHRIS 51. Background photo by David B. Stinson

FAST & FURIOUS 1989
HAYES & CERRANO
© CHRIS 51

SIMPSONIZED HELMETS

KANSAS CITY DUFF
SAN DIEGO BUZZ

DETROIT ITCHYS
JACKSONVILLE SCRATCHYS

SFL
SPRINGFIELD FOOTBALL LEAGUE

NEW ENGLAND *Jebediahs*

OAKELY-DOKELY FLANDERS

MIAMI *Blinkies*

CAROLINA SNOWBALLS

BUFFALO STAMPYS

Washington YELLOWSKINS

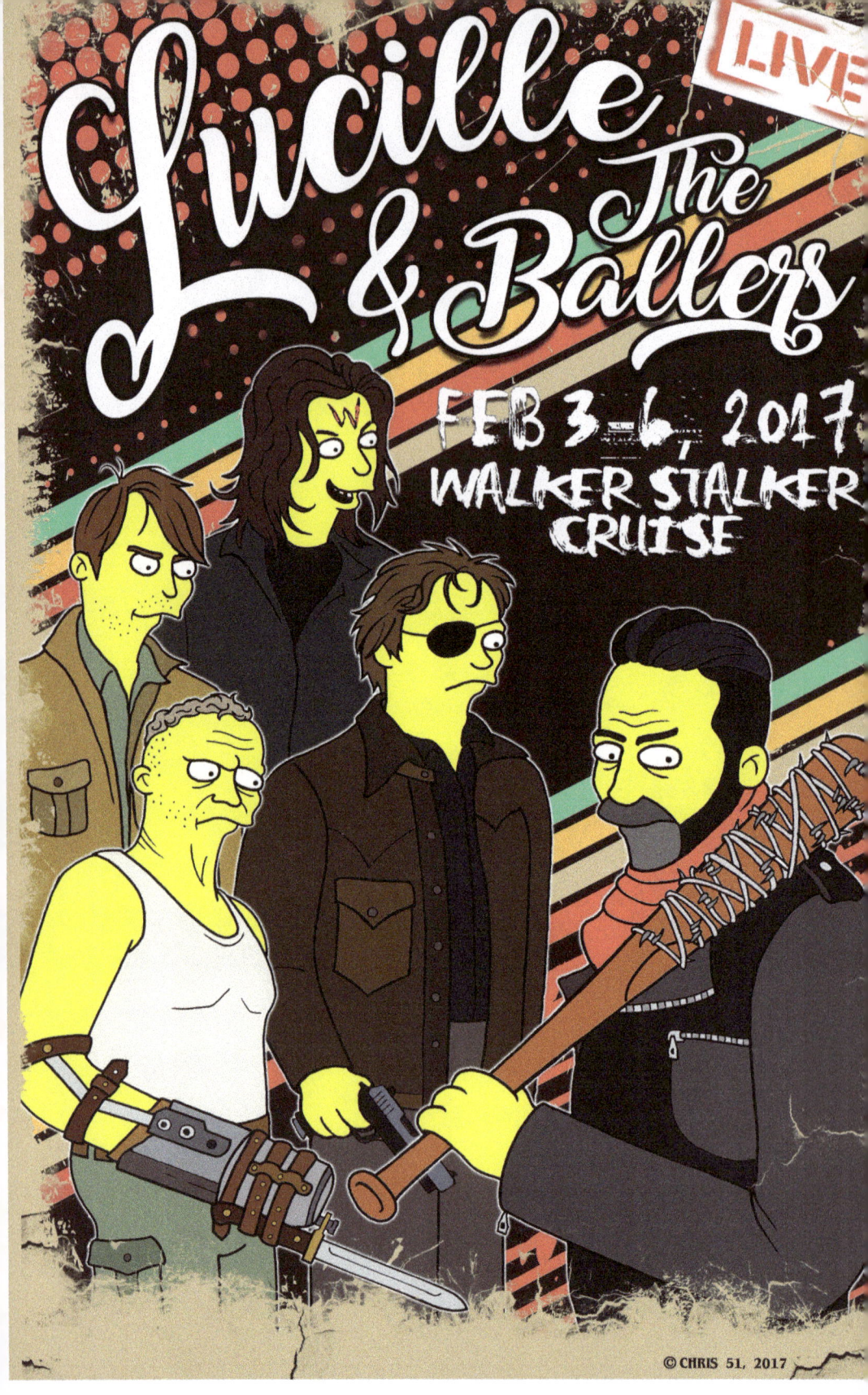

TATTOOS

TATTOOS

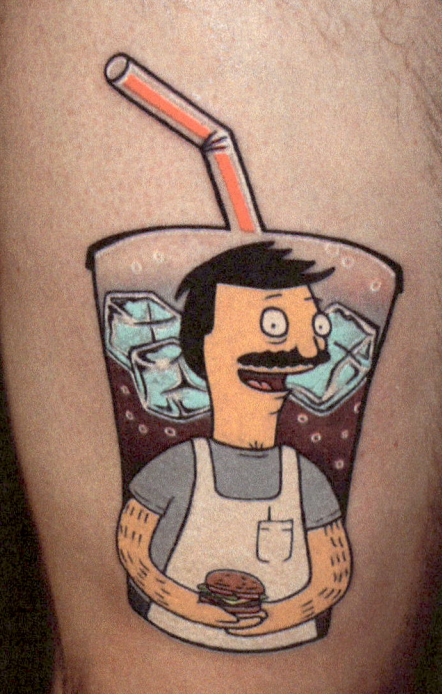

TATTOOS

51

FAR FROM PERFECT

The closest thing to perfection is probably The Borg. Their collective mind collaborates the greatness of every individual into one motivated team without defiance or selfishness. In the end, though, we learn that even The Borg aren't perfect, and it's their very drive for that unobtainable goal of perfection that makes them imperfect and flawed. Geeky *Star Trek* innuendos aside, we all have our faults, especially me . . . and that's never easy to admit or share.

Where I fail is in thinking that my way is always the correct one and in wanting to be and stay in control of every situation. I usually think I can do things better and more efficiently than others around me. And though, in the end, I usually do . . . there is always room for learning and especially for more humility (as you just witnessed).

I always open my mouth with the first thoughts that pop in my head, without regard to others' feelings. I used to brush this behavior off, thinking I was just being an upfront and honest person, but I have learned that sometimes it is best to just sit back, chill, and re-

My painting, "The Seven Deadly Sweets" seemed appropriate here.

evaluate my position by looking at all the angles and realizing that not everyone is built the same. All this is thanks to my wife, who is way smarter in the "emotional feelings of others" department than I will ever be.

I teach and I help, and I NEVER ask for anything in return . . . except gratitude, loyalty, and respect. And I dwell on these things when they aren't constantly given. I require too much recognition for my aide and exploits and get hurt when it's not all received. Sometimes I lose sight of the fact that I should do things for other people to make them feel better, not to make myself feel better.

Probably my biggest shortcoming is my fear of losing. I always push and push myself to be the best, be the first, and do the most, even to the point of personal alienation and addiction to success. I fear that if I take one single break, then the person right behind me will surpass me, and I will lose that opportunity I worked so hard for.

Growing up, I was taught that being vulnerable meant being weak. The captain must always have all the answers and never show fear, or his enemies will eat him alive and his crew will lose faith in his leadership. I'd like to say that I have matured beyond that antiquated teaching. . . but I haven't.

Recognizing and admitting your own faults is only half the battle—doing something about them wins the war. It is a war I fight every day.

But I don't have to fight it alone.

Geeks Unite!

SPECIAL THANKS

I preach a lot about helping others, and I rarely ask for any help in return. But sometimes there are those souls who can just do a better job at particular things than you can. You have to recognize those stars if you want your product to shine brighter than the rest. If you don't aim to be the best, then your sight is way off. And sometimes you need the best to be the best. Drop your pride and ask for help sometimes . . .

I would like to thank the following people and companies for helping contribute to this long ass book. They are my rocks...and they fuckin rock!

-Kevin Rohaley. My baby brother. We've had our differences, and we lead different lives, but we always come together when it counts, and we will always have an unbreakable bond. You are at the front every great childhood memory I have. Love you always, no matter what. PS-Steelers suck! Go Hawks!

-Joe Ricken. My best friend for almost forty years. Wow, who the fuck else has one of those for that long? You have always understood me and put up with me better than anyone. You have been the biggest part of my story since the beginning. I love you. Dee-

-Nate Hopkins. You are my brother. You stood by my side through the most changes in my life, together or apart. Our future lives were shaped during our time together. I trust you until the end of time, and love you unconditionally.

-Kyler Shinn. My homeboy. My everyday confidant and support. You've shown constant interest and attention in not only this project but in everything I do. I trust you until the end. Love you, dude.

-Casey Baker. My Cay-bay. The most fair & humble dude I know. Couldn't have held the Epic shop together without you! I love you, even though you love super-gay Aquaman.

-The GeeksterInk Legends. You are all my rock. I consider you all my best friends, and our tour has changed my life forever. You make my dreams come true in every city we do. I couldn't do it without you all.

-Joe Pomparelli. The only business partner I have ever trusted. You let me fly and you support my ground. Love you forever. You are a huge part of my story and my motivation. You're loyalty is second to none, you are my Italian Klingon.

-Josh Bodwell. Always there for me. Always with intelligent advice. Always wanting to be a part of my life and accepting my faults. Always working hard. Love you, man.

-Butch Patrick. You may be Eddie Munster to the world, but you will always be Papa Butch to me. You have helped me more than anyone to find my way in the entertainment world, and have always looked out for me like a father. Love you, dude.

-Robert Williams Photography. You have been there for me almost since the beginning, and I for you. Thank you for all those late nights after our normal day jobs, working together and trying to make waves. You are a true pro!

-Royce Myers. For believing in me and and having me be a major part of the best event Eugene, Oregon has ever seen!

-**Celeb Photo Ops.** Kitsie and Chris and their crew are second to none. Always helping and always caring about me and my crew. I truly love you guys. You are hard-working mother-fuckin machines . . . with big hearts!

-**Jason David Frank.** Always there for me. Always setting a good example. Always being a positive role model and inspiration to everyone around you, no matter their stature. Thanks for all those greenroom talks and advice.

-**Voodoo Doughnut.** The best at what they do, period! Thanks for always having the balls to try new things and the sweet power to make us all smile. You are true bakery artists. I always love your free doughnut masterpieces . . . hint, hint.

DICKTIONARY

Sometimes the normal English vocabulary is limited and just doesn't offer the proper words that ideally describe a certain subject, especially with the Tattoo Generation. So I offer you the Chris 51 dicktionary for a more easily tolerable and understandable literary adventure.

Ambidangerous
[am-ba-dane-jer-us]
adjective
-able to use both hands equally when performing a dangerous or awesome task.
"Rob Prior is ambidangerous when painting live"

Anticonformography
[ant-I-kuh n-for-mi-awg-ref-ee]
noun
-against the social and traditional standards and attitudes of normal photography
"He was all anticonformography against the old-school photographers"

Apprenticeshit
[uh-pren-tah-shit]
noun
-a person who works under another in a shitty environment and isn't taught shit in order to try and learn a trade
"Chris 51 went through an apprenticeshit to tattoo"

Artertainer
[ahr-ter-tay-ner]
noun
-humorous and skilled combination of an artist and entertainer
"Chris 51 is a rare breed of artertainers"

Artistical
[ahr-tis-tik-al]
adjective
-describing one who has skills and education in the standards of art

Artrection
[ahr t-rek-shu n]
noun
-getting a hard penis and visually stimulated over art
"I wake up with an artection when cartoons are on"

Assletes
[ath-leet]
noun
-an individual who sits on their ass for a majority of their career and only performs physical activity or sports on an extremely limited or required basis
"Epic Ink artists are professional assletes"

Cartoonisms
[kahr-toon-iz-ums]
noun
-a realistic person or image turned into a cartoon version of itself. A pun or description of a cartoon version of a noun
"Chris 51's artwork is full of Simpsonized cartoonisms"

Emporees
[em-poor-ee]
noun
-a person who is working for another person or business for pay that is about to loose that work and that pay
"the employee that kept playing on her phone instead of helping customers was about to become an emporee"

Heartwork
[hahrt-wurk]
noun
-The act of working hard at matters of the heart. Not giving up on love
"you're having problems but still in love, what you need is some heartwork"

Inkccident
[eenk-si-dun nt]
noun
-when your tattoo inks explode or spill in transit
"I opened my suitcase to find a major inkccident"

Personablality
[pur-suh-nuh-buhl-al-it-tee]
adjective
-having a pleasing and inviting personality, persona and personal appearance simultaneously
"Chris 51's personablality is off the charts with his clients"

Tattoombulance
[ta-toom-beu-lence]
noun
-an ambulance vehicle that has been retrofitted to serve as a mobile tattooing studio

STAY EPIC!

www.ingramcontent.com/pod-product-compliance
Lightning Source LLC
Chambersburg PA
CBHW061213070526
44584CB00029B/3821